SHE WORE A SCARLET RIBBON

Published in the United Kingdom by MPire Books of Crewe
email: mark@markpotts.wanadoo.co.uk
ISBN 978-0-9538877-9-8

SHE WORE A SCARLET RIBBON

A FAN'S LOVE AFFAIR WITH MISTRESS ALEXANDRA

Jules Hornbrook

MPIRE BOOKS

For Mike

SCHOOLBOY ERROR

Mistress Alexandra has a lot to answer for. She's evil, twisted, forever making my life hell. She's the leggy blond in red stilettos that turns everyone's head. Most steal a cheeky glance as she walks by, intoxicated by the cheap perfume. I followed her home. It should have been a one-off misdemeanour, but I went back for more. Now I think about her constantly, throughout the working week, more so as the weekend arrives, and then obsessively on Saturday mornings as kick-off approaches.

There have been good times, of course; the best if I'm honest. And yet over the years she's bled me dry of cash, made me miss appointments, forced girlfriends to back off and, in recent years, the wife hasn't been too happy about her being around.

I've tried to walk away; really I have. But she has been part of my life since primary school days, when friendships and allegiances are formed. Like a playground dealer she got in early and ensured that I was hooked, unable to shake the habit across the years.

My dad was complicit, introducing me to her some time during the 1976-77 season, although he was never happy with the subsequent path that I followed. I suppose he wanted that like-father-like-son continuity on the football front. You see, he was a Man United fan, all his life, still is, and he took me to Old Trafford in the early 70s, homemade red and white scarf and all. And there was always a flask of lukewarm tea and some ham sandwiches. Male bonding at its simple best.

The experience was amazing, especially for a small boy, swept along by the massive crowds, sat high up in the gods, the seating above the old Stretford End, looking down upon thousands of passionate United fans, heads bobbing up and down, swaying, pushing and singing as one. After the match, as 60,000 supporters flooded home like a red tide, I hovered down the steps, my feet six inches from the ground, as my last breath was nearly squeezed from my body. Dad did his best to keep me upright, but the crush was such that I often thought I was going to die before we reached the bridge that took us up and over the railway lines to safety.

I wasn't hooked, but the day out to Manchester from Holmes Chapel was always something that excited me. It was great spending some time with dad, listening to stories about his younger days around inner city Manchester. It was so different to my childhood. On football days he came alive, cast free from his shirt and tie working week, and his enthusiasm for United and the game in general was infectious.

Then we moved to Alsager, a few miles from Crewe, and dad made a schoolboy error. The trips to United continued, but he decided to fill a blank Saturday with a visit to Gresty Road, and everything changed. Before that Crewe had meant shopping trips and the occasional film at the Odeon on Market Square. Division Four didn't exist in my football world, and Crewe Alexandra was just a name mentioned by the posh bloke who read out the scores on BBC1 at five o'clock on Saturday afternoons. So it was like a different world when I pushed through that stiff Popside turnstile for the first time. There were just a few crumbling steps to climb, no corporate boxes and just the one tea bar at the back of the terrace. The masses became a few thousand, we watched from pitch level and I didn't know any of the players. We'd swapped Harrods's for the corner shop, downgraded in one fell swoop.

I won't recall my first game, all misty-eyed and emotional, because I can't remember it, or who the opponents were. I'm sure we bought a programme, as dad did at most games he attended, but it's probably sat alongside many others picked up at car boot sales and bought via the Internet over the years. So I can't be sure, and the exact starting point of my Alex obsession is vague. I just remember seeing the tiny ground, decrepit in places, everything seemingly in miniature compared to my usual high-rise matchday experience. There were no snaking queues, everyone had space to move and breathe, and you could hear the referee and obscene shouts from the other side of the ground, instead of a dull rumble that made Old Trafford vibrate.

I'd seen tiny kids carrying milk crates and stools onto the huge Stretford End terrace. They used anything to gain the extra inches to see the game through armpits and over shoulders. At Crewe there was no need. There was no crush or fighting for spaces, and you didn't need to crane your neck around hulking bodies. There was plenty of room for a couple of deckchairs if you really wanted. There was no crescendo of noise as the players took to the field, or scenes of hysteria on the final whistle. But I loved it, all of it. The intimacy was far removed from the vastness of United's stadium, and being able to get up close and personal with the players made it so real. Compared to the Lowry matchstick men I watched in Manchester, these guys were in full colour 3D, just a few feet away. I could almost touch them. They'd lean against the advertising boards during the warm-up, swap jokes with regulars on the terraces and sign autographs for eager kids. I was never fussed about the signatures initially, but being able to hear them shout instructions to each other was something completely new.

Before that, footballers only spoke on TV, fussing their styled hair and flashing pearly white teeth as they swatted the interviewer who fired banal post-match questions. Like stars of the silver screen, they were untouchable. At Old Trafford they were half a mile away. Here, at this place called Gresty Road, they were ordinary blokes, messy hair and bits of lunch stuck on their chin. Best of all, I could be part of it. That, and having the freedom to roam about the simple ground, across ramshackle paving slabs that masqueraded as terracing, was, without wanting to sound too daft, liberating.

So how did this temptress sink her claws in, luring me away from the mighty Manchester United? I don't think it happened over night, maybe across two or three seasons. Even then United's results were important to me, and dad always relayed the scores to fuel my interest. But stepping up to senior school, in my case Alsager Comprehensive, meant exposure to many new teams. Pencil cases sported various club colours, the first replica shirts were making an appearance, and we all bragged about knowing entire starting line-ups. There were lads from all over the area talking about Everton, Man City, Liverpool, Wolves, Stoke City and even Port Vale. Alsager was, after all, a Potteries commuter town.

Then, slowly but surely, a small band of young teenagers came together, recognising each other at the Alex ground, and realising that we all shared more than a passing interest in Crewe, despite showing allegiance to the bigger clubs when we were at school.

So the next step towards becoming a fully-fledged Alex fan was hopping on the train, sometimes the bus that connected Hanley and Crewe. It was easy, and that independence also felt good. We were unique, not part of a herd latched on to one of the top teams that only existed on television. So I found my place, I was up and running and the Alex was my team, something that I could call my own. That whole identity thing mattered to a kid keen to find his place in the grander scheme of things.

Looking back, even during those formative days, it was about the overall experience and not just the football. It was a group of lads thinking they were funny, expressing themselves and enjoying some time together. Girls were on the radar, but football always came first. If we weren't playing the game, on just about any patch of grass we could find, we chatted about it. Then on matchday we'd grab the 12.38pm train out of Alsager, knocking about the station when we arrived at Crewe, watching the flow of football traffic on the bustling platforms, playing the fruit machines, then on to Gresty Road to catch the stewards as they opened the turnstiles at 1.30pm. It was a challenge, being amongst the first into the ground.

There'd be ninety minutes until kick-off, but we'd watch the players warming up, practicing shots into the empty net. Sometimes they'd miss the goal (hard to believe, I know), so we'd retrieve the balls as they bounced along the cinders of the Railway End. Just getting that appreciative nod or wink from Peter Coyne, Mark Palios, Geoff Hunter or Dennis Nelson made our day. During the game we'd chat to workers from the railway that watched from over the wall, and if you looked up you'd see people on Rail House roof also catching the game for free. Theirs was perhaps the best vantage point in the town. It's no surprise that the club was always skint in those days!

Financial matters, however, were rarely on our mind. The football was a fun day out, a break from the norm, allowing us to put the day-to-day school lessons on the back burner. It was the late 1970s by now and big changes were afoot. Punks and New Romantics danced alongside the denim-clad rockers; the Conservatives were in power with Maggie Thatcher at the helm, and we had the first basic home computers.

Some things didn't change, and the Alex still finished near the bottom of Division Four. We didn't care, rarely checked a league table, just moaned about the result for an hour after the match as we grabbed chips and peppered mushy peas from the chippy at the top of Gresty Road, opposite the Royal Hotel.

Then, it was the train home. As thirteen-year-olds I suppose we didn't attract much attention from other clubs' supporters. Away games were not part of the deal just yet; we were considered too young to nip about the country without an adult. So it was Crewe and back for us, occasionally bumping into Stoke fans that arrived on the other platform as we rolled back into Alsager, usually around 6pm. Although trouble often flared up when opposing supporters met on stations and in town centres, we posed little threat to the Stoke lads. We got the occasional drunken remark, and if younger lads were tagged onto their group we'd sometimes finish our journey legging it down Station Road as they tried to impress the older blokes with their bravado. Luckily, we survived unscathed.

At Gresty Road it was the same. Pockets of trouble regularly broke out during matches, but it was never widespread disorder. We remained on the fringe, keen to be part of it alongside the older lads and men that should have known better. As impressionable kids I suppose we just slipped into the pack mentality that, ultimately, allowed football hooliganism to become rife throughout the English game. I remember the away fans being in the Railway End for some time, and then switching to the Gresty Road End when steel fencing was erected at many grounds in an attempt to contain some of the wanna-be hooligans.

Before the cages arrived, it wasn't uncommon to see fans from both sides leaping over the basic concrete barriers that separated them. There'd be a brief altercation, some scuffling and then calm when stewards and police pulled them apart. We didn't get dragged into the trouble, perhaps knocked about and swept along with the crowd if it happened near our spot. Sometimes there was no chance to get out of the way when the mob turned to run one way or the other. You often saw a few of the Alex 'leaders' belting along the top of the Popside, hunting down visiting fans who dared to infiltrate the home section, but it was usually handbags.

Outside the ground it was more likely to escalate, before the police could respond. When the boys in blue did arrive, you'd see the main culprits fleeing down Bedford Street, or cutting through Hewitt Street to get back onto Nantwich Road. By then the young lads from Alsager would be scoffing chips, excited to see the action unfold from a safe distance. When questioned at home, we'd always enjoyed a good game. There was never any mention of trouble for fear that our fortnightly pleasure would be stopped.

I sometimes wonder about young kids, taken along to games before they understand the rules, with no concept of rivalry or belonging. They just smile, laugh and clap along with mum or dad. Like religion, vegetarianism and schooling, assigning a football team can be something thrust upon a child, perhaps unfairly, but always with best intentions. When they are old enough, usually in the early teenage years, when that innocent kid forms opinions and begins to chart its own path, then the rebellion starts.

Football and allegiance to one club, however, is not something easily discarded. It's with you for life, a cross you have to bear. So I still have feelings for United, my first dalliance with the beautiful game. Not a bad place to start but, unlike many other kids, I switched my attentions to what most saw as a lesser club, a team that regularly propped up the other 91 professional sides. Re-election was an annual reality, although it meant little to me then. The trips to Gresty Road were something special; a secret shared with only a select few.

So that was that. For various reasons Mistress Alexandra took a hold of me, a pubescent still unsure of many things, but happy to follow a path that would take many fascinating twists and turns across the years. The journey was about to get very exciting...

CAREFREE YOUTH

The problem with football and other forms of entertainment is that they rarely come cheap. So finding the cash to feed my increasingly addictive habit was always a challenge, and some weeks it would split our small band of supporters if one or more couldn't find the price of a ticket. You'll be pleased to hear that this story isn't about to take a sinister turn, recalling a desperate period of crime that helped to support the obsession. No, I was a reasonably industrious kid and had money courtesy of a paper round as soon as the newsagent on Crewe Road (by the Lodge pub) would take me on. It was called Jones' then, later Cavendish, and the Hassall Road round did me fine.

I also earned a few quid at a tropical fish shop that operated out of Oakhanger, on the edge of Alsager as you headed towards Crewe. Some friends of the family ran the business, and within a couple of years there wasn't much that I couldn't tell you about guppies, cichlids, algae-feeding plecostomus or charcoal filtration systems. They were carefree days - no mortgage, no bills, and just the occasional exam to worry about. I was financially independent, certainly enough to get myself to most matches at Gresty Road. I was growing up, and I knew what mattered to me.

The season that saw my involvement with Mistress Alexandra blossom was, I suppose, my coming of age era. Still a boy, I considered myself a youth, an arrogant and opinionated phase in the years leading up to legal manhood. I was fourteen going on fifteen, with a little bum fluff on my chin. I even shaved once, without foam, to see if that would encourage some growth and give me the appearance of an older lad. It nearly took a layer of skin off my face!

Clothes, well, I didn't have all of the new clobber that constituted most teenagers wardrobes; that wasn't me. So I tweaked what I had to blend in alongside the slightly older footy lads who already sported branded trainers. They had the latest trendy jeans and jackets that were out of my reach, and not something my parents would entertain buying. Checking old photos, there was a nasty mish-mash of dated jeans, collared t-shirts with faded logos, dubious tank tops (looking back, a fashion disaster), a tracksuit jacket zipped to the top and, of course, the obligatory white sports socks. They were cool once.

Eventually, I wanted to look the part. So in addition to visiting Gresty Road, other free Saturdays were then spent in Crewe or Hanley shopping, having previously fought the parents and manufactured any excuse to avoid the weekly trek around the shops. In Crewe there was a decent selection of high street chains, plus *Posters*, an independent shop that also played plenty of cracking tunes while you browsed. A local guy, Albert, ran the boutique, and much of the clothing was out of my price range. There was a good vibe about the place, and without really knowing them I'd recognise a few faces from the Alex. The items I could afford meant a move away from the stereotypical football fan garb that I was happy to wear as a younger kid. The Alex scarf wrapped around my right wrist was long gone; football colours were now discreetly pinned to my collar in the form of a red, white and gold-trimmed badge – one of the classic round ones with a lion and a railway wheel.

The football Saturdays were certainly fun, and on a budget! It sounds such a cliché now, but the train, matchday ticket, a can of pop and some chips really did only cost a few quid. The demon drink was yet to consume us, admission to anything and everything was at junior rates, and you even had the chippy owner giving us the occasional freebie because we looked scrawny. Life was easy, with few responsibilities and no real concern that the Alex underperformed year in, year out. And yet that sense of belonging soon intensified and we all wanted more involvement. So by the end of the 1979-80 season, home games were a must and there was a hankering to start travelling away.

My big day on the road came with the first round of the FA Cup, a favourite with fans everywhere, including my dad. Getting to United away matches was never easy due to ticket allocations, plus he was a considerate man and knew that watching football every weekend would heap pressure on mum and the rest of our family. So when the Alex drew Altrincham in round one it ticked a few boxes. First, it was an easy drive to Moss Lane, as he knew the roads well and where to park near to the ground. Second, former United 'keeper Alex Stepney had joined Alty. Finally, a former United youth player, Peter Coyne, was now lining up for the Alex. It was perfect, and although I didn't get to sit with other Alex supporters on the official coaches I broke my away-day duck.

Seeing the Alex play away from Gresty Road was a big deal for me. It was discussed in great detail at school, the other lads incredulous that I was travelling to a cup-tie. They were jealous as I recall, disappointed that they couldn't tag along. None of their dads were particularly interested in the Alex or, in some cases, football. The result, however, was embarrassing; a limp 1-0 defeat in a match of few chances for our strikers. Losing to non-league opposition is never good, but with the Alex floundering at the bottom of Division Four for many seasons it gave credence to Altrincham's regular application to rise up into the Football League.

Dad's only stipulation about attending the match was that we stood with the home fans, a small concession I thought. This opened my eyes once more, as it was fascinating to hear other supporters criticising my team, picking fault with the manager's formation and suggesting that we should be turfed out of the league. Most amusing was the Crewe fans that stood to our right. For most of the first half they chanted 'Alex, Alex, Alex' when Alex Stepney was in goal at that end. He turned around a few times and applauded them. This gesture was then greeted with a mocking chorus of 'Arrrrgh!' from the Crewe enclosure. He looked baffled, and it took me a while to cotton on that it was just the usual Alex chant and nothing to do with him. Even dad thought that they must like him because of Crewe's links to United, in particular their famous 'keeper Harry Gregg who managed the Alex during my first seasons at Gresty Road. It was a lighter moment in an otherwise awful game for Crewe that saw pressure heaped on manager Tony Waddington.

The tail end of that campaign, another season of struggle, erratic results and regular defeats, saw us finish amongst the bottom teams yet again. I'd started to appreciate how serious the club's situation was, but the latter half of the season stood out for one reason - Bruce Grobbelaar, a goalkeeper signed around Christmas time, formerly of Vancouver Whitecaps. Other clubs had tried to sign the promising 'keeper, but failed due to passport and visa issues. For some reason the Alex gaffer pulled off a clever loan deal, assisted by the Crewe & Nantwich MP Gwyneth Dunwoody I later found out. The player's name and his Canadian club sounded exotic, and the new 'keeper started as he intended to go on – as an entertainer. If he wasn't dribbling out of the area or booting the ball into the stand, he was leant against one of his goalposts chatting to supporters. He wore a constant smile and was often seen meeting and greeting fans outside the ground leading up to a match, usually wearing a flash suit.

Then, when York City arrived at Gresty Road for the final match of that season, he surpassed himself. Perhaps the manager knew he was going, maybe Brucie had made his mind up and expected an offer from a major club. Whatever, with the Alex holding a 1-0 lead and awarded a penalty, the madcap 'keeper raced up the pitch to take the spot kick.

He scored, of course, and the ground erupted. It was hardly Argentina '78, but we threw a few bog rolls all the same, acquired from the train earlier that day. We'd never seen anything like it, and it just added to the magical experience that was slowly but surely consuming our young lives.

***

The following season didn't start well; I remember that because a bunch of older men were always moaning, berating the manager and players at every opportunity, and threatening to walk out at half-time. They never did, but took great delight shouting abuse until the final whistle. And they were not alone, as larger groups of fans had started chanting anti-club verses, their wrath aimed at the club's board of directors. That still meant little to us, but it was all part of the day as far as we were concerned, something we couldn't experience back in Alsager. I certainly didn't swear then, as my mum would have murdered me, washed my mouth out and stopped the weekly football. The colourful language was something we enjoyed on match days only.

There was unrest for several weeks during the 1980-81 season and I remember joining several hundred who piled onto the pitch after one game, all demanding chairman Norman Rowlinson's head. Wimbledon thrashed us 3-0, a real embarrassment to the club, its players and the supporters. I didn't have a clue what was going on, and that was probably true of 75% of the fans who screamed and shouted obscenities at the club hierarchy, banged on the advertising hoardings and waved banners painted with not particularly flattering slogans.

This was the *Rowlinson Out* era. It was the usual nonsense, and most pinned the blame for the club's woes on the chairman's shoulders. For a few weeks, as games neared the final whistle, calls for the supporters to go 'on the pitch' would intensify. The police and stewards had no chance of containing it, as fans lined up along the barriers ready to pile onto the playing surface. Other idiots like me followed, and life was made very uncomfortable for the directors who remained in and around the wooden seats of the main stand, looking on as their kingdom slowly fell apart.

Dad came along to a game during this uneasy phase and for some reason we ended up in the paddock, the strip of terrace directly below the seating. I'd never been there before and always saw it as the posh bit of the ground. Laughable, really, as the stand was shoddy and poorly maintained, but a few hundred red seats under cover gave the ground an air of respectability. And to be fair, it was proper terracing unlike the cracked three by two paving slabs across the pitch on the Popside.

Some of the comments thrown from the terraces that day, at the men in suits above, were, let's just say, rather unkind. I learnt a whole new vocabulary. According to one fella, he'd witnessed a bloke hurling an apple at the chairman the previous week away at Bury, the rogue piece of fruit hitting Mr Rowlinson on the head! Although I had no idea who the chairman was, it sounded hilarious at the time. I doubt he found it funny, and when further insults were traded that afternoon, I saw a particularly agitated man remonstrating with a large group of supporters near the centre of the stand.

'That's him. I wouldn't fancy his job at the moment,' my dad told me, pointing at a small man in a light grey suit.

Then a full-blown argument broke out and a few stewards raced to his assistance. Fingers were pointed and more abusive words exchanged, in both directions. Then everyone settled back to watch the match. It was fascinating, a microcosm of society rising up, reacting, voicing their collective opinion, before falling back in line. My dad tried to explain a few things to me at half-time, but it was still baffling to a young lad who understood little about the mechanics of football administration, boards of directors or politics. It was still just football to me, and the row was another exciting element of the day.

My birthday coincided perfectly with a home game the following week, against Halifax Town, with further calls for protest, but also a chance to meet some of the players. I went with the lads on the bus and managed to get a few autographs during the warm-up, plus a slap on the back from Ken Mulhearn, the new 'keeper who replaced the crazy Bruce Grobbelaar. That meant a lot to a kid, and I suppose we thought that our football days out made us pretty cool, certainly very different from our mates that stayed at home. And yet we were still star struck, in awe of the men who took to the field wearing scarlet Alex shirts, something we couldn't get our hands on.

We wanted our own heroes, players we could relate to and certainly not the ones on TV. The giant figure of Bob Scott, scary black mane of hair and all, was up there, but it was a wisp of a lad who started to attract my attention. Peter Coyne became a favourite not just because of his United connections, but because he had a knack in front of goal. Playing regular games for the school team, often against teams from Crewe, like Ruskin, gave me a whole new perspective on football. I understood about effort, and that some players didn't do a full shift. As a midfield dynamo – at least that's what I told myself – I was up and down the pitch, working hard. I also started to appreciate the finer details, and at Gresty Road I could see what some of the Alex players were trying to achieve on the pitch, with good running off the ball, some clever passes, making space and letting the ball do the work. Unfortunately, when you had a team made up of players past their sell-by dates, kids that didn't make it elsewhere and average, journeymen footballers, it's not hard to see why the Alex didn't gel.

So despite the team's shortcomings, I thought that Peter Coyne was a decent player who had a nose for goal. A few weeks after my birthday, the Alex played Hereford and I witnessed one of the best Crewe results in years – a thumping 5-0 win. Not only that, Coyne scored four in probably the most one-sided game I'd ever seen. As he turned to celebrate his fourth goal, a lad jumped over the Paddock wall and ran onto the pitch to hug him. Coyne became a cult hero amongst the supporters after that, and I was unbearable for weeks, telling my mates over and over that I'd always thought that he was a tremendous talent.

This period also marked the beginning of my programme obsession, but for a while I failed to appreciate the golden rules of being a collector. I often folded them, recorded notes about the players and scorers, and even tore out the pages with player photos to stick on my wardrobe. At the next home game I managed to grab Coyne's signature, hastily scribbled with thick marker pen on the cover of the programme. He was the centre of attention that day, called onto the pitch to mark the momentous occasion of an Alex player scoring four goals in one game. He was presented with a TV, still one of the most bizarre things I've seen before kick-off. Everyone applauded as the Alex striker struggled back down the tunnel with his prize, before a member of staff spared his blushes and took the set away before he gave himself a hernia.

That impressive goal haul was perhaps the highlight of an otherwise drab season. The only other distraction was another feather in the cap for Crewe supporters from Alsager. Tony Waddington was desperate to succeed at the Alex and used all of his contacts to bring half-decent players to the club. So when a Man United and Stoke legend signed around Christmas there was a real buzz about the place.

For us, it was additionally exciting because we knew the man - none other than Jimmy Greenhoff. Well, my mate Bizza knew him, later babysitting for his young kids. So by association we all knew the Alex striker and delighted in telling anyone who would listen. Greenhoff lived in the village, down by Alsager Mere, and we sometimes saw him jogging in his Alex tracksuit. In those days replica kits were like gold dust, so when Bizza rolled up wearing an Alex training top emblazoned with JG and the Bass beer logo we were green with envy. The official kit was so rare it almost caused a panic at the end of the season. The players saluted the fans on the final day and some tossed their shirts into the crowd. A few minutes later a sheepish Tannoy message asked supporters if they would return them to the club office, as they couldn't afford new ones. Somehow, I doubt that too many were handed back.

So as far as we were concerned, Greenhoff was the club's saviour. Promotion would be forthcoming and everyone from Alsager would be paraded around Crewe as heroes. It didn't quite work out like that. Jimmy scored four in eleven games, showed his class a few times, but was obviously playing out some of his final football days close to home, doing the gaffer a favour and earning a few quid. He was gone before the season ended and the Alex looked a sorry sight. We held local rivals Port Vale to a 0-0 draw on the last day in front of a decent crowd, but there were serious rumblings of discontent on the terraces. Worse still, Greenhoff went on to join the Vale. Suddenly, he was just someone my mate once knew.

In the tense summer of 1981, many inner city areas exploded when rioting, looting and anti-establishment demonstrations swept across the country. Crewe wasn't affected, but at the football club during the pre-season there was drama - off the pitch. Popular manager Tony Waddington was sacked during that summer and with it, many believed, went our chances of bringing better players to Gresty Road. There was outrage, something I hadn't witnessed in my short time as a supporter. Passion, aggression and pure frustration written over the faces of lads and men I stood alongside each week. So yet another manager stepped up, a chap called Arfon Griffiths. He was the fourth in my few short years as a fan, but it didn't mean much to me. A manager was just a manager. I didn't understand why something so simple caused so much fuss, but I was learning fast. I just wanted the new season to start.

THE GRADI YEARS

The crazy scenes before Tony Waddington's departure had a significant affect on me. I watched the local news with my parents, and there was a story developing at Crewe. After years of neglect, chaotic management and woeful results, the supporters had endured as much as they could take. I only witnessed this on match days, and towards the end of the Waddington era it seemed that the club was about to implode. But then I saw a feature on the BBC Northwest bulletin that asked if the club had a future. A reporter was at the ground, stood outside the main stand. It looked pathetic, flaky red paint, and advertising boards weathered to the point that you could hardly see the company names. The massive structure of Rail House filled the frame behind him, adding drama to his feature.

'Is this the end of the line for Crewe?' he asked, a railway cliché I'd hear countless times over the years.

It painted a depressing picture of life at the football club. That made me sit up and take notice. Things were much worse than I'd realised. All I knew was that I couldn't lose the Alex.

There was no in-depth book detailing the Crewe Alexandra history then, and I struggled getting newspaper snippets. I didn't know how previous seasons had played out, or that we'd had a few good years in the late 1960s. I just turned up to watch games, no comprehension of the turmoil behind the scenes.

Because of dad's childhood roots, each night after work he bought the *Manchester Evening News*, instead of the local *Evening Sentinel*, so I was lucky if the Alex got a few column inches in the sports section, usually when they played Wigan, Rochdale or Bury. The commentary was derogatory and it was obvious that my club was seen as a joke. That hurt, and it was then that I knew my supporting involvement needed to go up a notch. I started buying a copy of the *Crewe Chronicle* each week, sometimes getting a freebie because I still worked at the newsagents. The first clippings were squirreled away in an archive that would grow extensively as I craved more and more information about the club.

Suddenly those obscure statistics mattered. Attendances, goals scored and league positions became important. The increased numbers at certain matches also made sense - against Vale, Wrexham, Chester and Shrewsbury. The whole tribal/rivalry thing became clear. Gresty Road was our patch, no matter how scruffy it was.

Memories can be a funny old box of tricks, and it's easy to look back, reminisce and exaggerate things. But let's face it, the Alex ground in the early 1980s was atrocious - a mish-mash of crooked stands, uneven terraces, paddocks and cinder banks that wouldn't last two minutes in today's health and safety mad society.

The Railway End was an embarrassment, with a few token barriers to give weary supporters somewhere to lean, at least stopping them falling asleep. The gents' toilet was, quite simply, a painted wall with a trough to carry away unwanted fluids. You could peer over the wall to the railway lines, or swivel your head and catch the action on the pitch if the crowd got excited. If it wasn't a high-profile match (not many were) and the stewards were distracted, you could nip into the paddock from the corner of the Railway End, grab a drink in the tea bar and sometimes sneak up the wooden steps to the seats. That was decadence!

On the other side the Popside provided shelter, but not much else. Supporters had their own spot, dotted about the terrace, holding the same place alongside their mates for years, although the more vocal fans would swap ends at half-time to see the Alex goals banged in - often wishful thinking!

We scored a couple at home to Sheffield United at the tail end of the 1982-83 season, but still lost the match. The whole miserable experience left a sour taste in the mouth. The Blades brought abject embarrassment when the home fans were herded into the Gresty Road End to accommodate the Yorkshire invasion en route to promotion. They filled both the Railway End and the Popside, with supporters also scattered across the seats and Paddock of the main stand. Can you imagine that happening at many other grounds? No, and worse still we didn't fill the Gresty End that day, such was the despondency amongst supporters.

A further kick in the balls saw several Sheffield fans running though our supporters just after half-time. I never wanted to be wholeheartedly involved in any trouble, but the lads around you become an extended family and I felt real anger that day. The older lads did react and the sheer volume of United fans milling around Nantwich Road that late afternoon ensured that the police were kept busy deep into the evening.

That season ended with three depressing defeats and yet another application for re-election. By now I was fully aware of the implications, and waiting on news of our fate was an awful experience. Dad eventually relayed the details when he heard the announcement on a Radio Two sports bulletin. We survived, by the skin of our teeth. Some of the other clubs who voted seemed to have a soft spot for Crewe. Also, being a major junction for several rail lines made visiting Gresty Road an easy trip for most clubs. That must have been a factor, especially when Barrow, Workington and Southport were voted out, all of them a nightmare journey from anywhere south of Birmingham.

Still, the annual lottery was a vicious circle, and I was sucked into the relentless spin cycle. It had to stop and I wanted to play my part. So I went to every game after that, hoping that things would change, singing ever louder, tagged on to the Popside pack that made the noise and competed with the lads from the Paddock. It was the driving force of my week by now, schoolwork always completed but the last thing on my mind. Finishing in the bottom places of Division Four concerned me more, and it happened again the next season. This time Peter Morris got the axe, another in a long line of failed managers who passed through before he could get his feet under the table. It was hardly worth fixing their nameplates to the door, and the daily taunts at school intensified as the years went by. If nothing else, it was character building following the Alex.

***

Enter the Italian, a complete unknown.

'Who the hell is Dario Gradi?' a lad at school asked me when news broke of another managerial appointment at Gresty Road.

'You want me to speak to my old man?' he added. 'He's a carpenter. He could fit you some revolving doors at that club of yours.'

Another day, another jibe that I filed away, ever hopeful that eventually I might give the Stoke, United and Liverpool fans some back, perhaps in the distant future. We had no idea who Gradi was. He was a young man, certainly younger than many of our recent managers. He'd coached in and around London for several years, at a few different clubs. So why did he want to come up to Crewe? None of us got carried away by the new appointment, but dutifully attended the first match of the new season – a dreary 1-0 defeat at Rochdale. Something had changed; but nothing had really changed, that's how it felt. It was another cosmetic exercise to appease the disgruntled supporters.

Anyway, this new fella disappointed me from day one. Not because of the expected poor start away at Spotland, a ground substantially worse than Gresty Road in those days. That was industrial grey kind of grim, and Fred Dibnah should have been commissioned to blow up Rochdale's tumbledown shack. No, Dario Gradi ruffled my feathers for a reason much more personal than that. As the new school term started the football also began, and we got wind of a visit from an Alex scout who would be watching one of our early school team games.

In the event, it wasn't Gradi lurking amongst proud parents on the touchline, and we never did find out who came to assess us from the sidelines. However, after eighty odd minutes of a match that was - for schoolboy football - uncharacteristically even and goalless, we snatched a late winner following a crafty through ball from yours truly. I saw myself as a playmaker, a box-to-box midfielder with a good engine, comfortable on the ball and not scared of a challenge. How on earth did I ever slip through the net? The Alex scout obviously wasn't too impressed, as a few days later just one of our team was invited over to Crewe for a trial - the striker, the lad who'd knocked the goal in, from about six yards. I don't think he'd touched the ball before that.

So my impression of the Alex scouting system in 1983 wasn't good. To be fair to the Italian maestro, subsequent years of youth development and plucking rough diamonds from the non-league would vindicate his methods. Still, I've never forgiven him, and as Gradi's first season played out we all wondered when, not if, chopper Rowlinson would wield the managerial axe. Amazingly, it never happened.

Playing the game myself, by now I thought that I understood the finer things about football and became increasingly vocal from the Popside terrace. I'd like to think that my comments added a little balance to the general moaning that trickled steadily from a few of the older guys who stood around me. I'd lambaste sloppy passes from midfield, despair when defenders backed out of tackles and hold my head in utter disbelief when the strikers fired high and wide. But I thought it was constructive criticism. It dawned on me that Crewe Alexandra had a mountain to climb. It was blatantly obvious why we finished at the wrong end of the table every season. So it was heartening to see a newfound enthusiasm on the sidelines by the dugouts. I quite fancied transferring to the Paddock, to get closer to the gaffer and his coaches. I wanted to see how he ran the team and why we didn't get the results every supporter craved.

Thankfully, things started to change. The new manager brought in a few players and seemed to get the best out of them. It wasn't an overnight transformation, but there was a noticeable difference. We got a serious tanking in the away leg of the League Cup, losing 8-1 at Queens Park Rangers. That was expected; so few tears were shed when I heard the score on the evening news. Back at Gresty Road in the return leg, we enjoyed a rare treat; the Alex beat the Londoners 3-0, with a hat-trick from Dave Pullar, one of Dario Gradi's new signings. So there was growing belief that the man knew what he was doing.

That season, because I attended more games, a number of Alex fans started to look familiar. We didn't swap names, but accepted each other as members of an extended family, a tenuous third-cousin-removed kind of relationship. That, I have always thought, is part of football's appeal. You can be anonymous, part of a collective without signing up, never committing yourself to others. The common bond is the club, and they take your money whether they know you or not. Free to come and go as I pleased, I felt much closer to the Alex scene. Mistress Alexandra had accepted me, and suddenly I was watching a team that didn't lose quite so often.

There were also changes to the pre-match ritual during this period. If I claimed that drinking and football didn't come hand in hand during my seventeenth year, well, I'd be lying. Several pubs served us while we still wore the black blazers of Alsager Comprehensive, so in the more casual attire of the lower sixth form most establishments were happy to offer us alcohol. This inevitably extended to our schedule on Saturdays. Now, instead of waiting patiently on the platform, we enjoyed a quick pint of lager alongside the Stoke fans in the pub. They still dismissed us as big kids. We were, I suppose, but joining that adult drinking culture filled in the gaps of our evolving lifestyle.

In Crewe, it wasn't always quite so easy getting served. The Nantwich Road pubs were strict, and none of us could muster a decent fake ID badge. So we often stayed at the bar on platform six of the station. Mixed with other football supporters changing trains, I suppose being associated with grown men travelling up and down the country convinced those serving that we were old enough. So yet more of the innocence disappeared, we didn't get into the ground early, and standing on the terrace no longer meant enduring the stench of beer and fags. We just didn't notice it any more, as our clothes also smelt like a back street boozer. My mum was aghast. Dad wasn't a big drinker, but I think he knew that I'd progressed to the next phase of supporting my team.

PART OF THE PACK

Things had definitely improved at Gresty Road, but the jury was still out going into Gradi's second season. Some of the diehard fans were tough nuts to crack, and few read too much into a half-decent first campaign that ended with a respectable 16th position. For once, we didn't apply for re-election. There were no protests on the pitch and the usual suspects turned out for the first few games with a smirk on their faces. A full-blown smile was asking far too much. I was just glad to see the football back. A few summer jobs allowed me to save some extra cash, and I started working at a local bar – the Mill Hotel, off Crewe Road. Most of the lads had part-time work, so this meant that away days were possible - usually on the train.

In the league there was a mixed bag of results in the opening months, with unexpected wins and equally baffling defeats. A couple of younger lads had joined us, Higgy and Fletch, the next generation of supporters who chose the Alex ahead of Stoke and other bigger clubs. We travelled to Tranmere and watched the team taken apart on the field, and then received a similar offer in a pub after the match. We declined and were just grateful to escape in one piece.

Mansfield away was the complete reverse. It was another easy train journey for Dave, Bizza and myself, direct to Nottingham, then a change to get to the Field Mill ground. We won the match, enjoyed a few pubs near their ground and took part in a pool tournament just before kick-off. Dave made the final and was narrowly beaten by one of the locals, so the landlord invited us back after the match for sandwiches and beers. We got lucky and everything fell into place. About one hundred Crewe fans stood with us that day, but our next adventure to nearby Port Vale saw numbers swell to well over a thousand.

The trip to Vale Park represented my first big derby match, something we discussed at length with the more civil Stoke fans back at the pub on the Friday night. They despised their Potteries neighbours and recounted many tales of clashes between supporters at both grounds. My mate Bizza had been to a few Alex-Vale encounters with his dad and confirmed they were lively affairs. So on the Saturday morning I slipped a couple of magazines under my shirt as extra padding, and put my footy shin pads on just in case. I even borrowed a spare pair of Dave's Doc Marten boots. I must have looked like junior Robocop!

Although we disliked Stoke back then, they weren't particularly fussed with little old Crewe. So two of the City lads from the pub decided to join us that day as we hopped on the Burslem-bound platform. They were more interested in taunting Vale and seeing them lose, but it was amusing having them along for the ride.

It was probably the best train journey we made from Alsager. We timed it to arrive at around 2pm, and so had around 500 other Alex fans! Our Stokie mates from sixth form couldn't believe their eyes as the packed train made its first stop since leaving Crewe. We were part of an army. You could hear the singing long before the carriages came to a halt, fists thumping on the windows in appreciation as we applauded the train in. There was no chance of a seat. There were that many people on board that we were lucky to squeeze into the rammed carriages at all. The inspector had no chance getting down the aisle to sell or check tickets, so we saved a couple of quid as well.

At Burslem, there was a massive police presence ready for the train. Heading into the town for a few beers was out of the question. Instead, after a few barked orders from the most official looking officer, they marched us off towards Vale Park. The Alex chants started as soon as the escort made its way up the hill towards the ground, and police dogs kept other pedestrians and a few Vale fans well clear of the marching group.

Then we came to a junction with the main road. Bizza and I were at the front by now, in full flow and loving the songs that shattered the silence around the terraced streets. We helped a couple of Crewe lads unfurl a banner and carried one end so that it stretched across the road. Then a couple of Vale lads yelled out and gave us the finger, so we both happily returned the gesture. The traffic had been halted to get us clear of the area, and in the car stopped directly in front of the raucous mob were Bizza's mum and dad, on their way to Hanley. There was a wry smile on his dad's face, someone who had obviously been there years before as a young fan himself. His mother, however, was in a state of shock. She didn't look impressed. We moved on, fully aware that we'd been clocked. It was something to sort out later, after the match.

The day was only ruined by the result, a 2-0 defeat, but I didn't need the magazines or shin pads. The Vale fans went home happy; we had a laugh on the train and a few jars in the pub back in Alsager. I went home with Bizza later that evening, as moral support when he faced his mother. So I kept the padding on, just in case she went crazy. We had been part of the Alex pack, but now our tails were firmly between our legs!

***

Losing to the Vale was disappointing, but there were victories over other local rivals like Stockport, Chester and Wrexham during the first third of the season. That lifted everyone, but the Alex supporters craved some real excitement now that we seemed to have stabilised under the new manager. Burnley ditched us out of the League Cup in the second round, so all eyes moved to the FA Cup later in November, that holy grail that rarely saw the Alex get past the first hurdle. So when Northwich Victoria came out of the first round hat everyone was delighted. It was easy pickings and a short trip across Cheshire for the fans that drove over to the game, but a convoluted rail route for the trio that travelled from Alsager.

We got there, eventually, and Northwich's Drill Field claimed to be the oldest football ground in the world, and it certainly looked it.

With such a boast, I half expected some quaint medieval structure that once accommodated jousting and longbow tournaments. Instead, after a lengthy trek from the station, tucked alongside the River Dane we found an odd assortment of half-hearted stands, patchy terraces and grassy banks. Northwich was about one third the size of Crewe, and its football club had never progressed beyond the feeder divisions. League football was a million miles away. This should have been like taking candy from a baby!

That's what the massive Alex contingent thought, many of them drunk and enjoying being able to dominate a smaller town. Some went overboard that afternoon, and took things too far. The mob from Crewe caused plenty of trouble throughout the centre. Northwich, however, had its rough element, and for the cup game it was obvious that lads who normally followed Man City, Man United, Everton and Liverpool had decided to join their mates to take on the Alex. It boosted the numbers, and inside the tiny ground it looked like a swollen river about to burst its banks.

It didn't help that the visitors decided to stand in all areas of the ground. Some had cans of ale tucked under their coats, and the smell of alcohol was strong throughout the game. There was friction from kick-off, and the police were just happy to keep things contained and for the match to go ahead without any problems. Unfortunately, the crowd was bigger than expected and getting increasingly hostile as the game progressed. Things got a whole lot worse when Northwich took the lead and Alex fans realised that an upset was on the cards. While they celebrated the first serious altercations took place.

Barriers were kicked, the back of the stand took a battering as some Alex lads tried to break out, and several objects were thrown on the pitch. It wasn't much at first, just alcohol, frustration and excessive numbers resulting in the inevitable outbreaks of trouble. But when the non-league side took a 3-1 lead, with an impromptu flash of his arse from the Northwich scorer, the terrace exploded. Some of the hoarding in the corner gave way and bodies toppled like dominoes. Missiles were thrown across the fences, by both sets of fans. An older man who was stood directly in front of us suddenly grabbed his head. Seconds later a trickle of blood ran down past his ear, and onto his collar. A coin had sliced into his scalp, hurtling through the air from an unknown assailant, just a few yards from us.

There was fear, excitement and anger. Even the most passive supporter would have reacted, and there was a rush towards the barrier that divided the two sets of supporters. We were swept along, driven down the steps as several hundred Alex fans bayed for blood and dished out their own justice. Some of them spat into the air as they fired a volley of abuse past increasingly worried police officers. They had genuine terror in their eyes, just a helmet and truncheon to protect them from the agitated mob.

Things took a turn for the worse as some Crewe fans started pulling at the railings, so the officers stepped back to allow the dog handlers onto the terrace. That caused mass panic; dogs howling and straining at their leashes. The gates were opened and the Crewe section quickly started to clear into the streets.

The game was lost. There was disbelief and rage. Cars in the nearby parking spaces were kicked and punched. A large group of Alex fans congregated by one of the Northwich exits, a welcoming committee with no intention of swapping pleasantries. It was pitch black but for the pool of light provided by the basic floodlights and a handful of street lamps. Shadows darted in and out as the final whistle sounded, and then the masses poured out of the ground, half of them ecstatic, the rest livid, gutted and deflated.

Around 500 Alex fans had arrived by train and the police were keen to get them out of Northwich and back to Crewe - as quickly as possible. That was like herding cats. Most were hacked off with the result but wanted a beer in the town centre, and others wanted a scrap. They were going nowhere, and their resistance added to the mayhem. Fans dashed across the car parks, some tried to get to the coaches and cars, while some started to swap insults with the Northwich fans that took great pleasure winding us up.

The coaches took the hit first, as a shower of car park gravel rained down on the roofs. It was retaliation for the havoc caused earlier in the day. I remember plenty of young faces peering out of the windows into the gloom, looking terrified as aggressive Northwich fans banged in celebration on the flimsy metal panels. I didn't see any of the windows go in, but I did hear breaking glass a few seconds later. It was possibly part of the Northwich clubhouse, more random acts of destruction by aggrieved Alex fans, but we were gone, making our way back to the station. Some supporters broke away from the main group, legitimately trying to get to cars parked elsewhere in the town; others were intent of clashing with the Northwich boys.

There were no hiding places. First there was a chase over the bridge and I wondered if someone would end up in the river below. Then skirmishes carried on along the main road. It was a stop-start walk back into the town, constantly looking over our shoulders. Groups of Northwich and Crewe lads were everywhere, and in the darkness it was hard to make out friendly faces. By the cinema in the centre it was much worse, nasty one-to-ones and running battles that the police seemed unable to contain. It was mayhem, and one lad was hit by a van as he staggered into the road.

There was a train waiting on the platform, probably held back on police instructions. So we piled on, filling the carriages in seconds. It pulled away soon after, with a large group to the side of the station giving us a one-fingered send off. My heart was in my mouth as I heard that first window break, a thousand pieces scattering into the carriage before anyone could react. Another went a few seats away, the half-brick bouncing away down the aisle. The driver hit the brakes and two police vans screeched to a halt on the road, blue lights flashing and sirens wailing. A dozen officers chased a group of youths down the side street, but their efforts were futile. The younger legs were long gone, already hidden in the streets behind houses and businesses.

This wasn't back to square one, but the high expectations of two thousand Crewe fans had been dashed. I remember the first rumblings of discontent, that Dario Gradi obviously wasn't all he was cracked up to be. One lad in the seats behind us suggested that the manager would be chopped on Monday morning, as losing to non-league teams was no longer acceptable. I didn't have an opinion about the manager then; he'd done okay. But we'd lost a cup match to a tiny club who would forever remind us of their victory. It was a lousy feeling as the damaged train limped away into the night. Perhaps two hours later we got home, and all three of us were subdued as we popped into the pub for a pint. That was a big mistake, as our Stokie friends were already there and ready with the Mickey taking. They'd lost 4-0 to Everton that day, but the Toffees were leading Division One at the time. That was bearable; our defeat made us the laughing stock once again!

CALL OF DUTY

At eighteen, my life was a mix of further education, football, then out and about on Friday and Saturday nights, girls and beer thrown into the mix. It was a great time, and far too easy. However, the big wide world was calling. I had to make decisions, and there were plenty of choices when you left school in South Cheshire, whether at sixteen or eighteen.

Nearby we had *Radda* (Radway Green Ordnance factory), which offered technical and engineering apprenticeships. Otherwise, there was *Royce's* (Rolls-Royce, latterly Bentley Motors) or *The Works* (the then sprawling railway industry dotted around the town) in Crewe. If you chose further education instead, you went to sixth form or Dane Bank College. Beyond that, it was life as a tax-dodging student at university or a weekly pay packet doing whatever you could get.

I chose none of the above. After years of building my support for the Alex, becoming independent enough to attend home and away games, I decided to see the world with the Royal Navy. It was the first of many ridiculous decisions I'd make across my life. I had provisional university places at Liverpool and Birmingham, both perfect for travelling to Gresty Road and almost anywhere around the country. Instead, I went into the Armed Forces careers office in Hanley, chatted to a Lieutenant Commander with a magnificent moustache, and then signed on the dotted line. It was that quick. A life-changing decision made on a whim. Mum wasn't impressed. Getting to Crewe games would become a momentous challenge, especially as I would spend the first phase of my new career at the Naval College in Dartmouth, down on the south coast. I couldn't have moved much further away if I'd tried!

Absence makes the heart grow fonder, another old cliché but pretty damn apt after a few weeks of basic training. I was homesick, for sure, but knowing that an Alex game was taking place without me stood on the Popside was painful. It felt as though something had been chopped off. There was no Internet back then, no mobile phones and no copies of the *Crewe Chronicle* in the local paper shop. I was marooned, and for several weeks I hardly heard any football snippets. It was as though they wanted to drum the life out of you, create a robot that cared little for anything other than official duties. All I had was a crumpled fixture list cut from the paper and tucked into my bag before I left home.

So this was a transitional period of my life, and for a couple of years my relationship with the Alex was, to say the least, strained. Life is all about choices, and you sometimes look back wondering if you took the right turn. The girlfriend from sixth form ditched me, seeing no sense in prolonging a relationship that was doomed to fail because of the distance. So I got a *Dear John* letter before I even started my training! I think her mother influenced her, but she was probably right. I was more concerned about Mistress Alexandra; what would she think of me running away with bell-bottomed sailors? Still, I have no major regrets, as a few years in the Royal Navy taught me a lot. I just missed the Alex like a long lost friend.

The first contact with civilization and, crucially, how the Alex were doing came after basic training, when rules and regulations were relaxed. Sat huddled around an old TV in the shared living space became a Saturday afternoon ritual during my incarceration. That and a crackly radio was the only source of communication with the world beyond the college walls. We had so little time, and perhaps once a week you could go into the town of Dartmouth itself. It's funny, but I was seriously concerned that my disappearance from Gresty Road would have a detrimental effect on the noise generated from the terraces. I'd found my voice in the previous seasons and wasn't scared to pitch in with the long-standing lads who had led the chants since I started following the club. I knew a few names, the knowing nod was forthcoming from fans I saw most weeks, and although I hadn't lived in Crewe I'd started to feel part of the whole scene. So travelling down to the south coast was a wrench. Not seeing the Alex started to contribute to the growing feeling that I'd made a serious mistake joining the navy.

Luckily, you meet some decent people in the forces and make friends for life. One of my comrades, Karl, from Coventry, felt the same about football, and missed his team just the same. We were first to the TV on Saturdays as the BBC's Final Score programme began, eventually joined by about ten more who wanted to see the day's results. There were others, strange blokes that had no interest in footy, and if we weren't quick enough they'd be in position watching all manner of nonsense, usually on video. Then we'd be forced to grab the radio as the scores were revealed by one of the most recognised voices in broadcasting. The room soon cleared after James Alexander Gordon (a man with a near-perfect middle name) completed the top two divisions, but I'd stay rooted to the spot until the results had concluded with the dregs of the English game. It wasn't fun seeing my side floundering near the foot of the division, and Armed Forces ribbing soon kicked in. If nothing else, that harsh male environment ensured that I grew a thick skin to deal with any Alex-related insults that came my way.

A couple of months into my navy stint I got my first pass home, a chance to see the family and of course a match. So I made sure the weekend coincided with a home game, and that turned out to be Halifax. The training regime at Dartmouth was intense, a mix of serious physical workouts and upwards of eight hours in the classroom. So falling asleep during lessons, immediately after meals and certainly no later than 9pm was the norm. So on that first trip back home it was no surprise that I missed my stop. I woke up at Liverpool Lime Street and sheepishly got back on the next service to Crewe. The guard had seen it a million times, and coupled with my navy kit bag he waved me through without any extra ticket charges.

The Alex drew 2-2 against Halifax, memorable for the woeful attendance of less than 1,500 and a goal by David Platt. He arrived in the latter half of the previous season and showed early promise. He was another ex-United youth player, so dad also came along to check him out that day. I suppose Platty was the player I wanted to be, creative in midfield and with a nose for goal. During the game I watched him intently, analysing his movement and economical running off the ball. He'd dropped from the top of the English game to Crewe, and I wondered how he felt about that. Was he happy to get a new team, or just passing through? I was impressed that Dario Gradi had picked up such an obvious talent and I now wanted to see a stable team develop. I returned to Dartmouth with a few fancy tricks to deploy in my next training session. Sadly, I couldn't equal Mr Platt's high standards!

There were limited opportunities to get home over the next few months and it was a frustrating season that resulted in me seeing just six or seven games, most of them a draw or defeat for the Alex! When that happens, you start wondering if you're the jinx, a bad luck charm who should stay away completely. I think all supporters go through such barmy emotions at some point, and then run through ridiculous superstitious ideas to break the sequence of bad luck.

Ultimately, 1985-86 was bearable because of two fixtures that I could have reached by push bike. Torquay away was a sinch. I introduced fellow trainees Karl and Duncan to Crewe Alexandra that fresh spring afternoon, a gorgeous day that saw us catch a bus along the coast, past Brixham and Paignton before arriving at the English Riviera town of Torquay. The lads even agreed to stand with the Crewe fans, although finding them was another matter! I'd say there were thirty that day, just one official coach that wasn't full. That was no disgrace as the overall attendance was the lowest I had ever seen. Duncan and Karl were amazed that a professional football match could attract fewer than 1,000 spectators. There were 850; I know this because I counted them and scribbled the unbelievable figure on the back of my matchday programme. There wasn't much else to write home about. It was a tedious 0-0 draw; a game when counting the crowd was the perfect distraction. We played okay but couldn't find the net. It was also an off day for Platty, so after hours of building him up my navy mates couldn't understand what all the fuss was about. Man United were, they said, well rid of him.

Thankfully, there was something to cheer about at the penultimate game of the season. The lads who joined me at Torquay were intrigued and wondered if the Alex would ever score, and if the crowd could be any lower than last time. So we caught the train to Exeter, an easy trip from Dartmouth. Duncan was a West Ham fan, Karl a regular at Coventry. So it was no surprise that they poured scorn on the shoddy facilities at the lower league grounds they saw that season. I didn't care. It was another rare chance to see the Alex playing. I would have watched them kick about on a car park if nothing else was on offer. So we stood on the terrace alongside another coach load from Crewe, only a few of the faces familiar to me. Platty didn't score, but Gary Blissett and Chris Cutler did, and it finished 2-1 to the Alex. The bulk of the 1,700 crowd went home unhappy, as Exeter were not safe from the spectre of re-election. The Alex sat comfortably in mid-table, but I was feeling strangely detached from the club I'd spent so long supporting.

***

The following season saw me move around with the navy. Sadly, there was no base in Crewe, or anywhere near home for that matter. Most of my assignments were along the south coast. There was a bit of time at sea, some training at the Culdrose Air Base on the tip of Cornwall (a lengthy trek home, I can tell you), Portsmouth and even Plymouth. So my attendance at Crewe games was sporadic. I followed the results and received clippings through the post, but it wasn't the same. It was like losing a friend, a very good friend. I didn't know how the relationship could ever get back on track. There was no football counsellor to advise, just a rough-arse colour sergeant who sent me jogging around the parade ground in full military kit when he caught me chatting about the weekend results.

There was an additional headache for the clubs in Division Four this season. Automatic relegation from the Football League was introduced, something that would have given Alex managers nightmares five years earlier. Now, there was genuine belief that we were a much-improved club that shouldn't be sweating on the final few results. Sadly, too many points were lost on our travels and although we sat above the drop zone, in the final weeks we were far too close for comfort.

It was a largely unspectacular season as I watched from afar. Crowds were down, hovering dangerously around the 1,400 mark for many games. There wasn't much consistency on the pitch, and coupled with a tough economic climate many Alex fans voted with their feet.

The penultimate match, at home to Burnley, was on my list long before it became a must-win game. I had just finished a course at the air station, so I booked a few days off. On the day of the match, I headed to Penzance station early in the morning so that I'd arrive in Crewe around lunchtime. I was meeting mum and dad for something to eat, watching the game later and then staying over in Alsager for a couple of days. That was the plan.

Unfortunately, my train was delayed, and at 11.30am it became apparent that all services had run into trouble. There'd been a signalling failure and nothing was moving. An hour later I gave up, totally hacked off. There was no chance of getting back for the football, so I cancelled the trip completely. When I spoke to mum she couldn't understand why I didn't just come back home anyway. I was so wrapped up in the football disappointment that I didn't consider their feelings. As a thoughtful son, I fell well short of the mark.

So I missed a 1-0 win, a vital three points that lifted us clear of the dreaded solitary relegation place. That was fantastic, but Platty scored and I wasn't there. He'd been on a great run towards the end of the season, and each goal was tucked away while I scratched around for updates a few hundred miles away. At least the final game on the season was down on south coast, and Torquay in the May sunshine was an opportunity for Alex fans to let their hair down without fear of relegation. It was a cliffhanger for the home fans, as they needed the points to stay in the league. For both reasons, a big crowd was expected, and Karl, Duncan and another ten of the navy fellas signed up for the trip as soon as I told them how important the fixture was.

The weather that final weekend was amazing, and we got to Torquay early to soak up the atmosphere and enjoy a few drinks along the front. Even I was taken aback when we rolled into town just before midday. It was wall-to-wall Alex. Some old faces I remembered from my early teens were there, fellas I'd stood with on the Popside, families and friends making it a holiday weekend. It was only disappointing because I wasn't going to stand with Alex supporters during the game. The Royal Navy posse took a collective vote and decided to join the home fans. I protested, but as three of the group were Devon boys I suppose it was fair enough. All for one and one for all, or something like that. Still, the Alex badge was worn with pride, carefully tucked under my shirt collar.

It was also unusual to be stood amongst thirteen young men, perhaps ten of them not really interested in football. There were rugby lads, rowers and a couple of hockey players. Whatever floats your boat,

I suppose. They didn't get the whole football thing, but as we made our way onto the packed terrace their attitudes changed. The sun was shining, flags and air horns made it a carnival atmosphere, and the anticipation amongst the other supporters was infectious. They warmed to the occasion, and as a number of Alex fans were already stood alongside us on the home terrace, the navy boys all decided to back my team.

Because the stewards and police didn't bother trying to segregate the crowd, the first confrontations occurred minutes after the match kicked off. There were scuffles throughout the game, something that amused Duncan no end. He fancied joining in, for the hell of it. He was a decent boxer, a bit of a rough diamond come good. I talked him out of that, as it wouldn't look good on his navy record if he was rounded up. I also had serious concerns. Would I be guilty by association, banned from Alex games forever?

Duncan, a Londoner from the East End, thought the trouble was handbags at best. He had stories that would make anyone's toes curl. We sparred a few times during physical training sessions at Dartmouth and he wiped the floor with me. I got knocked down one afternoon and the Physical Training Instructor was typically sympathetic.

'Hornbrook, get your sorry arse off the floor. This is the hard knocks of life. Man up!' was the gist of his tirade.

It was simple: Duncan took violence to a much higher level than me. I punched and foolishly tried to stick to the Queensbury Rules. Duncan was ruthless. He'd hit low and trade blows when the bell went. The PTI laughed it off and told me to get on with it. So I did, and got knocked down again. I realised then that if I was a similar size and equal level of fitness, then the rest was in the mind. So the next time we sparred I raised my game and stood toe-to-toe, fighting fire with fire. Duncan loved it, we battered each other and the sadistic PTI was delighted. I wasn't knocked over again, but Duncan was always on top. He had a nasty edge that I couldn't reproduce. After all, I'd grown up in a small pond where the fish played nice. He'd swum with sharks all his life.

At football grounds around the country I have seen similar situations when supporters fall out. Smaller clubs are rarely on equal terms with the big city boys. Not because the numbers are greater, but because the levels of violence dished out by some are just too extreme for others to deal with. There are the odd exceptions, but lads from Crewe who think they're hard wouldn't stand a chance with kids who have grown up on the tough streets of Manchester. Similarly, those who think that Manchester, Liverpool and Birmingham have some of the toughest estates need to spend a few days around some of London's worst areas. Basically, there's always a bigger fish, prepared to go that one scary step further. Fists become bottles and bricks. Instead of ending with a punch, some think nothing of a stamp to the head when their opponent is already on the floor. Then knives and guns come into the equation. It's a horribly vicious circle.

So listening to Duncan was fascinating. Nothing fazed him. He pointed out a big lad from Torquay who seemed to be in charge of the local nutters. He was massive, wading through the crowd to pitch in if anything kicked off. Duncan wasn't impressed and picked fault with the fella's undisciplined and wild technique.

Eventually the police caught up with him, and Duncan and I stood about twenty yards away laughing our heads off. First, one constable asked the monster to follow him off the terrace. The naïve copper immediately had his helmet knocked off. So two more officers raced to his assistance and both were felled with one sweeping right hook. All three boys in blue then jumped on him, trying to drag him away. The big lad twisted and turned, trying to throw the policemen clear. They hung on, and for a few seconds it was like watching a windmill in action. They finally removed him when two more of their colleagues arrived, one with a particularly nasty German Shepherd that proved more than a match for the Torquay yob. The poor mutt took a kick to the head but returned the gesture by sinking its teeth into his leg.

It was a ding-dong match, with Torquay desperate for the points and the Alex actually trying to play football. The crowd made some decent noise, plenty of it coming from the Alex contingent in one of the corners. In fact, there were Crewe fans all over the ground. Every few minutes an argument seemed to break out, just pushing and shoving most of the time, occasionally getting a bit ugly.

Peter Bodak struck twice for the Alex and Torquay were on the brink. They grabbed a goal back, and then something bizarre happened that would prolong the match deep into injury time. It involved a dog again - another police dog! There were a few official mutts about that day, so I'm not sure if it was the same one that attacked the big Torquay fan twenty minutes earlier. Whatever, it reacted when a Torquay player ran over to take a throw-in. The dog lunged and managed to bite his leg. The player was treated for some time and the referee quite rightly added this to the end of the game. The ground went quiet apart from a few drunken Alex lads who continued to sing. You could cut the atmosphere with a knife as Crewe tried to knock the ball about and keep possession.

Then one misplaced pass and, you guessed it, they scored - about five minutes after the 90 had elapsed! The ground erupted and the Torquay lads went berserk. Almost dead and buried, they snatched a 2-2 draw and that point was enough to save their skin. Their fans poured onto the pitch and in the confusion it looked as though the referee might take the players off. Instead, he blew for full-time. We didn't care, the celebrating Torquay supporters weren't bothered, but I suspect that Lincoln City's fans were distraught as they were sent down to the Football Conference.

THRILLER WITH VILLA

Sometimes you just have to call in a favour. Stuck in Portsmouth, I was always going to struggle getting a ticket for the Villa cup match. The previous season was easily the most frustrating as a football fan, and trawling through programmes, newspaper clippings and ticket stubs found in the loft years later, I probably saw just five home games. The 1988-89 season didn't start much better in terms of getting to matches, but when the club announced that the Torquay and Carlisle games either side of Christmas would carry vouchers that could be used to buy cup tickets, well, I just had to hatch a plan.

Due to technical exams during December there was no way I could make the first of these games. So I called my mate Dave and asked him to buy two tickets. He only needed one, but I said he could use the other providing he kept the spare voucher. He obliged, but try as he might he couldn't convince any of our non-Alex mates to watch a match against Torquay on a Friday night before Christmas! Still, I got the token and just needed to get home to Alsager for the early January game with Carlisle.

Thankfully, I was granted a decent bit of leave either side of Christmas. Still in various stages of training, I wasn't required over the festive period. My time was my own, and there was only one place I wanted to be. I even managed to get hold of an Alex shirt, something I had never bought before. Replica tops were increasingly popular and living away it meant that I could fly the club colours with pride, and raise a few eyebrows back in Portsmouth.

Carlisle was bonkers, a decent game and packed with fans desperate to get the second voucher. The 1-0 win kept the momentum going, and the Alex looked a good bet to go into the New Year at the top of the table. But then it was all about the Villa build-up, and that evening was like a Roald Dahl *Charlie And The Chocolate Factory* moment. I had my golden ticket. Well, I had the vouchers I hoped would secure my golden pass. That involved a monster queue the following morning, a line the length of Gresty Road. But it was worth it. That moment when you get hold of a ticket for a sell-out event is very special. It's no different than the others, but the gold trim around the edge, the name of Aston Villa and that extra sparkle that comes with the FA Cup makes you stare in wonder. I still have countless stubs tucked away in the loft that I occasionally look at with great fondness. It's a sad affliction. Only other football fans would understand.

Because of the clamour for elusive spaces, the Alsager posse was scattered around the ground. One had admission to the main stand because his dad had connections. Another was over in the Paddock courtesy of a generous neighbour who couldn't attend. Another managed to grab a place amongst the Villa fans because his brother was a season ticket holder at Villa Park. So I joined a couple of others in the usual spot on the Popside, amongst a few familiar faces but also several hundred I'd never seen before! The cup, I realised, brought out plenty of supporters who otherwise didn't give a damn about the Alex.

There were a few changes around the ground by now. For starters, they had removed the old Gresty Road End roof. Let's be honest, it was an eyesore. And yet it was one of those things that gave our stadium identity. It was ramshackle, but it was part of the matchday experience for the few hundred supporters who called it home. The brick wall was replaced and a huge pair of iron gates appeared resplendent in red. The away fans were contained there, with high fences added to stop supporters getting onto the pitch. That worked, usually, but it was also a handy ledge that many jumped onto as they celebrated goals. Police and stewards would rush across, determined to stop them climbing over. They rarely did, just hopped back down and taunted their jailors. At the back there was a railing that daring fans would use to get the best view. They also attached their flags still higher on the barbed wire that topped the wall, marking their territory and claiming a moral victory.

These were the cosmetic changes before the more substantial ground improvements a few years later. The Gresty Road capacity was supposedly around 6,500 but against Villa the club declared the crowd as 5,500. It felt like seven or eight thousand had been squeezed in, with massive queues before the game started, and I suspect a few extra did sneak in that day. I always think back to the much-hyped Tottenham Hotspur game in 1960, when the attendance was 20,000. I wonder how many really saw that game?

Against Villa it was heaving, although the Railway End looked pitiful with just ball boys and a few police officers on patrol. The club wasn't daft though, and extra advertising boards had been dropped in place. I assume that the authorities had ruled it unfit, especially as it was an FA Cup game. It was no more than a rough bank that sported a fine grassy carpet in places, and a cheap one at that! Clubs couldn't risk the chance of accidents occurring, especially in light of several very sad disasters at other stadia in the late 1980s. With hindsight, the wooden stand at Gresty Road was a ticking bomb that thankfully never went off.

The big talking point was the return of David Platt, sold to Villa for a few hundred thousand pounds the previous year. I had worried that his departure would set the club back, as he had become the heartbeat of the team. Instead, it allowed players like Paul Fishenden and young Steve Walters to prosper. So old boy Platty trotted out and waved to fans as he emerged onto the pitch with his new colleagues. He was applauded by both sets of supporters and was visibly touched by the reception.

He wasn't happy a few minutes after the match started. Attacking that barren open end, Mark Gardiner thrashed an unstoppable left foot volley past the Villa 'keeper. He was just yards from the Popside corner that was filled to bursting point with supporters hoping to see Alex goals scored at that end. As Gardiner peeled away to celebrate we surged forward, hardly able to move but ecstatic to have taken the lead so early. Everyone had talked about a potential cup shock, but few really believed it. So any opportunity to go wild wasn't going to be missed. As the crush continued, long after the restart, it felt as though the basic concrete barriers in front of us would buckle and give way. Few cared, and the only worry was that some of the smaller kids amongst us had been caught up in the frenzy.

Not long after that, with several youngsters moved away from the corner for their own safety, we had more to celebrate. Gardiner was buzzing and whipped a tantalising cross deep into the six-yard area. A few Alex players charged in, putting pressure on the Villa defence. The 'keeper hesitated, and before he could react the ball hit the back of the net. It was an own goal, a forced error as one of the big Villa defenders tried to head the ball clear. We were in dreamland, and two-nil up against the Villa. It didn't get much better than this.

If the match had ended at half-time, then our fairytale cup run would have continued unabated. I enjoyed a quick pie and a cuppa from the tea bar with a very excitable bunch of mates. Then we headed down to the Gresty end of the Popside, wondering how many more we'd score. Several hundred others had the same idea and we couldn't get close to our usual spot. So we moved to the back and looked down on the amazing cup scene below us.

We enjoyed a lesson in football after the break, sadly from the opposition. Villa made changes and came out fired up. Apparently, Villa boss Graham Taylor told his players that they had got themselves into the mess, so they could get themselves out of it. What a pep talk that turned out to be. Former Alex hero Platty grabbed their first. The Popside fell silent and watched the Villa fans jump onto the fencing as he popped up at the back post to score. Anyone else would have been lambasted, cursed by an enraged stand of wounded Crewe fans. Not Platty, he was applauded by some. Others considered what could have been if he was still wearing an Alex shirt. After all, we knew what he was capable of. He'd returned to haunt us. We just needed to hang on to our slender lead.

Containing a top-flight team is never easy, and sometimes attack is the best form of defence. We tossed that theory aside, and became stifled in midfield and lost our heads at the back. Things got frantic as we hung on in the second half, but watching our basement division players digging deep was fantastic. In a masochistic way, it was almost as exciting as the first period. We fought like dogs, but Villa equalised and it was a question of when not if they'd win. A draw would have been deserved, a great reward for our determined first-half efforts. But life, and football, is rarely fair. Villa's third saw Alex heads drop. Platty didn't celebrate his own goal, but jumped on his team mate's back after their winner, something that riled plenty of lads stood on the Popside.

Gutted doesn't properly describe the emotions as the game ended. We never thought we'd progress to round four, but there is always one unexpected result that shocks the pundits and ruins football coupons. It just wasn't our turn. Thankfully, there was plenty to look forward to in the league.

PARTY TIME

Losing to Villa was disappointing but it didn't seem to bother the players. They bounced back and carried any despondent supporters with them. This was a cracking season, with excitement on all fronts. The Alex squad seemed to be up for anything. We even made it through to the northern section of the Sherpa Van Trophy, narrowly beaten by Bolton after extra time. But it was the league campaign that encouraged me back to Crewe much more after Christmas. I was sent on a few navy placements that didn't involve any weekend duties. So the rest of the season became a whole lot easier getting to games. I also got lucky and met two fellas, Andy and Steve, who drove up to Crewe from Guildford, so I split the petrol costs and enjoyed some good football chat on the way to matches.

During those discussions we talked more and more about the emerging players, something none of us had really considered in the past. Crewe youngsters were representing England at youth level, and the best of the latest crop were already making their mark in the first team. Rob Jones was getting a few chances, and we'd seen the first flashes of brilliance from Steve Walters. He had everything, except maybe a little more height. But that didn't matter, as he was tough, comfortable on the ball, a sublime passer and a great finisher. He was a Crewe product, and a local lad to boot. If this was the end result of the new-fangled youth system then everyone was happy.

Walters was embedded in the team when Wrexham arrived at Crewe for a Friday night match, with ex-Liverpool legend Joey Jones in his second spell with the club. As their team bus rolled up a few young Alex fans raced over to grab his autograph. I wasn't fussed; my book of players' signatures was stowed away back at mum and dad's house. That innocent lad from the late 1970s was long gone. I just hankered for a beer before the match started. So did a few of Walters' mates, a group of lads we got to know over Christmas. They were full of it, often with free tickets and access to the players' lounge courtesy of their buddy. But it was their relationship with the young midfielder that fascinated me. They were seventeen and eighteen years old, only a few years younger than us. They did what men our age enjoyed doing on a Friday and Saturday. So did Mr Walters, and I realised more so than ever that the players out on the pitch were just the same as us, not superstars. So for me, they were no longer on a pedestal, but as long as they did the business on match days I'd forgive them any misdemeanours.

That night, against Wrexham, the Alex players were superb. I love floodlit games, just something about the atmosphere that goes hand-in-hand with shadows and blasts of chilly air – especially in those late winter months. Wrexham were contenders that season and the added English-Welsh rivalry made it a typically heated contest, especially with over 6,500 in the ground. The inflatable sheep bounced around the Popside and the visitors' enclosure, the usual songs were sung with added fervour and the police had to keep a few over enthusiastic fans in line.

On the pitch, the occasion seemed to affect the Alex players. So at two-nil down in the first half, you can imagine how much the Wrexham lads loved it. They were hanging off the fencing behind the goal, a barrage of abuse thrown in our direction.

Then came the fight back. It was just what we needed, a massive boost that suddenly silenced the Gresty Road End. Paul Clayton and Paul Fishenden stood tall that night, and grabbing a 2-2 draw when all looked lost convinced us that we had the bottle to go the distance.

It was nights like these that the two-way relationship between fans and players became increasingly important to me. Moaning about the performance and the results is easy, but I wondered how many times the players thought that the supporters had let them down. They needed our backing, and we drove that incredible comeback against Wrexham from the terraces. Well, we did our bit.

The amazing form continued up to Easter, and the Alex old boys we met in the pub before games talked about seeing their club win the title. They'd witnessed good and bad over many decades, even enjoyed success in the late 1960s - but never a championship. I wasn't bothered; promotion was good enough for me. I'd been conditioned to accept failure, and didn't expect any success having seen over twelve years of struggle and mediocrity, although recent seasons under Dario Gradi had been much better.

Then everything ground to a halt. Another bumper home crowd against Rotherham rolled up expecting our march to victory to continue unhindered, but the majority went home disappointed. The Millers turned us over 3-1 that day, reinforcing their title-winning credentials. It was a wake-up call that wasn't heeded. Perhaps the Crewe players bottled it, some of them too young to handle the pressure? It was the start of a nine-game sequence that saw the Alex win just once. It sounds ridiculous, but I had sleepless nights. We'd started to believe our own hype and promotion was ours. To throw it away now was unthinkable. I had to avoid the sports pages at one point, as analysing the Fourth Division table was making me ill.

As if Gradi and the players suddenly realised what it meant to us, they produced the performance of the season against Burnley. It was the final home game, a must-win match to have any chance of taking the third promotion place. I had a week off and was back up in Cheshire. So in the late afternoon I was sat in the Brunswick enjoying a pint with Dave and a few locals, discussing our chances against a Burnley team with nothing much to play for in those final weeks.

As kick-off approached, we cut through Hewitt Street from behind the Barrel pub, then on to Gresty Road. It was a beautiful sunny evening and I'd expected a carnival atmosphere, but there was an eerie stillness about the streets. There were no flags, banners or balloons, just apprehensive faces. What surprised me most was the attendance that evening - only 3,500 when I'd expected five thousand or more. Perhaps the dip in form contributed, and maybe others didn't want to see the team fail when so much had been promised. We'd been ready to party for months and someone had cancelled the gig.

Ninety minutes later I leant against the Popside barrier watching the Alex players do a lap of honour, a thank you to the home supporters for backing them over ten months. Everyone was smiling, as that night's game ended 4-0 to Crewe. It was an exhibition match, the kind of football we all craved. Moreover, it meant that a good result away at Tranmere that Saturday would send us to the Third Division. Kenny Swain shook hands; Dale Jasper posed for a photo with two excited teenage girls; and Stevie Walters hi-fived his mates who called out to him from the terrace. I was emotionally drained. But there was one final matchday to prepare for.

***

Prenton Park was an impressive place in the 80s when it was full. It was a proper football ground, a blast from the past that deserved to stage big games. Tranmere sat in the shadows of Everton and Liverpool for years, but for once they were about to celebrate some success of their own. There were vast terraces, a decent amount of seating and that unique stand behind the goal with Bass beers emblazoned on the central section of the roof. This was the noisy home section, and a handful of their lads had the best view that day, sitting precariously at the bottom of the 'V' where two sections of roof met. We stood at the other end, in glorious sunshine on the open steps. Huge blue railings marked our area, penning us in like animals. They were cages designed to contain the trouble that had been a feature of the decade. On that final day there was no animosity, just expectant supporters all hoping that they'd be celebrating on the final whistle.

It didn't start well for us, and when Tranmere took the lead midway through the first half it would have been easy to throw in the towel. There wasn't a chance of that, and the Alex players lifted the large Crewe contingent with a determined fight back. Paul Clayton, Andy Sussex and Mark Gardiner were immense. All three of them looked over to us when we won corners, fists clenched, urging us to sing up and keep the faith. They were frustrated and knew that we were suffering. There was a constant crackle of radios, sport bulletins updating those who could bear to listen, hoping to hear that Scarborough and Scunthorpe were losing. That was the least of our worries; we needed to score.

Our moment didn't come until the second half. There was a great period of pressure that revived our spirits, and it felt as though the breakthrough was coming. It was one player in particular who kept us going. And for me, Gardiner was the main man, a mop of blond hair trailing in his wake making him instantly recognisable – even from distance. Of the games I managed to see, he always looked the most likely to score, or feed others with goal scoring opportunities. So it was no surprise that he was voted player of the season.

His industry that afternoon saw two or three Tranmere players trying to block one of his surging runs into the penalty area. One clumsy moment, several outstretched legs, and he was taken down. Penalty! We started celebrating immediately. But the Tranmere 'keeper was determined to spoil our party, and he dived the right way to save Paul Fishenden's spot kick. One second we had a foot back in the promotion bus, the next we were clinging for dear life on the edge of a cliff. The Tranmere fans went crazy, as if they'd won the division and not finished second. Hundreds jumped onto the pitch and about fifty surrounded Eric Nixon in the goalmouth, as though the 'keeper had won the game for them.

He hadn't won anything yet, and with the clock ticking it was Paul Clayton who slipped past him a few minutes later, before coolly shooting into an empty net as a despairing defender slid across the goal line hoping to reach the ball. Clayton peeled away and raced to the Alex bench. Even the usually calm manager was bouncing up and down with the Alex staff and substitutes. Then they looked to the fans - a chaotic mass of red and white bodies, some with tops off, most screeching as loud as they could, some crying tears of joy. Then the singing started and the tempo of the game eased, the two teams aware that both could enjoy promotion. We didn't know it at the time, but Gradi was about to substitute Clayton just a few seconds before he scored. Leaving substitutions until the last minutes would become his trademark!

What mattered was that several thousand Alex fans could finally celebrate the club's first promotion for twenty years. It was a feeling of exhilaration, relief and freedom. We had done it, not just the players. A few supporters raced onto the pitch when the referee confirmed the 1-1 scoreline, a result that no doubt broke other fans' hearts around the country. That didn't matter. This was our day. The gates at the front of the terrace opened and thousands poured onto the pitch. Some climbed up the high fences, others onto the floodlight structures. Any vantage point was taken to enjoy the party unfolding on the pitch. Players and fans of both clubs mingled in a football love-in, the likes of which I'd never witnessed before.

On the train home the carriage sang for the entire journey back to Crewe. Flags and scarves were draped out of the windows and the various towns and villages on the way back wondered what the fuss was all about. At Crewe station, I was shaken awake by a mate. I'd fallen asleep a few minutes earlier, completely shattered, and drained by the emotional roller coaster of the last few weeks. It had been frustrating, worrying and painful at times, but also absolutely wonderful. We had been promoted.

GREAT EXPECTATIONS

The summer after promotion was a busy one - a whirlwind of planning ahead for the exciting new season, changing jobs and being ditched by another girlfriend. Navy life wasn't for me long term, so I decided to cut my losses and leave before I finished my specialist training. That way I wasn't fully committed and there was no costly buy-out involved. I had moved between bases and assignments for three years, finally landing in Portsmouth at HMS *Nelson*. I met Karen there, at an officers' mess party. She came along with a friend, and after a brief introduction we hit it off. Everything was hunky dory, especially when I decided to leave the service and stay in Pompey. She liked that, but not my regular disappearances up north to Gresty Road, or to other grounds around the country. She thought I was seeing someone else, having an affair. In a way I was, and the Alex was something Karen couldn't accept. I was given an ultimatum: her or the football. I didn't answer, just raised my eyebrows. She knew the answer, and walked away in disgust. We never spoke again. Mistress Alexandra just smirked, knowing that she had me by the balls.

The new career was pub management, an assistant manager with a major chain. I impressed as a barman over two or three weeks when I was deciding what to do after leaving the navy, so they took me on. I struck a deal with the couple that ran the pub, such that I'd always work Friday nights but have Saturdays off, plus one other day in the week, often a Tuesday that tied in with most midweek Crewe games. So my days with the Alex were safe. It was great timing, as we became a surprise package in the league and also progressed in the FA Cup.

The early rounds even saw us fend off determined challenges from non-league clubs. Congleton and Blyth Spartans turned out to be enjoyable days instead of the awful embarrassments endured in previous years. But Chelsea away in the third round was mouth watering. It was an easy journey from Portsmouth, and an excuse to stay over with Bizza and a few of the London-based lads. Between us, we had a decent knowledge of the capital, knowing where to drink, places to avoid, and how to get there – without getting stuck on the busy tourist routes.

One pub on the way to Stamford Bridge grabbed our attention with a superb real ale offer. So we enjoyed a few beers that morning, sitting in the sunshine and catching sight of the first Alex fans arriving in West London. It was a real party by lunchtime, with over a hundred sat in the beer garden. Home and away Crewe shirts from every season were on display, caps, flags and scarves adorning the younger supporters. There was no hostility; as the Alex remained an unknown force under Dario Gradi in his early years, a small town team that the bigger clubs were happy to welcome to their grounds. You could wear colours without fear. Chelsea fans mingled, and some talked about cup games from the 1960s and 70s. There was even time to chat about Gradi's links to Chelsea, when he was their coach.

Typically, I got a little carried away and jokingly tapped a glass ashtray on the counter, calling for service when we needed a top up. It was high spirits, in no way intended to offend. The manager didn't see it that way and despatched a couple hefty bouncers in our direction. I needed to calm down, apparently; else I'd be learning to fly. That was the gist of it, eloquently delivered by the two burly gentlemen in dark overcoats. I quickly decided against a cheeky riposte, that I had already flown Sea King helicopters.

So I behaved myself, ordered drinks and placed a fifty pence piece on the pool table. Now that was an eye-opener, when one of the locals already on the table suggested that I doubled my deposit. More used to 20p and 30p games back home, I broke my £1-a-game virginity that early afternoon. One pound, for a game of pool in a pub! I nearly dropped my pint. To be fair it was the most luxurious table I'd seen, more like something you'd see in a plush snooker hall, wooden surround, a new block of chalk, tips on both cues and three working lights suspended perfectly above the immaculate green baize. All very nice, but we didn't have a second game.

Instead, being fond of the odd flutter, Bizza suggested a punt on the match. It was no surprise to see the Alex installed as underdogs, but

20-1 for a 1-0 Crewe victory was too good to be true. We both slapped £10 on the Alex and headed to the ground, with another London lad called Martin who was shaking his head in disbelief that we'd wasted our money. We mingled with others making their way to the game, and realised what a huge deal the fixture was. The streets were teeming, a real big-match feel as we approached the ground. Programme sellers littered the roads near the turnstiles, barking their hoarse sales pitch every few seconds; hotdog vans were parked on every corner and kids sat on walls watching the crowds roll by, some of them asking if we had a spare quid!

Stamford Bridge was no oil painting in 1990, long before the club's resurgence courtesy of Ken Bates and, later, Russian Roubles. But it was a substantial football stadium; old corrugated roof stands, sweeping terraces and a track around the pitch. It looked and felt massive. The Alex fans were housed in the open end, perhaps three thousand of us that day. It was magical, and the attendance of more than 18,000 was easily my biggest away day as a Crewe supporter.

The action kept us on our toes for 90 minutes. It was end to end, the Alex more than a match for the hosts. They showed touches of higher-division class, and a goal was always likely. But we frustrated them, hassled them all over the pitch and surprised the Chelsea faithful with our determination to play football.

And then it happened. Stevie Walters, the baby of the team, collected the ball on the edge of the box fired through several defenders into the corner of the goal. The resultant surge down the steep terrace was like nothing I had experienced before. It was crazy, every one of the travelling Alex fans going berserk. We were beating Chelsea. Walters didn't know what to do. Because of the oval-shaped stadium, there was a ten-metre stretch of grass between the goal and the away terracing. He ran behind the net, skipped over an advertising board and headed towards us. Then he stopped, wondering if he should venture any further. He punched the air and headed back, eventually congratulated by his team mates who wondered if he was going to return. I looked at Bizza, and then we both grabbed the crumpled betting slips from our pockets to check they were real, that we really had bet on the Alex to win 1-0.

The next twenty five minutes were pure torture. The home fans were agitated and you could cut the atmosphere with a knife. I think we'd already planned how to spend the winnings when Chelsea's Steve Clarke tucked the ball away and the rest of the stadium erupted around us, just relieved to have finally scored against lowly Crewe. That's how it finished, a stunning effort by our players, but not quite enough on the day. And yet there was an empty feeling as we trudged through the London streets back to Bizza's flat. The bet was insignificant, although the cash would have been great. We had come so close to ditching a top side out of the cup, but failed in the dying minutes. That's what mattered and hurt the most.

***

After the Saturday night out in London I returned to Portsmouth ready for the Sunday evening shift back at the pub. The replay was on Tuesday and presented a whole different set of issues for me. Trains, well, you could forget trying to get back to Portsmouth any time after about 6pm. So it was a stopover in Cheshire or nothing. That wasn't the only problem, as pubs don't run themselves. The manager and his wife were away that week, and the dutiful assistant manager was expected to keep the ship on a steady course. There were several excellent bar staff on hand, but the brewery insisted that a member of the management team was always present. There was only one option – to shut the pub and travel up regardless.

It was worth every penny and every second of the reprimand that followed a few days later, although the match ended in disappointment. Gresty Road was compact in the early 90s, and it made for a brilliant atmosphere on cup nights. Chelsea's big name players looked apprehensive and their manager, Bobby Gould, looked on from the tiny away team's dugout as the cameras followed his every move during the warm up. That was special, knowing that millions would be watching from their armchairs, most backing the underdog. An upset was on the cards and the nation was going to see it. Before kick-off I tried to muscle in on a Granada Reports interview that was taking place outside the chippy. Rash predictions of two, three and four-nil to the Alex were being made by fans delighted to be in the spotlight. Everyone was brimming with confidence.

It was never likely to be a high-scoring game, but both sides really flew at each other in the first half, creating some great chances. Dean Greygoose played a blinder in the Alex goal, stopping several efforts from Chelsea strikers Kerry Dixon and Ian Durie. For Crewe, Francis Joseph caused panic down the right in front of the Popside and sent in a series of teasing crosses that lanky Dave Beasant did well to hold.

Kerry Dixon scored the inevitable opening goal, but the Alex refused to lie down. Then, for a few brief seconds, we all thought that we had equalised. Joseph rounded the big Chelsea 'keeper and stroked the ball into the empty net following a clever breakaway move. Chelsea were caught napping. I was still hugging a random stranger when we realised that the linesman had his flag in the air, waving it like a lunatic. I wanted to reach out an grab it, hope that the referee had missed it. But he didn't. Joseph was offside, but we kept on fighting. Even Stevie Walters was in the thick of it, bustling about the Chelsea box hoping for glory once again. It didn't happen, and Dixon slipped another past Greygoose with about ten minutes left on the clock. We sighed, while the Chelsea fans climbed up the Gresty Road End fences and raised the volume. It was painful watching them celebrate. They hadn't dominated, but it was obvious that they had enough quality to see out the game. They did a professional job on us.

This game really stands out for me because I think we deserved something. I've always worn rose-tinted spectacles where the Alex are concerned, but we gave Chelsea a good game. Only the dominant Beasant kept them in it, with his long reach, lucky gloves, curly perm and all. They had class throughout the side, but we really pushed them. When the second goal flew in I looked at the Chelsea fans going crazy, and beyond them were the terraced houses of Gresty Road. The old roof had been removed from the enclosure, and it made me smile that people in the upstairs windows of the houses were looking down at the action, although they could only see one half of the pitch. Maybe they had been spared some of the pain.

It was a great night wherever you stood or watched from, and certainly no disgrace losing to Chelsea. I stopped in Alsager that night, but headed south the following day to face the music and explain to the brewery why the pub had been closed. Let's just say that the area manager was not impressed, and my days as a publican were numbered!

***

Success in the cup competitions, especially when you're a small club, often has a detrimental effect on the bread and butter league games. Unusually for us, the Chelsea disappointment was soon followed by the most amazing unbeaten sequence. The Alex surged up the division, with notable wins over Blackpool, Huddersfield Town and Rotherham. It was ridiculous to even consider it, but another promotion was possible.

Gresty Road was looking much better, with some work done to the Railway End meaning that all four sides of the ground were back in use. The average attendance was up, a noticeable rise thanks to bigger teams coming to Crewe and some older supporters back on the scene now that the dark old days had been put behind us. I was still travelling from Portsmouth, but hardly missed a match. This was the best run I'd known as a supporter. Then one Monday night in April 1990 I got a phone call from Bizza.

'Let's go to Bristol tomorrow,' he said, 'meet you there about 5pm for a few beers, some food and a good natter about promotion.'

He had the bug. In fact, a lot of Alex fans caught it. The bandwagon was in full flow, almost unstoppable. Winning fever had flushed through the fan base like an epidemic, and almost everyone was infected. Only a few level headed types resisted. They harked back to other false dawns. But this time there was serious chatter about the Alex becoming a real force in the Third Division.

Next up was Bristol City, a relatively easy journey for me. I also received some good news through the post that morning. I had great expectations of my own having decided to return to education. My place on a degree course in Middlesbrough was confirmed for September later that year. I'd had enough of flitting between temporary jobs in Portsmouth, but quite why I chose Boro is beyond me. I put it down to some gypsy blood somewhere down the line, as I seemed determined to live in all four corners of the country. That was all in the pipeline, and the incredible first season in Division Three promised so much more. So I caught that train and met Bizza with plenty of time to take a look around the city before the game.

We didn't need anyone to hype Crewe Alexandra's chances that evening, but the Bristol fans we encountered around the bars at teatime were extremely pessimistic. They were convinced that the Alex would turn them over. If only! The next few hours were an exercise in putting things in perspective. Amazingly, it was 0-0 at half-time, but that was the lull before the storm. One, two, three, four… that was the Bristol City goal tally, a painful but brilliant exhibition of finishing. It wasn't a one-way game, by all means, but we were beaten from early in the second half. The only consolation was a long-range strike from Aiden Murphy to lift deflated Alex hearts. It was a wake-up call. We were not ready for another promotion. For the first time in months, the train journey home was a miserable one.

Ultimately, we couldn't quite take the pace alongside the frontrunners. We ran out of steam. Notts County beat us the following week despite a huge Alex following at Meadow Lane. We still believed, but the team that eventually finished third were too much for us. Although we beat Walsall and then held second placed Bristol Rovers to a draw, it wasn't enough. Further defeats ruled out any slim chance of a place in the play-offs. It was an amazing ride while it lasted, but back-to-back promotions were beyond the reach and resources of a modest club from Cheshire.

The final game, at home to Wigan, was a great send off. The campaign had petered out, but the players could not be faulted for their effort. An exciting 3-2 win was the reward for those who turned out at Gresty Road on the final Saturday. I felt proud, as did over three thousand Alex fans who applauded the players as they saluted the supporters and threw boots, shirts and sweaty socks into the crowd. I realised that it was fine to demand better, to aspire and hope that one day we'd sneak into the upper echelons of the football league. I'd just have to be patient...

OFF THE HINGES

Don't get me wrong, this book is not about football hooligans. But looking back, the early part of the 1990s was an angry time, and some Crewe games involved violent incidents. Older faces from the late 1970s and early 80s seemed to have reappeared, and some Alex fans were no shrinking violets. Compared to some clubs, however, I'd always thought that the numbers wanting to be involved in trouble were relatively low. That was certainly true when you consider the size of the town. But in a season that saw games with Stoke, Tranmere, Birmingham, Shrewsbury and Chester, the number of ugly encounters started to rise considerably.

By December 1990 we'd won just a handful of league games. It was a hugely frustrating time, especially as we'd enjoyed such a fantastic first season in the Third Division. Losing is always hard to stomach, and the relentless defeats took its toll. The disappointment on the pitch soon engendered resentment, and when other fans taunted it didn't take much to light the fuse. Losing at home to Chester was messy, and Stoke fans ran riot around the town to compound our misery when they beat us 2-1 at Gresty Road. In the space of a few months, our world seemed to fall apart and some reacted badly.

Thankfully, there were plenty of distractions to lighten the mood. The League Cup came first, a two-leg affair that brought good revenues through the turnstiles but stretched the smaller squads. We beat Grimsby thanks to an away goal, setting us up with a not-to-be-missed encounter with Liverpool. It meant a hectic, pocket-busting period of league and midweek cup games for supporters, but standing behind the goal at the

Anfield Road end, looking out into the vast stadium illuminated by enormous floodlights was such a proud moment and . The Alex tackled a side that had topped the English leagues and lifted European titles. It was the stuff usually reserved for fairy tales.

Then Andy Sussex scored. I looked at the bloke next to me, wondering if he had seen what I had just witnessed. Andy Sussex had scored, we were 1-0 up at Liverpool. I hugged the guy beside me, and we both did that awkward football supporters' dance, jumping up and down together in a manly embrace. It usually ends with a firm pat on the shoulder, a signal that you should both let go.

I remember Liverpool fans applauding, many with a soft spot for Crewe. They showed great respect for a tiny club trying to play football. But they knew that the storm was coming, a Liverpool onslaught and five goals for the home side. It didn't matter. We'd scored at Anfield. We were winning, briefly, at Anfield, and many top-flight clubs will never be able to say that!

Two weeks later, back at Gresty Road, they only managed four. We all joked that we would eventually beat them if enough games were played. Sussex did his reputation no harm, scoring our only goal again in a match that remained 0-0 until half-time. I didn't see my Anfield dance partner that evening, so I celebrated Sussex's strike as normal with the lads. We had two fantastic nights, and yet there was a realisation that the Alex and the country's top sides were a million miles apart. The euphoria of promotion at Tranmere seemed a very long time ago.

The Liverpool games were only a starter, and a few weeks later several hundred Alex fans took their places on the open terrace at Lincoln's Sincil Bank for the FA Cup opening round. I dropped my keys that day, but the Alex won 4-1. Then, about three minutes from time, a fella tapped me on the shoulder and asked if I knew anyone who had lost a bunch of keys. Apparently, they had been passed around the block of Crewe fans for half an hour!

We leapt comfortably over the Atherstone United banana skin in round two, and then cruised past Bristol Rovers in the third round. It was my first year at college as a mature (ish) student, supposedly concentrating on my studies, but there was no way I was missing a single game, and the Alex marched on past Rotherham in a tense 1-0 win at Gresty Road. The Wembley songs echoed around the ground and the awful league form was forgotten.

The reward in round five was a trip to West Ham's Upton Park. Round Five! It still sounds unreal, but we stood there on the huge terrace in East London, singing the roof off the away end. Check Marco Criscuolo's *Crewe Alexandra Match by Match* statistical epic and you'll see that the Alex lost 1-0 to the Hammers. You had to be there to appreciate how close we came, almost nicking a goal and claiming a significant scalp and a spot in round six. It just wasn't our day. Jimmy Quinn killed us off nearly eighty minutes into the game and there was nothing left in the tank. No amount of vocal encouragement could push the players any further, as they all gave 100%. So did we, and it was no disgrace walking away from the ground that day. Even the West Ham fans were full of praise. Another proud memory, providing you could put the prospect of relegation to the back of your mind.

***

With hindsight the painful run in the league was perhaps due to the hectic schedule brought on by involvement in the cups. In terms of our Division Three status that season, our fate was effectively sealed with an abysmal run of results in March and April 1991. The slide stopped briefly with an unlikely midweek win for Crewe away at Grimsby, although the Mariners still went on to be promoted. Suddenly, there was hope. There was a chink of light at the end of an otherwise dark and dreary tunnel that looked set to take us back to Division Four. Some had already conceded; others, with that awful affliction of misguided optimism, battled on and refused to give up on the players. At Birmingham a few days later, hearts were racing – for several reasons.

The healthy Crewe following was in tremendous voice that day, and it was amazing going to a big stadium like St. Andrew's and dominating proceedings from the terraces. Although Birmingham is the second city, with a population of over one million people, the City fans had deserted their club following several seasons of poor results. So to see only 6,000 in such a large arena was a shock.

Crewe's Rob Edwards did the business on the pitch, scoring twice to give us another three very unexpected points. For me, it was also a chance to meet up with Bizza and Geoff. Both had studied in Birmingham together, a few years earlier, and we'd all met up for Alex games since we went our separate ways. We'd almost resigned ourselves to the drop, and the run-in was just a series of days out without worrying about the football. Of course that all changed with back-to-back wins.

So we left the ground in buoyant mood, ready to grab beers and a pizza near the Bullring shopping centre. Unfortunately, we got sucked into the police escort that was leading a large number of Crewe fans down to New Street station. The Brummies were not happy, humbled by Crewe, their season effectively over and no chance of even a play-off spot for their once-mighty club.

So they piled in. I was lucky to stay on my feet when a lad to my right received a punch to the head, his assailant coming from nowhere before the police line could react. I broke his fall, but he didn't look in good shape. The Alex fans started to scatter as a massive group of the Birmingham Zulus appeared and charged through the police. The batons came out, but it was too late. Pockets of trouble flared along the road, with a few Alex lads fighting back. We peeled off and headed to the city centre, with a few Crewe faces behind thinking it was a good idea to follow us. Then another mob appeared, baby hoolies hoping to become Zulus one day, looking to pick off groups of ten or less. They were younger than us, but outnumbered three to one none of us fancied the odds, or our chances in side streets that we didn't know.

We made it to the main shopping area, just a couple of kicks and punches taken as we tried to loose the Brummie toe rags. We dashed into a bar, and watched as some of them raced past. That was that, we foolishly thought. Bizza headed to the bar to order some drinks just as a street bin came flying through the window. A police van arrived and collected the culprit in seconds, but the bar manager gave us a dirty look and pointed to the door. He didn't want anyone in his bistro that attracted trouble. So we left, wondering what awaited us outside? Geoff still lived on the edge of the city, so we decided to head there. Police were swarming all over, trying to round up any 18-30 year old males who fitted the football profile. The three Alex lads who followed us looked bemused as we said goodbye, and they cautiously set off in the direction of the station.

So a terrible second half to the season was in danger of becoming one of the great escapes, especially when the Alex beat Rotherham in front of a bumper Gresty Road crowd. Staying in the higher division was important, and three victories left us flying high and confident that we could win the last two games. It was another bout of that inexplicable fan belief, when all sense and logic go out of the window.

Sadly, Chester away later that week was the match that decided our fate, although the damage was done over a frustratingly inconsistent season. It was a far cry from the excitement that almost took us to the play-offs twelve months earlier, or the confidence that bubbled away leading up to this match. The great progress made under Dario Gradi was about to be undone.

The hosts no longer played at Sealand Road, so it was an unusual journey for the 2,000 Alex fans that hoped to see us preserve our Division Three status. Chester shared Moss Rose with Macclesfield Town while plans were afoot to build a new ground. It was a dump then, not a lot better years later. Only small parts of the ground enjoyed cover, the terracing was poor and the other facilities were woeful.

My mate Bizza played a blinder, heading to Boro for a night out on the Friday so that we could drive over together for the football on the Saturday afternoon. As with any best-laid plans we didn't get up until gone 11am and hastily threw some things together before hitting the road. Typically, there was plenty of traffic, road works and even a brief problem with the car. The omens were not good. So as we parked up, about half a mile from the venue, the match was already under way. Loud cheers, rival chanting and then a goal celebration could be heard as we made our way to the ground. There's nothing more frustrating, not knowing who has scored, especially when so much depended on this one game. There was a massive Alex following that day, so the goal could have been ours. Then a second roar went up, that unmistakable outpouring of passion when your team has scored. Our quick walk became a sprint and we covered the last hundred yards like fine-tuned athletes.

We couldn't hand over our cash quick enough, and we both punched the air when the turnstile operator told us that the Alex were winning 2-0. He was lying, winding us up, and playing on the fact that we didn't know which way the goals had gone. Another Crewe fan revealed the truth, his hangdog expression a dead giveaway as he sloped over to the tea bar. We conceded another, and by half-time it was obvious that many supporters had given up hope. There was talk about pitch invasions, anything to get the game postponed. That didn't happen, but tensions continued to rise as the second half played out. A few morons did get onto the pitch, but they were quickly dealt with.

We scored, courtesy of young Craig Hignett, but it was scant consolation. At 3-1 down we looked dead and buried. The crowd was already agitated, our status in the division hanging by a thread, and the Chester fans were baiting us, delighted to see us struggling. Tempers became frayed as Alex supporters stood waiting for the inevitable relegation to be confirmed, something that had been on the radar for several weeks. I looked behind the mass of Alex fans and, beyond the back wall, you could see people perched on the upper balcony of the *Silkman* pub, enjoying every minute, pint glasses in hand, bouncing up and down in celebration. I wouldn't have minded, but Chester had nothing riding on the game. They were safe. Getting one over Crewe was all that mattered, sending us down, ruining our season. I suppose we've done the same over the years - hoping that Chester, Wrexham, Stoke, Vale and Shrewsbury would fail, meaning heartache for their fans.

This time it was our turn, and they loved it. I turned away from the game and looked to my right. There was a disturbance by the exit gate. Around twenty Alex lads pushed forward, trying to get out of the ground. They weren't looking for trouble, initially, just desperate to escape a match that was heading for defeat. Waiting for that awful moment, when the referee's whistle confirms your fate, is hard to take at the best of times, but with your rivals revelling in your misery it's magnified until you're fit to burst. There was still another ten minutes to endure.

That anger, that seething rage that builds within you, manifests itself in many ways, more often than not in outbursts of violence. That eventually happened at Moss Rose. The Alex fans wanted out at any cost. Stewards and police moved forward and made it quite clear that nobody was leaving early. They wanted to contain the Alex contingent. That was a red rag to a growing number of fired up bulls. I stood there behind the goal with Bizza, deflated as our time in Division Three ebbed away. But I couldn't leave. There was always a chance, no matter how slim.

Neil Lennon was still barking orders, trying to motivate the tired legs around him. Jason Smart and Aaron Callaghan were weary warriors at the back, beaten three times and all-too aware that their careers were heading to the bottom division once again. Rob Jones still had the energy, and offered hope as he burst down the wing overlapping Mark Gardiner who looked completely spent. They'd given it everything but it wasn't enough.

Suddenly the crowd roared, not in celebration but as Alex reinforcements arrived to boost the numbers by the gate. There was a surge, pushing, shoving and screaming, agitated voices shouting out. More police raced over from the adjacent stand as tempers flared, punches were thrown and bodies fell to the floor. The token stewards moved aside, their paltry matchday pay not worth risking life and limb for. The Alex mob was in full flow and the gates rocked. It took a few more bodies, but the hinges finally surrendered. The gates fell and a few hundred poured out onto the car park and into the street to the rear of the stand. Chester supporters applauded, but they were mocking us. Other Crewe fans threw in the towel and slipped away when they realised that an escape route had opened up. The beer monsters on the balcony gave the finger, while others showered the disappearing Alex fans with abuse.

Most of us hung our heads as the final whistle sounded a few minutes later. We were beaten, and the Alex players collapsed to their knees. There is no feeling like it, as though the sky is about to fall in. Suddenly it's not just a game. It's a year of your life wasted, details etched in your mind that you'll never forget, unhappy memories, multiple defeats and opportunities spurned. The force that drives you throughout the working week has kicked you in the gut. You know the emptiness will pass, eventually, but that's no consolation when you're walking away from a football ground deflated, beaten and despondent.

I paid no attention to the scuffles that developed around the ground as a few Chester idiots did their best to incite as many people as possible. What was the point of it all? There were no words spoken as we wandered back to Bizza's car. There was nothing to be said. The final home game against Mansfield would be meaningless, a knockabout to fulfil the fixture list.

Minutes later, sat in the car, both of us silent, I shed a few tears. I tried to hide them, cover the streaks on my cheek with a loud sniff and quick wipe of the sleeve. But Bizza knew, and gave me a shove, a friendly nudge to reassure me.

'We'll be back,' he said, trying his best to lift me.

He was right, and as always there was the new season to look forward to, but I suspected that he was hurting just the same inside. So we wound the car windows down, slipped on a tape and listened to Morrissey at full blast as we sped off to Alsager. The miserable Smiths front man was the perfect company as we both dipped into melancholy mood...

BEEHIVE STING

College worked out well for me. This was long before the nasty spectre of annual tuition fees and hefty student loans. The country hadn't maxed out its credit card and there was still enough in the pot to offer a free education for work-shy students. I arrived with a bit of money stashed away, and as a twenty-something I also qualified as a mature student. Crucially, this meant that I secured an additional grant.

During my first year, after a boozy night out around the pubs and a few of Middlesbrough's after-hours venues, I walked into one of the nightclubs and took a job. Bar work was a doddle, and I knew that my student cash would eventually run out, so I decided to stem the flow early. Unlike other freshers, I had priorities: namely the Alex.

By now I'd lived in a few towns and cities, and I always went along to the local footy if I couldn't get to Crewe games. Boro's Ayresome Park was no different. It was much like Portsmouth, a huge old ground that had seen better days. The Holgate End was like twenty Popsides put together. It was heaving with men wanting to let off steam, chant, shout and fight, and generally forget about work. So Tuesday nights, when travel to Crewe was almost impossible, I'd stand alongside lads I met at college, local boys who had Boro running through their veins. They were sensible, deciding to continue their studies without jeopardising their football obsessions. I wish I'd done the same!

Players like Bernie Slaven, Tony Mowbray and Stuart Ripley turned out for Middlesbrough, class acts that would later play at the highest level. They also knew how to lift a crowd, and the baying masses at Ayresome Park demanded nothing less. This didn't happen back at Crewe, certainly not on the same scale. A guy on a psychology course often chatted to me about behaviour at football grounds. He was studying the reasons behind violence on the terraces. He reckoned that it went hand-in-hand with working class, inner city areas. It was all about identity and belonging, according to him. Crewe had its rough areas but nothing like Boro, Sunderland or Newcastle. So you'd see snapshots of similar behaviour at Gresty Road, just substantially toned down. It was food for thought, and I watched on with interest as we travelled to a few games in my first few months in the North East.

Work in the nightclub was great, as it gave me time for a cheeky pint or two with mates in the early evening before heading to work around 9.30pm. My shifts were usually on Thursday and Friday nights, but it seemed the logical thing to do. It kept the money coming in and stopped me spending when other students were already bleeding their accounts dry. It was a simple equation that allowed the football travel to continue. So I didn't grumble about a few unsociable hours. The late shifts would invariably end with drinks or a house party, meaning that Saturday morning train journeys started with a sore head. My ambitious idea to use such travel time to study was soon forgotten, as the criss-cross tracks that connected the North East to Yorkshire and then on to Lancashire and Cheshire soon provided some great early morning football conversations. I even came across two Alex fans, Jamie and Mark, who occasionally joined me as we changed trains at York.

From an early stage my circle of friends used the student union bar and its facilities, but also the *Star & Garter* pub that sat conveniently between our house and the university campus. We drank there most days, be it lunchtime, a full afternoon session or during the evenings. It was run by Noel, a real Boro lad. He had something of a reputation around the town. In fact, for a number of years he was considered the 'top boy', not just at the football but also across the whole town, a crown he'd held since knocking out the previous 'leader' when he was just seventeen. He took a shine to us, which was good news, and within a few months three of our group were working the bar or looking after the door on busier nights. He also sponsored our university footy team, which enjoyed great success against the other departmental sides. It was a bizarre set up, with students mingling with some of Boro's most infamous, the brassiest local girls on Saturday nights, plus the occasional appearance from comedy man Bob Mortimer. He'd used the pub for years, but we never saw Vic Reeves. Next door there was a club with no windows, with doormen the size of tree trunks. Not a nice place, but reassuring that Noel had asked them to look after us if we got into any bother!

Something else happened during my time on Teesside; I started to feel isolated and distant from the club I loved. I'd been away from Cheshire since leaving school, and although I'd clocked up as many home and away games as many other Alex fans I still felt like an outsider. I knew several pockets of supporters but never became a regular with any of them. My core group of mates from Alsager had gone their separate ways - living in Manchester, Birmingham, Liverpool, Oxford and London. So unless a couple of us got together, arrived and managed to meet up ahead of a match, then I would stand on my own. Like having neighbours you never get to know, there was a nod, a wave and the occasional exchange of Alex chat. I was there for the football but rarely enjoyed the social side of things with other Crewe lads. My life was spent on trains to and from games, with a few beers only possible when I got back to Middlesbrough.

This remote supporting existence forced my hand after my first year; I had to stop the rot and take some action. A number of the other lads at college seemed equally frustrated and missed seeing their own teams in action. So a mini society was formed, informal but very active. The easiest option was to tag along with local Boro lads who we met at college, so the Middlesbrough games became a good substitute that filled a gap, especially during the week. But before long I'd managed to coerce lads from all over the country to accompany me to the Alex. They just wanted to see a few games, enjoy the match atmosphere and have a good day out with the lads. We travelled to Scunthorpe, Blackpool, Darlington and York – all relatively easy by train from our Teesside base. At Scarborough my new jacket caused plenty of amusement. It was almost orange, quite a vivid colour, one of those ill-advised student purchases, and I stood out like a sore thumb. Within five minutes of the match starting the Scarborough supporters targeted me while the action on the pitch failed to grab their attention.

'Who's the gay boy in the coat?' they sang for about fifteen minutes.

The rest of the lads thought it was hilarious and left me alone on the terrace to take the abuse. I played up to this taunting, and it was all light-hearted. There was no hassle that day, and we met some local fans in a pub after the game. True to form, they continued to take the Mickey – assisted by the bunch from Middlesbrough. I didn't wear that jacket to the football again!

The most memorable day - for all the wrong reasons - involved another easy train trip across country, about 90 miles from Middlesbrough to Carlisle. It was an FA Cup game, so a decent crowd was expected. Six of the lads from college fancied it - Eddie a Liverpool fan, Dave (Nottingham), Daryl (Newcastle), Matt (Leicester), Brent (Coventry) and Boro lad Ian. We started early with bacon butties from the station café, and a pack of lagers purchased the night before especially for the trip. It was always strange heading to Crewe games like this, especially to somewhere like Carlisle. The train was full of shoppers, day-trippers and a few walkers heading to the Lake District. Oh, and a bunch of raucous students supping ale at 9.30am.

In Carlisle I recognised a few friendly faces from Crewe. It added to the occasion, introducing my college mates to everyone, all honorary Alex fans for the day. By early afternoon we had a lively group having a laugh. Then a couple of blokes fell out over a few spilt drinks. It happened by the bar, well away from us, but it was obvious that Alex and Carlisle fans were involved. Violence is everywhere in society, but at football the sheer numbers involved often give match days a sinister undertone. Carlisle town centre was teeming, and as we progressed from pub to pub, towards the ground, the atmosphere changed noticeably. It started with families and shoppers, having lunch alongside us and other Alex supporters, and then became wall-to-wall football fans at the Beehive close to the ground.

From here the day went quickly downhill. It was my round, so I squeezed through to the bar to order some drinks. The lads found a bit of space in one of the adjoining rooms, near a pool table. I'd seen busy pubs, especially the cheaper boozers that are always rammed solid in the hour leading up to kick-off, but the Beehive was ridiculous. It took ten minutes getting served, and during that time I saw tempers flare. There were a couple of big lads on the door, but they'd been letting anyone and everyone into the pub. I reckon two hundreds blokes were crammed inside, probably a fifty-fifty mix of Carlisle and Crewe. You often find supporters side by side, but this was a recipe for disaster. For starters, the older Alex faces had appeared, the ones who limit travel to local derbies and cup days out. Basically, the bigger occasions when there's a chance of trouble. Most had been drinking for three or four hours, including our group from Boro. It was always likely to end in bother.

What happened next took everyone by surprise. I got back with the drinks and watched two lads being dragged outside by the bouncers. My mate Eddie said that he'd just seen them coming to blows.

Then it happened. A roar went up that meant one thing – a group of Carlisle fans had decided to steam into their rivals. It started in the centre of the main bar area, a mass of bodies dragged to one side as perhaps five or six started trading punches. It spilled into our room immediately as a couple of Carlisle lads took out Crewe fans they had been watching. There was no room to move clear. Most tried to stand their ground, keeping themselves upright as bodies slammed into them from all angles. Within thirty seconds, unless you recognised a face, it was impossible to tell who was on which side.

Then the chairs and bar stools started flying. A window went through, and two policemen who had been showing their faces a few minutes earlier rushed inside. Other officers joined them and the pub doors were locked. They wanted to contain the violence and identify the troublemakers. That was the wrong decision. A few glasses and bottles had broken during the early part of the melee, but events took a horrendous turn a few seconds later. Three of our group had been jostled into the main area, fending off a few idiots who fancied taking pot shots at anyone – whether you wanted trouble or not.

Then I heard another pint glass smash. I looked to the right, about five yards away, and watched a raised hand holding a shattered glass stub. An anonymous face full of rage stabbed the top of five, six or seven unguarded heads. There was blood squirting everywhere, and screams of agonising pain. Some of the victims retaliated and another series of sickening sounds were heard as glass connected with bone and flesh. Bodies fell quickly. Worse still, injured men were then punched down or smashed over the back with broken furniture. It was carnage.

My mate Eddie appeared five minutes later. He'd taken an unprovoked punch to the head and wanted none of it, locking himself in a toilet cubicle before the scrapping escalated. I didn't blame him, and a couple of our lads looked visibly shaken. They'd wanted a day out on the beer, not a full-blown pub riot. The situation remained confused for fifteen minutes. They eventually let people outside, in twos and threes, and then kept everyone in a large group on the pub car park. A dozen ringleaders were identified, lads from both towns. They were cuffed and hauled off to waiting police vans. The worst part was the aftermath, victims on the pavement outside, bleeding heavily with just a couple of medics trying to attend to dozens of serious cuts. The police eventually escorted the rest of us to the ground. There were a few bruised egos, but they were the lucky ones.

Apart from a few nasty isolated incidents over the years, that pub ruck was probably the worst football-related violence I've ever seen. For the record, the Alex won 2-1, but there was little talk about the game that day.

***

As we didn't get roped in with the Alex fans after the match, able to prove that we lived in Middlesbrough, we went back into the town centre. But by six o'clock we'd had enough of the dirty looks. There was a simmering resentment. Two Carlisle fellas had been badly hurt and Crewe fans were blamed. We had two Boro lads with us, plus a Geordie with one of the strongest accents you can imagine, but this cut no ice. We were strangers. They didn't want us in their pubs, or their town. So we drank up and hopped on a train to Penrith, a town a few miles south of Carlisle, on the A66 that heads back to Teesside. It was another stop-off as we tried to make the best of a strained day out.

Maybe we were unlucky, or maybe we had trouble written on our backs that evening. The first pub we tried saw us chased out by locals who just fancied kicking off with strangers. The next, a tacky pub-club arrangement, was no better. It was almost comical, but Eddie was punched on the back of the head for the second time – as he was on his way to the toilet! He'd been dancing with a girl and the boyfriend wasn't happy. Eddie landed nose first and sported a huge graze and a black eye for days. It wasn't funny, but we couldn't stop laughing at his misfortune.

To really cap a ridiculous day, we missed the last train back to Middlesbrough. Drunk, tired and one of us a little wounded, there was no other option. We hopped in a taxi that broke the collective bank, but delivered us home around 2am. It was just another crazy away day!

POPSIDE TRUMPET

The daft thing about football fans is that shocking results, exorbitant prices, poor facilities, embarrassing FA Cup exits and painful relegations are soon forgotten. We're a bunch of Muppets, gluttons for punishment. No matter how bad things get there's always the new season just around the corner, with the chance of better times ahead. We are eternal optimists, even though we moan, grumble and complain for ten months of every year. It's as though we're all fitted with reset buttons, returned to factory settings when August comes, when everything is suddenly shiny and new.

With university holidays particularly generous (four months over the summer wasn't unusual) it was easy catching the start of the new season. There was nothing to stop me taking in every game - as long as I'd left a few quid stashed away. So August 1991 had added spice, with a couple of incredible pre-season friendlies - against FC Utrecht and Real Valladolid. World class players arrived in Crewe, and some of those star names were perfect gentlemen. They signed autographs, performed tricks and skills for the kids as they warmed up, and then met supporters to shake hands after the games.

It was a major coop getting such teams to stop off in Crewe, but it didn't grab the town by the balls. Seeing a bunch of smouldering, hairy blokes from the Spanish league didn't do it for the local lasses either. Even Columbian international Carlos Valderrama, complete with enormous curly perm, failed to attract the full house that the club craved. Only 1,500 turned up, probably a shock to the big names used to red carpets, full-capacity stadia and jet planes. I always wished that I'd met their coach and captured the image as their players climbed down the steps and stared at a football ground no bigger than the terraced houses in the surrounding streets. Utrecht didn't encourage many more, but at least we could taunt our rivals who had watched the usual pre-season dross, friendlies against tiny clubs from nowhere.

Being back in the basement division wasn't ideal, but I always got the feeling that it gave the club the opportunity to regroup and build upon the success of the 1989 promotion. There was a decent squad, an abundance of young players eager to debut in the first team, and with cash in the bank from a few player sales the first phase of ground improvements would soon take place.

The thought of upgrading Gresty Road excited and terrified me in equal measures. Like a pair of comfy slippers, chucking them out was a daunting and painful prospect. How could you improve something that fitted like a glove, even though a couple of the fingers were missing and the stitching was coming away? The Popside was my second home, where my life made sense and the supposedly important stuff could be forgotten. It was awful; a poorly maintained pavement best describes the conditions tolerated by fans who paid to stand on its uneven slabs. Those two dozen terrace steps, however, represented a place where hundreds of fans came together. You wouldn't give strangers in the street the time of day, but standing shoulder to shoulder on that dull expanse of grey concrete forged friendships that last for life. There were no birthday cards exchanged, not even a drink shared with some of those anonymous faces. But we knew each other, with a simple nod usually enough to welcome new arrivals into the fold. It was my social club, my hangout, my street corner, and I didn't want it to change.

In those early 90s there was yet another link to my Alsager roots that made the Popside a cool place to stand. I met up with Richard many times after we left school, especially down in London where he studied at one of the prestigious music colleges. He wasn't a keen footy fan during our younger days, certainly not part of the group that regularly travelled to Gresty Road on Saturdays. But when he returned home a few years later he started coming along, and his contribution was unique for one special reason - he played the trumpet, and was happy to do so at matches!

Now this was no run-of-the-mill horn blower, like the Portsmouth numpty who annoyed the hell out of everyone with his tuneless honking and infuriating rattle when he came to Crewe. Oh no. Richard was classically trained and could adapt any composition to fit the mood, mimic terrace chants and taunt Burnley, Rochdale and Bury fans with blasts of the *Coronation Street* theme tune. From the uplifting sounds of the *Superman* opening sequence, to the sombre *Last Post* if the Alex were losing. He had something for every occasion. It added colour and incredible sound to our terrace experience and wowed visiting supporters who didn't know what had hit them. For a few years he made the Popside extra special and it was brilliant standing alongside him.

At Gresty Road, drunken Alex fans would stagger over and leave requests, as though he was the DJ at a family get together in the Crosville Club. He usually obliged, and the crowd was visibly moved as they caught the opening notes of a terrace favourite, like *Blue Moon*.

On our travels we encountered a few grounds where jobsworth stewards refused him entry, power-crazy nutters that allowed their positions of authority to go to their heads.

'That's an offensive weapon mate,' they would suggest when he revealed the contents of his protective black box. 'You might hit someone with that,' they accused.

It was over a grand's worth of musical engineering. He had no intention of hitting anyone with his beloved trumpet, although he came close to smacking a few idiots with the instrument's heavy case on more than one occasion.

A few supporters at Gresty Road took exception to the trumpet playing, probably because they wished that Richard had joined them over on the Paddock or up in the seats. Like so many things in life, I suspect they were jealous. He became a real Marmite figure the following season, loved by those who sung beside him but despised by others who thought he got more attention than he deserved. It was sour grapes, and they didn't like seeing him interviewed by TV and radio commentators. When the club awarded him a free season ticket for services rendered it nearly tipped some over the edge!

The 1992-93 league campaign couldn't have started better, and Richard took his place once again to help lift the players. We smashed four past Torquay in glorious sunshine on the opening day, and the modest following from the south coast had a horn of their own. But the red and green party blower was no match for our semi-pro musician and it was tucked away as the Gulls wilted under pressure from a strong Alex line-up. It was fun, and when results went our way, the weather was balmy and the atmosphere top notch, we couldn't ask for much more.

Next up were Rochdale, and the season will always be special to me for the brief but exciting run in the League Cup that started with a stunning four-goal salvo from the Alex strikers. They all scored in the warm early evening sunshine, fluent moves and deserved goals for Tony Naylor, Craig Hignett and Phil Clarkson. Jim Harvey chipped in with a rare strike, a swan song for the experienced old head before he moved into management.

The second leg was, without being too derogatory, a formality at Spotland. A steady 2-1 victory gave us an impressive aggregate win and another chance to beat the mighty West Ham United, just a couple of years after our harsh FA Cup defeat at Upton Park.

Anyone who has played the game, at any level, will tell you that hearing words of support from the sidelines really spurs you on. The same applies when you get flak. I remember getting stick from one gobby manager when I played college football around this time. I became more determined than ever to prove him wrong. I suppose different things drive people in many different ways, but his criticism lifted my game. The trumpet and our singing was a huge boost to the players, so Neil Lennon once told me. With his endorsement, there was no chance we could let them down. It was our duty.

Positive chanting from the sidelines is surely the best encouragement, hearing your name sung by hundreds of Alex fans? So we did, game after game, celebrating each and every player in turn, noise reverberating around those rusty Popside girders above our heads. It was a drunken collective that believed we could match the best choirs in the world. The reality was that an alley cat quartet probably held a better tune, but we didn't care. We gave 100% for the Alex, stood on that terrace as though we were positioned for one last stand. It could have fallen down around our ears and we would have carried on, doing our bit for the club.

Our vocal support was tested when the happy Hammers came to Crewe, the tie all square after a surprising 0-0 draw at Upton Park in the first leg. It was the only scoreless game of the season for the Alex, and the fact that Crewe had shut out a host of internationals suggested that an upset was on the cards at Gresty Road. The East Londoners filled the only uncovered area of the ground, and started the night in fine voice.

At the other end, the newly-built family stand opened for the first time. That was packed with supporters fascinated to see what the facility offered, but more so because tickets were in such short supply. The club had invested in the stadium at the end of the 1991-92 season, and the weary old Railway End was transformed from eyesore to modern cantilever stand in a few short months. It was compact, but resplendent in red and boasting a restaurant area that looked out onto the pitch. It was more Wendy's than Waldorf, but at last the club had something resembling a corporate area. With the tidy block of new seating it certainly transformed the ground, three sides now covered from the elements.

Then Richard whipped his trumpet out and the *Eastenders* jingle soon silenced the visitors. They were gob smacked, but mightily impressed when he kick-started their *I'm Forever Blowing Bubbles* anthem. They sang along and accompanied his impeccable playing. That kind of camaraderie brings fans together, and the match took on a party atmosphere after that.

For Billy Bonds' West Ham side, Julian Dicks, Trevor Morley and 'keeper Ludek Miklosko were the big name opponents, but the Alex didn't afford them any courtesy. It was feisty out on the pitch, and although it wasn't a dirty match the referee had his yellow card out several times.

That didn't ruin the flow, and at times it was like watching a tennis match, end to end every few seconds.

We also had a good game on the Popside that night, an awesome array of tunes to keep spirits high. There was a growing feeling that we could win the match, and when Tony Naylor drilled a low shot into the net we almost tumbled onto the pitch. The top corner was packed and the mass of supporters seemed to move as one, side to side and regularly surging down the steps. You can appreciate why the authorities wanted to bring in seating, but those terrace moments were carefree and fabulous. So when Craig Hignett smashed a second past Miklosko we rolled out all of the terrace classics. We thought that we were on our way to Wembley. It was, quite simply, a sublime night.

To achieve that seemingly impossible dream of playing in a major final at the national stadium, we had to keep winning, starting with victory over Nottingham Forest in round three. It was a one-off match, no longer two legs by that stage of the tournament, and I think that suited us fine. It was one night, just ninety frantic minutes with over 7,000 watching from the sidelines, most of them backing the Alex. It was an incredible scene, lights on from the start as winter bullied the last days of autumn and the rain started to fall. It was the perfect setting for another cup upset. Forest didn't fancy it.

I sang myself hoarse that night, easily my best ever performance as a supporter. If I wasn't nudging Richard to fire up his trumpet, I was doing my best to whip up our corner of the ground, our little patch of Popside that encouraged the volume to rise as song after song rippled down the terrace. Until that night, I'd never felt so confident about beating a team from a higher division. The players looked on top of their game, with Craig Hignett scoring goals for fun, while Neil Lennon and Stevie Walters looked a match for any midfield at any level.

So when Forest scored there was a brief pause, disbelief that the script had been changed without our knowledge. That just fired us even more. The noise was relentless, a seething mass of young men roaring the Alex on, determined to support them to the end.

So when the whistle sounded I was light headed, a spent force. I could have done no more, and as one the Popside had given everything. We were the extra man. It just wasn't enough on the night.

That Forest match was the high point for me, an incredible experience that had everything. A superb build up, great mates in the pubs and alongside me on the Popside, the Alex playing some amazing football and equal to a top flight club, plus an atmosphere like any First

Division ground. It wasn't always like that, of course it wasn't. But that night, that special night was top drawer. We had two more years ahead of us before the seating was installed, but if I could roll back time it would be to the night against Nottingham Forest. Okay, so maybe with us winning 1-0, that would be perfect.

BORO BUS TO WEMBLEY

At college in spring 1993 it was nearly exam time, mocks already done and dusted, and revision for finals underway for those prepared to buckle down and put normal distractions to one side. That wasn't for me. I wasn't blasé, but I knew I'd score okay in the June exams. Missing the play-off final was never an option, no matter how many brain cells were destroyed shouting, singing and drinking myself stupid for the cause.

Luckily, a whopping 40% of my final degree grade was based upon the dissertation, a monster study featuring a business topic of the student's choice. For me there was only one option: to incorporate football and marketing, and somehow include the Alex. *Selling The Game* was my masterpiece, a combination of statistics, research, interviews and good old-fashioned waffle that compared the marketing merits and commercial operations of three professional football clubs - Sunderland, Middlesbrough and Crewe Alexandra. So when I'd convinced my tutor that such a study was possible, and that it would make decent reading, I was up and running.

The core research was straightforward and within a few weeks I'd spent time with people at Middlesbrough and Sunderland, gathering data and making comparisons across the two top divisions. The Alex proved tricky, perhaps because it was a much smaller outfit, maybe because they were suspicious. It took a few letters (this was before email), phone calls and finally asking around one match day. It worked, and my persistence saw me invited to the club offices. The Alex chairman, John Bowler, walked in and sat with me at the kitchen table, a cup of tea each and a look of disbelief that someone wanted to examine the administrative mechanics behind the Alex. He has always come across as a mild mannered man, thoughtful, cautious and yet passionate about the things he does. He impressed me that day, and despite a few disagreements between us over the years, I have always admired him for what he has achieved at the club. He and Gill Palin, the then club secretary, couldn't have been more helpful, providing all the information I needed to complete my dissertation.

So my Alex analysis sat alongside details from Middlesbrough, plus some superb input from Sunderland chairman Bob Murray. Even then, before the Wearsiders built the Stadium of Light, he was bursting with pride about his city, where he wanted Sunderland to be and what could be achieved with the right business model at the club. That was the theory stuff, but in his swish offices at Roker Park, he unveiled an impressive scale model of the new stadium that was, at that point, just a dream. I was one of the first to see it, and watching him enthuse about Sunderland's potential would have restored anyone's faith in the people who run the game. He handed me VIP tickets for the weekend's match vs. Southend, and I saw an up-and-coming Stan Collymore grab the match ball with a MotM hat-trick as his side beat Sunderland 4-2. Bob Murray was amongst the first to shake the player's hand, and joked that he'd love to see big Stan in red and white stripes. That never happened, but his magnificent new stadium was a reality within a few years.

Completing my football study was great fun, far removed from the dreary daily lectures, but the course work was the last of my worries as promotion fever intensified. The build-up could not have been better. It rained goals at Gresty Road, and as the season came to a climax I was glued to the house TV as Final Score reported incredible wins over Carlisle and Colchester. I only managed to see perhaps three of the last five games at home, but had no intention of missing the play-off semis when we secured our place in the top seven with a 4-1 win over Barnet.

We hammered Walsall - home and away - and the buzz amongst supporters was, to coin a cheesy phrase, absolutely electric. We were unstoppable. We couldn't stop scoring goals, and the defence wasn't too generous, ably marshalled by Dave McKearney, Shaun Smith and the very hairy Stewart 'Deirdre' Evans. The lanky fella had played up front for two seasons, without much success. A stroke of genius saw him dropped to the back, where he found his calling. With Neil Lennon, Stevie Walters and Tony Naylor looking good, everything was set for an end-of-season spectacular, a day to remember for the rest of our lives. The main concern was getting down to Wembley for the showdown with York City.

Over my three-year college stint I'd been to numerous games with other lads on my course, people who shared the football bug and wanted to see some action at Boro, Hartlepool, Darlington, Sunderland or Newcastle. So we attended loads of games together, but some of the best days out involved Crewe matches. Amazingly, despite dust-ups at a few matches, including the messy day at Carlisle, there was a willing bunch who wanted to join me on the path to promotion.

One of the local lads, Ian, from the tough streets around Ayresome Park, said he'd sort the transport, sufficient to take ten of us down to London in comfort. He knew a bloke at the pub who knew a bloke, and so on. It would cost just £10 each, including petrol, so nobody was complaining. We should have, as a suspiciously feeble beep of a horn signalled his arrival at 7am on the morning of the match. I'd been up for hours, woken the lads from the house and made other calls to ensure that everyone was ready.

We raced outside when Ian arrived, excited and expectant, somehow believing that a Hollywood limousine would be waiting. It wasn't, nor was it a minibus. It was a bulk standard crew bus (pretty apt name I know, but somewhat uncomfortable). The front cabin had two passenger spaces alongside the driver, with one seat belt, while the back was a sparse void adorned with two wooden racks that ran the length of each side of dented metal. Four hours sat on hard racking! There was a spade tucked under one of the benches, and Ian had attached a homemade banner to the roof, partially draped above the windscreen and tucked inside each of the front doors to hold it firm. It read 'Crewe Alexander on tour' which was close enough I suppose, a good effort under the circumstances. I didn't have the heart to criticise the spelling, as he meant well. So we all piled in and made the best of the rather primitive conditions as we rattled down the motorway before most students saw the light of day.

The good thing about football tours is the humour, an ability to overcome the most extreme conditions, and the fact that a plentiful supply of beer was usually on hand, the perfect anaesthetic for a sore backside. We had it in abundance - lagers, bitters, cider and a dodgy bottle of cheap vodka. The playing cards came out, and we were off, down the M1 before the traffic started to build up. A bunch of lads in a van never makes an attractive spectacle, but pulled over on the hard shoulder less than one hour down the road we cut a sorry sight. One being sick, two taking a leak and one doubled up with cramp. Ian, the driver, stood having a fag. And yet we got there, eventually, with two pit stops at services en route, some gesticulating at York City fans and a near miss with a lorry as we almost took an exit in error.

The best bit of the journey was that moment when the twin towers came into view, above the London skyline of apartment blocks and businesses as far as the eye can see. You know you're almost there, that the day proper is about to begin. We made it around noon, leaving far too much time to hit the north London bars. We didn't need topping up, but the demon beer monkey had been released and everyone except the driver was hell bent on liver abuse. Not big, not clever, but the norm for students and away day footy fans.

Thankfully, as we neared the stadium, the pubs were at bursting point and some had strict door policies. So the flow of booze slowed and we didn't become too drunk or disorderly. One weird moment, in a bar not far from the nearby Wembley Park tube station, saw a group of unfamiliar Alex fans supping cocktails. Now I'd acquired a taste for red wine during my time at college, but cocktails! The concoction was called a *Blue Moon*, named after our terrace chant that was eventually claimed by Man City fans. Anyway, Vodka, lemonade and a generous dash of Blue Curacao looked nasty and tasted even nastier. We washed the sickly lining from our mouths with a cold lager and then pushed on to cruise Wembley Way and meander around the stadium, soaking up the atmosphere and getting ready for the action ahead. The numbers didn't quite match my last visit, some ten years earlier with dad when Man United played Brighton, but it was every bit as special, if not more so as I watched thousands of Alex faces, smiling, excitedly chatting and enjoying the moment.

The serious chanting started as the numbers continued to swell and the pubs began to clear, hardly any animosity, just healthy banter with York fans and a few neutrals scattered amongst the masses. Then flags and banners materialised as more of the organised Alex coaches arrived from Crewe, a riot of red and white, air horns blaring and a dazzling array of crazy hats made and purchased especially for the occasion. I bought a programme and immediately wondered where I'd keep it. It was huge, twice the size of a normal matchday rag. Folding it was out of the question, as putting a crease down the centre of such landmark memento would be frowned upon. So I slipped it between my favourite 1990 Synchro-sponsored Alex top and a t-shirt, tucked just above my belt. It was safe, my hands free to grab a pie and punch the air when the Alex scored.

All that remained was to climb those steps into the stadium; the hairs stood up on the back of my neck, as that expanse of green appeared when we reached the summit and looked down into the arena. Thousands of bodies stood to attention by their seats, waiting for that moment when the teams march out onto the hallowed turf. We didn't wait long, and Dario Gradi led his players out wearing a typically workmanlike tracksuit while his counterpart, York manager Alan Little, looked stiff in his new suit. The Alex team emerged in that strange blue and white-flecked shirt, but they could have worn fancy dress for all I cared. It was an incredibly proud moment watching them walk out. And yet it was surreal; Alex players being presented to royalty at Wembley, something usually reserved for the top-flight stars, and something we'd only ever seen on TV. Now it was our turn; the Alex had made the big time!

The game, however, was a blur. Not because of the beer, as that had long since worn off. It was more the frustration, wanting to see the goal that took us up a division, desperate for the referee to end our pain. It didn't happen. Every second was tense, the Alex players looked nervous, mistakes were made and we just couldn't score. I sang myself dizzy, determined to do my bit, start as much of the singing as possible. And yet it was very different from the weekly experience back at Crewe. The hundred-plus regular singers from Gresty Road, the ones who crafted new verses and led the chanting on both the Popside and the Paddock, were scattered across thousands of Wembley seats, pockets of noise here and there, occasionally accompanied by the masses. Only the standard tunes sparked some serious volume, with *Blue Moon* even sung by my extended family from college.

Then time evaporated. The ninety minutes were up; the match was even at 0-0 and another thirty minutes of additional stress beckoned. The players looked knackered, we were physically and emotionally drained, and nerves jangled. Just one strike, a scuffed goal, deflected shot or lucky header – anything to end the pain.

But York scored, at the end of the first period of extra time. Neil Lennon couldn't block a low shot that ultimately beat Mark Smith, and the Irishman was gutted, stamping the turf in frustration. It was all over. The players looked dead on their feet, heads bowed. A few fans crumbled immediately, crying, unable to see a way back for Crewe.

It must have been some rousing words from Gradi and Kenny Swain, the assistant manager back then, because the Alex came out all guns blazing for the second period. We suddenly looked a threat, pushing and probing, daring York to open up. But they were in no mood to be charitable and sat back, defending in numbers. The clock ticked, a deafening soundtrack to our final seconds at Wembley.

Then it all changed again. A stupid handball gifted us a penalty. Dave McKearney stepped up, the world and our hopes rested on his shoulders. He didn't disappoint, slotting the ball past York 'keeper Dean Kiely to level the scores. He raced over to the Crewe fans. He'd saved us. We loved him. And then it really was over. The game was done, more penalties beckoned, and few could watch.

I didn't turn away. McKearney picked the same spot, Shaun Smith blasted high into the roof of the net, but when Gareth Whalley missed our third kick, I knew that it was curtains. Ashley Ward's conversion counted for nothing, as York didn't miss their fifth spot kick, boasting a clean sweep of five well-taken goals.

The losing felt bad enough that afternoon, almost worse than relegation away at Chester two years earlier. There was a moment of anger, then hatred and jealousy as I looked to the jubilant York fans singing and dancing a few hundred yards away. But there was something else as I stood watching York celebrate, an empty sensation, a feeling of isolation although several good mates surrounded me. I wasn't with Crewe people, nor would I be heading back to Cheshire to drown my sorrows with them. It all boils down to moving away in my late teens, ripping up the roots that kept me close to the club as a youngster. Not for the first time I felt like an outsider. I'd done my bit, bringing nine non-Alex fans along to boost the numbers, all sharing my passion for Crewe Alexandra that day, but ultimately they were not distressed as I was.

That emptiness led to tears as the Alex players looped around the perimeter of Wembley's vast pitch, themselves emotional in defeat but grateful that we'd been there with them - all 12,000 of us. I raised my hands above my head and slow-clapped my appreciation as they walked by, socks around their ankles, holding scarves thrown by other supporters and stopping to chat to those by the barriers.

It felt like the end of the world but I knew we'd be back, hopefully the next season. My mate Ian wrapped an arm around my shoulder. There were no words, just a mutual understanding. He'd been there, in that pit of despair with Boro, several seasons earlier, when the administrators locked the gates to Ayresome Park. And yet he was still standing, Boro were back from the dead and football goes on. We grabbed the others and headed to the van, keen to escape some of the traffic that would be heading north.

It didn't end there of course, as no college days out with the lads were straightforward. I was gutted, distraught that we'd lost. Those around me gave me some space, perched precariously on those wooden torture slats. Then they rallied and did their best to drag me from my depression. The England national team was in action that evening, away in Poland for a World Cup qualifier. So a quick decision was made to head off the motorway at Nottingham, find a pub, and then grab food as we watched the game. Ian wasn't impressed, but we'd have made one or two stops on the way home anyway, so this would only add an hour onto the journey. He grudgingly agreed and checked the map.

There was no point scouting for a decent pub, so the first boozer with a sign advertising the England match got our business. It wasn't the best, but a vibrant bunch of locals welcomed us and soon lifted the mood. They ribbed me, about being an Alex fan, as a handful were Notts County supporters and our paths had crossed in the past. But they meant well. I even left the Wembley matchday programme for the landlord, to add to his collection of other football memorabilia dotted around the main bar, stuck to the walls and hanging from the ceiling. I have no idea what the pub was called, but somewhere on the edge of Nottingham there's a piece of Alex history, splashed with beers and tears, maybe still on display. We left as England's World Cup '94 dreams suffered a blow, only managing a 1-1 draw with the Poles.

Back on the motorway the day took another bizarre turn as Ian pulled off for petrol. As we left the service station we noticed a hitchhiker trying to attract the attention of lorries and cars. He was having no luck, so I suggested giving the lad a break and a lift up north. Stuart was going to York but had nothing to do with the football; he was just studying in the beautiful cathedral city. He was cautious at first, unsure about hopping into the back of a van that stank like a brewery, amongst other things! So it was probably kidnap, but he soon got into the spirit and tucked into some of the cans that still littered the floor. He had such a laugh in the back of that tatty crew bus that he decided to return to Boro with us. It saved Ian another drop-off, and we got to the student union bar around midnight, sweet-talking the door staff to let us in for a few cheeky late ones - like we needed any topping up!

Stuart had a riot, realised that college drinking could be taken to a higher level than he'd previously seen at York, joined us for the obligatory kebab and then collapsed on the floor of our lounge. I woke at lunchtime the following day and he was gone, just a note saying thanks for a crazy night. We never heard from him again, so I hope that he made it back to York in one piece. Hopefully, he'll have Crewe Alexandra as one of his second or third favourite teams.

SLOW BOAT TO... LIEGE!

Occasionally, things just spiral out of control, and if you're game for almost anything then crazy things can happen. Something very strange occurred after college, and as usual there were Alex connections. It all started when I surprised the hell out of a former girlfriend by honouring a date we'd made after my finals. It wasn't a date as such, more like old friends getting together to see how things had panned out after leaving Middlesbrough. My course had finished but she had a working year in

France, with an aviation firm, to complete her degree. So it was more a moral support thing, a friendly face going out to visit her.

Sadly, I had very little cash. I was back at home in Alsager after completing a few temp jobs in Middlesbrough during the summer, and I managed to see most of the opening games at the start of the 1993-94 season. But that wiped out my remaining money. So in early September I headed to London to stay with a mate, to figure out my next life move and earn some cash. Then I remembered my promise about going to France.

So it was a last-minute decision, well, a last-minute realisation that I'd promised to see how she was getting on. So I called at 6pm, chatted, and then agreed to head down the next day, arriving in Bordeaux around 5pm to meet her after she finished work. I didn't tell her, but I intended to hitch hike. It was the only way I could afford it, leaving myself a few quid for food and drinks when I got there. So I decided to start immediately, getting to Dover to catch a late ferry, leaving a full day to reach the south of France by Friday afternoon. Simple.

All went well and I managed to jump in with a lorry driver who said he'd take me to the edge of Paris. On the ferry, however, I looked at a map of France. I traced the A10 autoroute that dropped south from the A6 near Paris, followed it down, and then a bit further down. Sheeesh! It was over 500km to Bordeaux. It was a good job I'd set out a day early!

I made the rendezvous, at a café on Place Gambetta, with about fifteen minutes to spare thanks to a generous driver who dropped me in the heart of the city. We had a fantastic weekend, and then I made my way back home on Monday morning. I wanted to get back to Crewe for the weekend, as the Alex had a home game with Darlington. So I figured a day's trek back to Calais, over to Dover and on to London, before making my way back to Cheshire some time on the Wednesday or Thursday. Plenty of time, I told myself.

Best laid plans, and all that... I landed at Dover quite late on Monday evening, too late to make it back to London if I wanted to catch the last trains or tubes from the edge of the city. So I dived into a bar to assess my options. I include this sidetrack because, from the moment I stepped into the pub that evening, proudly wearing the latest Alex top, I was 'that Crewe fan' to about fifty Cardiff City supporters. Now relations between Cardiff and the Alex have not been too hot across the years, and as I faced the bar that night I did wonder if I'd get a severe pasting. That would have been harsh, almost alien to footy hoolies whose code dictates that there's nothing very clever taking out a single opponent. I was no threat, knackered from my long journey and only after a beer.

The pub was packed for two reasons. First, the tail end of a Monday night *Soccer Special* was being shown on Sky TV. Second, the Welsh lads fancied a few beers before they caught a late night ferry. They were already in raucous mood and their holdalls, rucksacks and bags littered the pub floor.

'Bloody hell, it's a Crewe fan,' was the opening gambit by one of the group.

He came striding over, pint of lager in hand and a bit of a swagger, and then offered me his hand. I'd seen this in pubs many times, where the handshake suddenly becomes a head butt. So I was ready, conscious that he might be out to impress his mates. He wasn't, and Tom turned out to be a decent lad, just a tad drunk. He was one of the more vocal of the large group, effectively one of the younger 'firms' with a bunch of other mates tagged on.

This is how things panned out. They were off to Belgium, to see Cardiff play Standard Liege in the Cup Winners Cup. It was the mother of all booze-ups, a chance to follow the Bluebirds in Europe. I was envious, as I couldn't see the Alex ever getting that opportunity, unless they let us back into the Welsh Cup again. The lads were buzzing about the trip, and within ten minutes they'd talked me into joining their expedition. I had a few clothes in my bag, about £20 in cash and a credit card, and I desperately needed a shave and a wash.

None of that mattered. In fact, Tom boldly predicted that I wouldn't need a penny. He'd been on numerous trips with Cardiff, where the sheer numbers and boisterous nature of their fans meant that most figures of authority just wanted to get rid of them. As a result, tickets and passes didn't come into the equation. So we drank up and headed to the ferry.

Sure enough, with a mob of Bluebirds singing, shouting and generally causing mayhem in the ferry terminal, it wasn't long before a few police vans arrived and we were ushered onto the ferry. Not a single ticket was checked, although a couple of the Cardiff lads did have them. I still felt a little uneasy, and wondered if the whole trip was going to be the ultimate stitch up.

Things progressed to an all-out party when the ferry set off to Ostend. A couple of stag parties were already in the main bar, so an additional one hundred tanked up Welsh men was potentially a recipe for disaster. A couple of police officers had joined the ferry, probably because of the numbers involved. I also got the feeling that a few of these lads were known faces, probably wanted for misdemeanours elsewhere. At one point, pints were flowing without a penny changing hands as the overstretched bar staff struggled to keep tabs on drinks ordered, or indeed keep an eye on beer pumps at each end of the long bar. It was chaos, but trouble free because everyone had a constant supply of alcohol.

On Belgium soil it was a similar scenario to Dover. The police were now out in force, ready for the imminent invasion. I heard several officers speaking French, telling their colleagues to simply get rid of the hooligans, get them onto trains and out of the terminal. My modest French was to be an asset and a curse over the next few days. Still, we were quite literally herded into the carriages and the train set off to Liege as first light started to break.

The football banter during the night was brilliant, and the Bluebirds' hatred of Swansea made any Alex rivalry with Vale, Stoke or Chester look like neighbours squabbling over whom should cut the hedge. They really meant it, and some of the stories about matchday clashes sounded like scripts from horror movies, just without the fake blood. They talked about meeting with a few Alex lads over the years, bust-ups on station platforms and a couple of skirmishes around the Nantwich Road pubs. But it was all good humoured and there was no bitterness. I was the token Crewe fan, and over several hours every one of them came over to check me out and take a peep at my Alex top.

I'll keep this short as it's starting to go way off topic, but the carnage in Liege was a sight to behold. At least another hundred were already roaming the streets when we arrived, filling the cafes that served breakfast and beers. Some were rolling drunk after a night on the ale; others were keen to catch up and threw it down their necks like there was no tomorrow. Tom told me to follow him and a few of his closest mates to a B&B. There, one of them signed in, before fifteen piled up the stairs to ditch their luggage. I considered this for a moment, but decided to leave mine in the train station lockers. After all, it was only for the day and I had visions of losing my few possessions. By now I'd swapped my shirt and resorted to wearing just my Alex pin badge, as a few of the less social Bluebirds had given me some seriously filthy looks as we got into Liege. I didn't think any of the lads I'd met would stitch me up, but I was still pretty uneasy about the whole situation. Then things took a nosedive when I spoke with a few of the Cardiff boys at the next bar.

'What time's the match,' I asked one of them.

'Think it's 7.30 mate, tomorrow night,' he replied.

'Tomorrow night!' I repeated, jaw on the floor.

It was, a Wednesday evening kick-off, and we'd arrived in Liege around breakfast time on the Tuesday morning. Another 36 hours with a bunch of crazy Welsh men!

The mayhem around the bars soon got out of hand. One lad would order drinks, pass them around, and then walk away leaving the bar staff scratching their heads. Receipts and tabs were left on the bar, but nobody collected them. It must have taken three or four hours before the owners realised that they were unlikely to be paid. That's when tempers flared, but unfortunately the Bluebirds were topped up and ready to fight anyone.

Around midday, the first window went through. About seventy lads were doing the *Ayatollah*, a head slapping ritual as they bounced up and down. It was something they'd done on the terraces for a few seasons, and now it was performed when groups of fans got together in pubs. The Belgians didn't know what to make of it, or them! Two barmen challenged one group about settling the bill, and within seconds all diplomacy – and a large table – had gone out of the window. A few locals stepped in to help the staff, but they were no match for the large numbers of Cardiff fans – every one of them prepared to pitch in when required. It soon spilled onto the street, and similar happened in a number of bars fronting one of the picturesque public squares.

The police were on hand but you could tell that they were waiting for back up. It came, with a series of vans screeching through the crowded streets with sirens blazing. There were a few running battles in front of the bars that had been damaged, but the police were seriously togged up in full riot gear. They weren't shy about using their batons either. I got cornered with about fifteen Cardiff lads, including Tom. That's when I decided to flex my second language, especially as Liege is a French-speaking district of Belgium.

Five minutes of grovelling followed, a series of apologies on behalf of various youths, and trying to explain to the officers that my Cardiff amigos were unable to speak any French, and that they had been confused rather than wanting to avoid paying the bill, or cause trouble. I was an unlikely hero, an Alex legend that would extend into South Wales long after the trip.

It didn't last. Incidents happened all day and into the evening, with more of the same on the Wednesday – the day of the game. By then there must have been 500 fans in town, with Liege nutters making the whole situation much worse. Then, leading up to kick-off, it went bonkers down by the train station. I was relatively sober, as I'd kept off the beer as much as possible that afternoon. But the police were indiscriminate, charging down groups of four, five and more, batons connecting with anyone who dared move or fight back.

Then the water cannons came out, and seeing fans swept off their feet and lifted into the air remains one of the strangest things I've seen before a football match. To cap a truly unforgettable experience, as we approached the stadium (without tickets) about fifty riot police waded in and cornered about thirty-to-forty supporters, me included. I was mixed in amongst a group that had just trashed another bar. Guilty by association, I was cuffed to a long metal railing beneath one of the stands. Suddenly, my French cut no ice. Others were taken to a different building nearby. The shame of it all, especially when they called me Cardiff hooligan scum!

So after all that, a day and a half with the Welsh lads, I didn't even see the match. Liege won 5-2 that night, and the police made a point of feeding us details as the goals went in. It was like a dripping tap, slowly torturing us as we stood there in the cold. They cracked jokes in French and had a great time seeing us suffer. After the final whistle, they stuffed us on buses and then forced us into the train station. I got my bag, just, after another garbled conversation in Franglais. So ditching my holdall in a station locker was the only good decision I made that trip!

Back in Dover, I stepped off the ferry and made a sharp exit for the main terminal, hoping for a lift back up to London and then on to Crewe ready for Saturday's match. I grabbed a few of the tabloid newspapers from a kiosk, keen to check that I hadn't been snapped alongside my unlikely Welsh friends. Their antics were splashed all over the front and back pages. Some of them were hastily rounded up as we passed through the terminal, British spotters ready for some of the usual suspects.

A thought struck me as I watched another lunatic being led away. Most of the Alex fans I knew loved to party, and they knew how to enjoy themselves on their travels. There are occasions when we all have a few too many drinks, often at the football, but there's something that stops most people going too far. That, I decided, applied to most Crewe supporters. With Cardiff, however, there was a significant core of men (and they were, mostly) who took things to a different level. Smashing up bars, assaulting police officers and attacking other groups of supporters en masse was second nature to some of them, certainly some of the lads I'd seen over two crazy days in Belgium. Their actions would probably see them banned, cast aside by their club. They would also drag their club's name through the mud once again. Thank goodness this didn't apply to the Alex. I didn't look back as I walked away, and headed to the truck exit point hoping for my first lift of the day.

Three weeks later I went into a pub, a Welsh boozer. As luck would have it, the fixture list had us away at Cardiff and it was too much to resist. I travelled over with two of the London lads, on the train rather than hitching for once. It was out of the way, more a city centre bar than a football pub. Then a bunch of Bluebirds came in and the mood changed. There were a few other Crewe fans by the bar, all wearing red Alex tops. Hardly targets for the Cardiff boys, but a few comments were thrown across the room. We were dressed in jeans and plain jackets, not even Alex badges on show. So when two of them came striding over towards us there was a brief panic. Had they been listening to our conversation, or did we just stand out from the locals? Neither was true; it was Tom and one of his mates, and he had recognised me from the other side of the pub.

This is one of those never-ending stories, as in March 2005 Cardiff visited Crewe for another league encounter. I popped into the Brunnie for a cheeky pre-match beer and guess who was stood at the bar? I shook hands with Tom once more, chatted, swapped stories and memories, and then headed our separate ways to watch the match. It's just one of those daft football friendships that will never die...

A SCORE SETTLED

Like elephants, football fans never forget. Being relegated by Chester hurt like hell, and that emotional day was the last time I shed a football tear. Revenge was always on Alex fans' minds in subsequent seasons, and I developed an irrational hatred of our Cheshire neighbours.

We beat them in Autoglass Trophy and FA Cup games, and then the following year at Gresty Road in league action when they returned to the bottom division. So the tail end of the 1993-94 campaign got pretty feisty when it became apparent that Chester would be one of our main promotional rivals. We had them in our sights throughout the season, and that chance to really even things up was enough to drive even the most placid supporters.

The Alex had a decent post-Christmas spell and managed to stay close to the frontrunners during the run-in, with games against the leading clubs still to come. The only disappointment was the team's failure to top the table. The Alex were something of an attacking force, almost gung-ho at times, and the football was always exciting. If the goals against column showed two or three conceded, we expected to see two, three or four banged in by Tony Naylor, Darren Rowbotham and Ashley Ward.

One bizarre match put a huge dent in our promotion aspirations.

Alex 'keeper Mark Smith got sent off after 19 seconds away at Darlington in early March, another whacky match I managed to attend from afar. You spend hours travelling to the game, full of hope, and then watch your goalkeeper force a team reshuffle after the first minute. We lost, which was no surprise, but that enforced change obviously unsettled the team, as further back-to-back defeats followed to put promotion chatter on the backburner. It wasn't until new stopper Mark Gayle arrived that fortunes changed and belief returned. In fact, Gayle was one of my favourite goalkeepers - tall, dominant in the area and someone prepared to bark at his defenders. He was the lean, athletic type to Smithy's more comfortable physique. And he managed to stay on the pitch for 90 minutes!

There was certainly a decent vibe about the club during this era, and players and supporters enjoyed good relations. Driven by men like Neil Lennon, confidence oozed from the club and it rubbed off on us. The squad had great balance, young and old, homegrown and journeymen. There was also plenty of pace and a few stoppers to break up play, really frustrate the opposition. Most of the players were happy to mix with the fans, around Gresty Road on match days, and in the Alexandra Suite after the final whistle. They were down to earth, enjoyed a pint with us, took criticism and gave a little back when they disagreed with our comments. We were all in it together. Some of my trips from down south were arduous, but it was nearly always worth it, those sessions in the Alex Suite made the days very special.

The penultimate home game, a Tuesday night match against Wigan, was a classic. We needed a win as three tough games followed, all against contenders, and the top of the table was horribly congested. It was a nasty run-in and the mother of all long shots, but we could still lift the title with four straight wins and other results going our way. It was fanciful thinking, and amazing that it was actually possible after some inconsistent results. Above us were two local rivals – Shrewsbury, who we held 0-0 at Gresty Road a week earlier, and Chester, our final opponents. It was all set up for a fantastic last few weeks. I manufactured numerous excuses to spend maximum time in Cheshire, desperate to be part of another promotion. Missing the remaining games just wasn't an option.

Wigan didn't roll over, but we played a massive part that evening as the vocal encouragement reached new heights and unsettled the visitors. Crowds were average that season, but our band of singers were packed like sardines, all delighted to be the twelfth man, doing our bit with some incredible chants. And being part of that swaying, intimidating mass was intoxicating. With every attack, foul or contentious moment we staggered down the steps like drunken warriors, desperate to see the action, clinging on to anything around them. Before the advent of all-seater grounds, a decent crowd at Gresty Road could be very off putting. We were up close and personal, inches away from the match official running the line. I remember a few of the Wigan players that night, looking anxious as they stepped back to take throw-ins. They didn't want to get too close, as they got blasted each time they came anywhere near us. It worried them, and they quivered as they attempted to take throw-ins. We were part of the team that night, and that bond was electrifying.

Eventually, they were broken down, and a goal from Neil Lennon was particularly sweet as we started to dominate the game. He raced over to the Popside, thumping the air, swinging wildly like a punch-drunk boxer.

'Come on,' he growled through clenched teeth.

Hundreds answered his call, and a couple of stewards pulled him clear of the mêlée, as delirious fans clambered by the barriers desperate to embrace him. He was wired, a one-man midfield tornado tearing up everything in his path. He was certainly on a mission, and you could tell how much he wanted the promotion that season.

It eventually finished 4-1, going up looked odds on and Alex fans were already in high spirits. There was the customary end-of-season pitch invasion, despite pleas from a desperate official voice over the PA system. It was futile, as hardly anyone could hear him and few cared. Promotion was within touching distance - just three away games to go, with nine points up for grabs. Jumping on to the grass, dashing down the line like the fastest winger and touching the players made it very real. Neil Lennon loved the attention, and if he weren't on the pitch he would have been with us. You could see the excitement in his eyes, a big kid that shared the same dreams of every supporter. He knew what was possible, and he realised what it meant to us.

After a few minutes we climbed back into the Popside as the police and stewards started to clear the pitch. There was time for a pint in the Royal, and I think I wore out my copy of the programme that night, pouring over the league table, working out possible outcomes and trying to predict our finishing position. I had a lift back to Alsager sorted, but I cancelled, as there was too much going on around Nantwich Road. There was no way I was missing the post-match beers that would extend late into the night.

I didn't get back until the early hours, spent up and unable to get a taxi. Shanks' pony came to the rescue and I eventually walked through the door just before first light, absolutely knackered but thinking only of promotion as my head hit the pillow.

Unfortunately, nothing ever goes smoothly when you follow the Alex, and a few days later at Rochdale we lost 2-1 and slipped out of contention again. It was like trying to climb a greasy pole, never quite making it to the top. I couldn't get up to Spotland and spent the entire match chasing Teletext updates back at home, my thumb worn out as I refreshed the page constantly. One game, one lousy defeat and everything changed. The next morning was spent analysing every inch of coverage given to Division Three, but the Alex hardly got a mention in the Sunday papers, and that made it worse. I was driving myself crazy. There was no midweek game, so it was a full week spent torturing myself with statistics, wondering if we'd blown it again.

So Wycombe at Gresty Road couldn't come soon enough. I hardly slept on the Friday night, instead succumbing to an hour's kip in the back of the car when I travelled back to Crewe with a few London-based mates early on Saturday morning. It was Wycombe's first season in the league, so they were relative unknowns. They were up there, looking for points to nudge themselves into the automatic promotion places. So it was a massive game for them as well.

Some aggressive Lewis Hamilton manoeuvres on the motorway saw us back in Cheshire by 11.45am, and the next three hours were spent cruising the pubs, chatting non-stop football with the early Alex arrivals and the visiting supporters that didn't mind mixing it with a few northerners. In fact, those Wycombe lads stand out as some of the best fans I have met. Level headed, ambitious but realistic about their club's chances, respectful of others, keen to see football played on the deck and full of admiration for what the Alex tried to achieve. They were a top bunch, and it was a relaxed atmosphere from start to finish. Wycombe had come up from the non-league, so I suppose their support was still developing. Just like the Alex losing fans to Liverpool, Stoke and the Manchester clubs, for years young Buckinghamshire lads had travelled into London for their football, or headed to Oxford, Reading or maybe Luton. Now they too had a club to be proud of. They were on the up.

Mutual admiration and platitudes aside, there was a game to win. The team taking three points would secure third spot with one game remaining, so perhaps the chilled pre-match atmosphere was just what the fixture needed considering so much was at stake. Of course, everything changes when the referee's whistle signals the start of the game. Ninety minutes of nail-biting frustration, willing the ball into the net, hoping for lucky deflections, goalkeeper errors or penalty decisions in our favour. It didn't help going into the interval all square, Ash Ward grabbing Crewe's goal. We wondered if that would be enough, if taking a draw would still give us a chance the following Saturday?

Most football fans are pessimistic, always fearing the worst unless their team is three or four goals ahead. As far as the Alex team was concerned, we needed five goals some games. If a lead could be thrown away, the Alex would. Perhaps it was the attacking nature of the side, always looking to break clear with Tony Naylor scampering down the left, or Darren Rowbotham using his pace, guile and extensive catalogue of tricks to slip past defenders. It was exciting, no doubt about that. And yet at the business end of the season we just wanted a win.

So it was a relief that Neil Lennon was at his imperious best, a true gladiator leading the men around him, always by example. Others were equal, like Steve Macauley and Gus Wilson, both no-nonsense players who knew that there was a job to be done. And yet it was a player with real flair who will be remembered as the saviour that day.

Ash Ward also knew how to mix it, and at over six feet tall he was no shrinking violet. That combination made him stand out in the basement division, and goals the following season would see him earn a deserved move to Norwich City. However, it was his winning goal against Wycombe that mattered to us. He scored a beauty, we hung on to the end, and endured several desperate minutes of injury time when many turned their backs, unable to watch the final seconds.

The ball was now in our court. Win at Chester and we were up! There was even chance to wish the Wycombe lads the best of luck for their final game. We owed them that, and they were gracious in defeat.

Then, it all boiled down to one match. The defeat at Rochdale had ended any lingering hopes of the title, but it also left us four points adrift of Chester who had been strong in the final weeks. They were already promoted and able to enjoy the day. So the game was about making sure we took the third promotion place and, if possible, dented Chester's season. Petty stuff, but we owed them one.

***

In Chester we were presented with the well-trodden route of pubs from the station, weaving into the touristy town centre, before making our way to the ground. Of course, they had a new stadium and this was my first visit. So we headed over a little earlier than usual to check it out.

Not far from the Deva Stadium, as we wandered about looking for another pub, a car pulled up alongside us. The initial reaction was that a bunch of Chester nutters were scouting the streets for Alex fans, hoping to find a bit of trouble. The car was basic, a bit tatty around the edges, so it was a surprise when the window rolled down and Neil Lennon stuck his head out to ask for directions to the ground. Shaun Smith, Gus Wilson and Steve Garvey were also in the car, hoping they'd asked the right people. They, like us, were completely lost. We did our best to help them, although we'd not yet found the new ground ourselves. We just pointed them roughly in the right direction and wished them all the best for the game.

There's always been a fierce rivalry between the two clubs, but the build up to kick-off that day wasn't as tense as usual. It was strangely relaxed and a little unnerving if I'm honest. The Chester fans carried banners into the ground and released hundreds of blue and white balloons. They'd had a rough time, forced to travel nearly forty miles to home games at Macclesfield, so this was a fresh beginning for them, and promotion was a superb way to celebrate the new era at the Deva Stadium.

We couldn't join in the fun, as there was work to do. We'd beaten Chester 2-1 at Gresty Road in November, so doing the double was a perfect way to end our season. In fact, securing that final win was essential, as a draw would have left us at the mercy of the play-offs once again. We'd been beaten by Scunthorpe in the semi-final two years earlier, and then left Wembley emotionally drained a year later. So nobody fancied a third gamble in the end-of-season lottery.

A few minutes into the game, Ash Ward broke free and should have given us the lead. He didn't, and the first goal went to Chester, scored in front of us. We stood motionless as the rest of the ground rocked, fearful that it just wasn't our day. Their supporters weren't bothered that we had started to dominate the game, and they sang relentlessly about their charge up the divisions.

They should have been worried, as Tony Naylor was a constant threat. It was his inch-perfect free-kick that levelled the scores and he could have grabbed a hat-trick if luck had been on our side. That would have been just rewards for a marvellous season for the tricky winger. He hit three at home to Hereford back in October, and although we lost at Leeds in the FA Cup he'd scored an amazing solo goal to send us into raptures at Elland Road.

The Alex looked stunning that season, in a kit that resembled the Union Jack flag. Looking around the packed terrace at Chester, those shirts were everywhere. They were worn with pride and carried the hopes of thousands. It certainly felt as though our momentum would see us win the day, but wave upon wave of Crewe attacks were stubbed out. The Chester players were intent on finishing their season on a high.

It helped that the Alex attacked our end in the second half. Each time the ball crossed the halfway line the volume increased, willing the players forward, sucking the ball towards the Chester goal. It had to happen, and finally two thousand supporters clad in red, white and blue soared into the air as one. Ash Ward glided past defenders that looked rooted to the spot. He pushed the ball inside, then onto his right foot, as effortlessly as a magician palms cards, and then he lit the fuse. It was no slow burner, as he unleashed a rocket into the top corner. We went mental as the net bulged. Ward raced over, some couldn't resist leaping onto the pitch and even the Crewe dugout exploded with joy.

We knew that was enough, but only the referee's whistle could confirm the promotion. Those final minutes were hell, those desperate nail-biting moments when you want time to fly. Then the dream became reality. Chester fans applauded, a little miffed but still delighted that they'd gone up. We were on cloud nine. We had beaten Chester to secure promotion on the last day of the season. It couldn't have been scripted much better. A score had been settled, but only until we met them the following season. Football grudges are never forgotten for long.

So for twenty minutes supporters of both clubs mingled on the pitch, congratulating players, singing and dancing on the lush grass. Ash Ward was carried on fans' shoulders like a god, Neil Lennon threw his sweaty shirt into the crowd and a conga started in front of the goal. A few went over the top, trying to grab souvenirs from the ground. That was stupid, and the police were quick to collar a few of the offenders. It was just high spirits, as supporters don't get many moments like that. The players disappeared and only returned for a lap of honour when things had quietened down. They walked out with bottles of champagne, no boots, some stripped to a pair of shorts, worn out but keen to share the moment with supporters who were now running through the back catalogue of Alex songs.

I turned round and my mate Ray was gone, dragged away by stewards and police. It was the usual over reaction that resulted in some heavy handed tactics. They wanted to make a point and removed about forty Alex lads, employing a sledgehammer to crack a walnut.

We met Ray later, when he had been released. He'd been thrown inside a police van, no charges, just detained in one of those sterile portable units for an hour after the match, cuffed to a railing with a zippy clip. No damage done, but he'd missed an hour of amazing celebrations in the pubs back in Chester town centre.

All that remained was the journey back to Crewe, a pint and a takeaway, and then on to Alsager. By now, I'd moved to London and looked as though I'd be staying there. But there was no way I wanted to return to the capital where our promotion would mean nothing. The boys were in party mood, and we managed to get a few late ones, after hours in the *Alsager Arms* as usual. We didn't leave until 3am, as Anna, one of the barmaids we knew well, joined our drinking games, and was happy to keep serving until we dropped. I crashed on her floor that night, as I didn't want mum thinking that I was treating the house like a hotel. Turning up at that time would have been out of order; especially when they didn't know I was back in town. I'd intended to call earlier that day, but became wrapped up in the occasion.

So I kept a low profile and woke with a stiff back the following morning. I also had a very sore head as the sun crept through the lounge curtains at stupid o'clock, so a couple of bacon and cheese oatcakes from Barry's Pantry was the best cure before catching the train back to London. The Sunday papers made fantastic reading and I soon forgot any discomfort. The Alex had secured promotion with a dramatic last-day victory, so for once we enjoyed plenty of coverage in the nationals. I fell asleep on the train, but you can't go wrong when Euston is the end of the line.

LONDON CALLING

'Choose life… but why would I want to do a thing like that?' said Mark Renton, lead character (played by actor Ewan McGregor) in the brilliant *Trainspotting* film that came out not long after my arrival in London. Thankfully, I didn't follow the fictional Scotsman down the heroin path, but I did choose a rather unconventional post-college career in London. Indeed, becoming a care assistant for young adults with Cerebral Palsy raised a few eyebrows, I can tell you.

Of all the things that I could have done, this was perhaps the least likely. I should have sent a CV and copies of my dissertation to football clubs around the country, secured a graduate starter job in the commercial department somewhere around the leagues. I didn't, probably because I secretly hankered for some involvement at the Alex. The case study whetted my appetite and even then I believed that I might be able to help improve things, offering a few new ideas and some fresh momentum. That was never likely to happen, such was the modest operation behind the scenes at Gresty Road during those dark days in the lower divisions. It wasn't quite a one-man band, but it was run on a shoestring. I could, however, have gone elsewhere, but maybe there was more to it than that. Working too closely with another team could have offended Mistress Alexandra, made her jealous with rage. So in another rash and foolish move I shelved any ideas about football administration and hit the bright lights of London.

Still, a job was a job, albeit a voluntary position. It came with a meagre allowance for food and, thankfully, an all zones pass for the underground system. But, and it's a massive BUT, it also came with accommodation, that priceless commodity in one of the world's most expensive cities. It was a start, something to build on, but feeding my nasty football habit called for additional ingenuity if I was to attend as many games as possible. The train was expensive, but if I could get to games in Crewe there was always a way to work the system and get back to London.

And so began the start of a very fruitful spell of hitchhiking - free travel, the chance to meet some wild and wonderful characters, but a potentially dangerous undertaking. It started a few months earlier, with trips to the girlfriend in Bordeaux when I realised that trains and ferries came at a significant price. So negotiating the busy south London routes to Dover, getting to know wagon drivers who were happy to take you through customs, on to Paris, around the mind-blowing Périphérique and then hours and hours down the A10 to southwest France... well, it certainly hones your hitching skills.

Heading north, up the M1, M6 and home to Alsager was a piece of cake. The freebie underground pass took me as far as Edgware, and I soon discovered a quick route to a slip road that fed the start of the M1 motorway.

Top tips for wannabe hitchers: have a shave beforehand, don't look too scruffy, and carry a reasonably smart sports bag. It worked for me, and the varied cross section of drivers who were prepared to stop never ceased to amaze me. There were young students, lorry drivers, sales reps, elderly ladies and, occasionally, fellow football fans. As anyone who knows me will tell you, I like a good chat. So conversations were lively, often centred on football, and I'd like to think that a few of the people I met still look out for Alex results.

One hitchhike involved the first round of the FA Cup, something I rarely missed, no matter where I was based around the UK. The Alex had a home tie with Gresley Rovers that autumn. I decided to double-up and see the parents on the Friday night, grab a few beers with mates, then on to the match the next morning. I'd made a few tough trips already that season, including horrendous journeys to Hull (where we lost 7-1) and Birmingham (a slightly less harsh 5-0 thrashing). The match at St. Andrew's was a Tuesday night fixture, and as well as being chased by thirty Blues fans after the final whistle (for no apparent reason) I didn't get home until 5am! So a casual stopover was a much more leisurely approach, and most Crewe fans looked to the cup clash with non-league opposition as light relief from the heavy-going league campaign. For me it was like a weekend break, just on a budget.

Unfortunately, getting back that Friday night didn't go as planned. I made the usual starting point in good time, around 3.30pm, which meant getting back to Alsager around 7pm. More often than not I'd bag a lift up the M1 and get out at the Watford Gap, unless the driver was northwest bound. Then, with a cheeky M6/Crewe sign displayed at the service station, I'd usually find a driver heading to Manchester or Liverpool who would drop me off at the Little Chef by junction 16. From there, dad would come and collect me or a friendly face of old would recognise me and drop me off in the village.

Things looked dubious when I got off the tube. Dark clouds hovered above me, looking particularly menacing, before they finally dropped their load. After a five-minute wait on the slip road I was drenched, soaking wet and looking pretty miserable. Now this works two ways: first, someone will take pity and stop because it's raining, not because they regularly give lifts to hitchhikers; or, second, everyone whizzes past because they don't want a steaming wet, smelly passenger sat beside them for a couple of hours. On this occasion, the latter scenario played out. I was stuck. I looked like a drowned rat. I was going nowhere.

By five o'clock I considered doubling back, ditching the whole idea and getting home to the warmth of the flat. But I'm no quitter and I really didn't want to miss the cup match. Thankfully, my patience was finally rewarded when a flash, bright yellow Toyota MR2 screeched to a halt a few yards down the road. Aficionados of sports cars and hitchhiking will appreciate that this was no match made in heaven, especially when you consider that the car was loaded with two burly men. There were only two seats, plus a shelf at the back suitable for a briefcase or a couple of shopping bags. I stood motionless for several seconds, unsure what to do. Were they serious?

'You getting in or what, mate?' was all I heard, a gruff voice posing a brief question, tossed casually from the window.

Nobody got out. I had no idea what they looked like, or who they were.

In the end, it was a case of beggars can't be choosers. The clock was ticking. I was wet, very wet. They were, it transpired, heading back to Liverpool, their accents a dead giveaway. So I squeezed into the back, sideways, with my bag on my knees. There was a suspicious looking black holdall stuffed behind the driver. I had no intention of asking what was inside. Then, for ten minutes, not a word was spoken.

Now considering this was a sports car, it wasn't very fast. The fella driving kept crunching the gears, and it did cross my mind that the bloke's name might not be on the vehicle registration document. Then, without warning, he pulled over onto the hard shoulder. They both got out. It was mid-November, nearly 6pm by now, pitch black and still raining. I had visions of ending my days in a bin liner, propping up a motorway sign, just a few daisies marking the spot on another anonymous stretch of grass verge - the tomb of the unknown football supporter! They didn't even let me out to stretch my legs. Thankfully, they were just checking the engine. They had encountered problems driving through London and had decided to take things easy. It wasn't what I'd hoped for, as a stop-start journey home beckoned, but at least I wasn't about to get murdered!

The Gresley Rovers match was definitely worth the effort. It was a romp, a cup game to really kick-start the rest of the season. The Alex hit seven that day, with Ash Ward smashing a deserved hat-trick and Darren Rowbotham grabbing a brace. In the Alex Suite afterwards we met Rowbo, a regular in the bar, friendly and easy to talk to. He also spoke his mind. He jokingly suggested that Ward's final goal was greedy and that he should have passed – to him! A few other players wandered in that early evening, and they were all brimming with confidence and convinced that the Alex could be a force in the Third Division. The cup win was a springboard, and some rash predictions were made ahead of the Christmas fixtures. That was always heartening coming from the lads on the pitch, rather than sound bites from the manager who often seemed to be watching a different game. The players were on our level, aware of the trials and tribulations of being a supporter.

Two weeks later, in an Auto Windscreens match at Chester, Ash Ward hit another hat-trick as we thrashed our local rivals 6-0. The following week he was gone, sold to Norwich in a deal that brought significant funds into the Alex but stripped fans of one of their favourite players. It never rained it poured!

***

After most Saturday matches, if I was heading back to London, there was an hour to spare before I raced down Gresty Road and along Nantwich Road to the train station. I hitched back, once, but soon realised that things were different in the evenings – especially on Saturdays. Less people were prepared to stop, unless I found an Alex fan heading my way. But there was an easier option. Around 6pm, the trains were packed with supporters from many different clubs, and if it didn't happen on Crewe or Birmingham New Street stations there would usually be an altercation of some kind in the carriages down to London. With another chaotic mix of allegiances converging at Euston, the police and ticket inspectors were kept very busy. It was chaos, and getting rid of football fans was top priority, whether they had valid tickets or not. So I hardly ever bought one. It was such a rush, you understand, that there was no opportunity to queue up without missing my connection south. I always had cash, plus my student railcard that hadn't expired. So I was prepared to pay, but very rarely had to part with any money. Back in London, the tube pass kicked in and I'd be home within the hour.

Fare dodging, and let's face it that's what it was, soon became tiresome, and I wanted the freedom to follow the Alex as and when I pleased. So the care work eventually led to a full-time position with a guy who provided services for people with disabilities. But it still didn't pay enough, certainly not enough to get to more than one or two games each month. That was torture, hearing details of the games I missed second hand, reading reports about our steady climb up the table, or news about the up-and-coming Danny Murphy who excited everyone with his assured play and eye for goal. So after six months I knew that I had to join the rat race, get a proper job and wear a suit.

As so often happens, a chance conversation eventually provided that link to earning a decent salary. I'd popped into a recruitment agency to ask about a temporary job but left with an interview to become a recruitment consultant, in the financial district of the city. Another less than obvious career choice, but a salary I really couldn't refuse - and commission to boot. I got the job, and landed in a male-dominated environment that meant non-stop footy chat, after-work beers and more. Perfect.

If nothing else, based in the capital there's always a bus, tube or mainline station to get you to your football destination. However, as any Alex fan that's travelled to a London game will know, a seemingly simple hop, skip and a jump across the city on any of the above can take hours. Squeezed onto overcrowded tubes, pushed and shoved on buses by rude and obnoxious Londoners who know how to play the system, or forced to stand on trains that are always full can be a nightmare. An expected 20-minute trip on the District Line (the green one) once took me longer than an express journey from Crewe to Euston! Many a time I'd join other London Exiles and head across the capital to a match. We'd arrange to meet friends from Crewe at various pubs, but nearly always arrived last, sometimes with only sufficient time to just make kick-off.

My move into recruitment was, thankfully, perfectly timed, and the second half of the 1994-95 season threw up four relatively easy journeys on top of the usual trips back to Crewe – Brighton, Brentford, Wycombe and Orient. The seaside jolly was easily the standout match, but with it came complications. I'd met a girl, as you do, but she was more friend than girlfriend. Except that she didn't cotton on to this. I told her that I was off to Brighton, to watch the Alex, and she wasn't happy. She had a strange notion that Saturdays meant shopping in the West End, and declined the offer to join me by the sea. I don't know why I offered, as taking girlfriends to the football never felt quite right. So I left it at that, took the train to Brighton and got there early enough for lunch and a few beers. A few of the lads turned up and we listened to a new Oasis tune on a pub jukebox, and then again. One local put the new single on constant repeat, pumping money in as though he was playing a fruit machine. I've always liked a bit of Liam and Noel, but there are limits. We left him to it as the track started once more, and then headed to the Goldstone Ground, ready for some football action.

Brighton was a club in serious trouble in the mid 90s; not on the pitch, but because of money worries and some complicated planning wrangles associated with their proposed new stadium. The old ground was crumbling, and it was a sorry sight seeing a pocket of their fans on a terrace that was sectioned off because of its condition. We had a great day out, singing most of the match and hoping for a decent result. It was stalemate, looking like a draw, but then Robbie Savage popped up with the only goal of the game. He was never one to miss out on a good celebration, and he almost landed in the middle of the Crewe fans as he charged over to join us behind the goal. He was still playing a forward role then, without much success most games. So his strike that afternoon was a collector's item, and much appreciated by the travellers. It wasn't until Savage switched to a more central midfield role that he came into his own, but watching him scamper around up front was a treat, that trademark blond hair somewhat shorter then, but still impersonating a headless chicken. He was always great value.

As we left the ground I checked my mobile phone for messages, one of the early units about the size of a brick. It was all part of the city boy deal, poncing around accountancy and legal firms taking calls from the office. But it proved handy at games, meeting up with the lads and sorting out train times. However, it was a little conspicuous, so I'd turn it off and leave it in my jacket pocket when we got to the pub, and certainly before we headed to the football. On this occasion, crazy girl from London had called to say that she'd decided to join me and had arrived at Brighton station.

'Where are you?' she demanded to know.

Five minutes later another message had been recorded, telling me that she'd taken a taxi to the ground. I was impressed with such initiative, but a few minutes after that she'd left a particularly agitated one-liner.

'Meet me outside NOW or you're in big trouble,' was the gist of it.

Just then one of the lads mentioned that he thought he'd heard my name mentioned over the Tannoy system during the half-time interval. Sure enough, as I listened to the next voicemail I had to hold the phone away from my ear. She was livid, screaming down the line.

'If you're going to ignore my messages you might as well forget it. I'm going home,' were her final words on the matter.

She didn't call again. But hey, Robbie Savage scored!

***

There was another Brighton link, as my boss at the office was also a Seagulls supporter. This was fantastic when I fancied a footy chat, but not when business came first. He was certainly a company man. The Alex were playing Hull at Gresty Road on a Tuesday night in early May, a crucial match as we chased an automatic promotion place. I even had a lift to Crewe sorted with a fellow Londoner.

Unfortunately, the annual office awards night was scheduled for the same evening. The boss knew all about my dirty little secret and regular liaisons with Mistress Alexandra, and also the lengths to which I would go to see a game. But there was no budging him. I had no chance of getting the night off, or the following day for that matter. So I grudgingly got togged up, DJ and shiny shoes, and joined the office team at the rather plush Grosvenor Hotel for the lavish function and presentations. The free drinks flowed, fancy canapés arrived more efficiently than buses, posh frocks lined up to be admired and the top performers from the previous year stepped up for back slapping and fat cheques.

Luckily, I had made plans. Cliffy, a mate with a mobile phone, would send text updates to my brick at regular intervals. I'd get up-to-date coverage and still enjoy the night out. Everything went well, at least until I'd knocked back a second bottle of bubbly with the office mob. I'd had a couple of text updates, but then it went quiet. There was nothing for the last thirty minutes of the match. It was nearly 10pm, I was rolling drunk, and squinting at the phone wondering if I'd disabled some function, or if the signal was so weak my mate's messages hadn't come through. So I disappeared from the function suite and nipped out front to phone him, get the final score and a few details about the match.

I made the call on the pavement outside, next to another lad who was having a fag. He was a Birmingham City fan, from one of our other offices, almost as drunk as me and with a big mouth on him. He reckoned that Alex fans had turned him over at Gresty Road early that season; that was when Phil Clarkson and Danny Murphy gave us a 2-1 win, as I smugly pointed out. He wasn't impressed, and two minutes later, as I was still trying to get some sense out of Cliff on a very crackly line, he took a swing and knocked the phone from my hand, caught me in the eye and then grabbed hold of me to break his fall. Now I'm pretty tolerant, but I hadn't even heard the final score yet. So I smacked him back, hoping he'd disappear and leave me alone. He didn't, and a few minutes later when two fine officers of the law walked past we were still scrapping on the floor, DJs in tatters and one of my shoes in the road. I can only assume that the hotel reception called the police, which was fair enough. They didn't want two drunken football yobs rolling about the hotel forecourt.

I spent the night at Vine Street station, in the cell adjacent to the Muppet from Birmingham. Detained for our own good but, thankfully, not charged. The daft thing is, they released us at 6am, together, and wondered why we exchanged a few words outside. I held back at the request of the duty officer. He seemed impressed by my attitude, until I asked him if he knew what the Alex score was from the previous evening. He told me to bugger off. I did, changed, and rolled into work with the makings of a black eye. The boss just looked at me, shook his head, and carried on with his bacon butty. The Alex won 3-2, I discovered later that morning.

SUPER DARIO LAND

Living in London can be a drag, but it gives you access to all manner of stuff, and off Tottenham Court Road, tucked away by boutiques, restaurants and ticket agencies, was a cracking book and magazine store called *Sports Pages*. It did exactly what it said on the tin, with shelves, cupboards and giant displays offering every sporting publication under the sun. Crucially, there was a huge selection of football fanzines available following a boom in the culture during the early-to-mid 1990s. I bought a couple to flick through on the journey home one day. Ten minutes later, sat on the Northern Line tube back to Tooting, I was doubled up laughing at off-the-wall articles, cartoons, jokes and fan-perspective rantings. They were brilliant, unofficial, fresh and entertaining. Both rags - *Over Land And Sea* (West Ham) and *Brian Moore's Head Looks Uncannily Like The London Planetarium* (Gillingham) - were read from cover to cover before I joined flatmates for a beer at the Wetherspoon pub, *J.J. Moon's,* by the Tooting Broadway station. Then, amongst a bunch of friends who didn't care less about football, I couldn't stop talking about these fan magazines all evening.

I returned the following day and quizzed one of the lads who worked at the shop. He was a West Ham fan; clued up on just about everything football, and he even recalled the FA Cup encounter with Crewe at Upton Park as though it had happened the day before. He knew his stuff. Crewe Alexandra, however, did not have a fanzine, he was sure of this. I was gutted.

There was one, it turned out, but a guy called Len who briefly produced a rough and ready publication called *The Railwaymen of Gresty Road* never thought to distribute his humble offering further afield than the bus stop on Gresty Road. We exchanged details one miserable afternoon stood outside the ground, and I sent him a few articles. It didn't last long, but I'd had a taster and really wanted to be part of something that reached out to the supporters.

Then a young fella called Huw combined his love for the Alex with the latest desktop publishing skills he'd fine-tuned on his fancy Apple Macintosh computer. The result was *Super Dario Land*, a slim but well presented fanzine that spurned five issues across its first season of publication. I didn't notice a copy on sale at home games until early 1994, but when I finally got hold of issue #5 with an amusing cartoon cover, from a lad in the Alex Suite who was about to toss his copy in the bin, I knew that I wanted to be more than just a reader.

It took a while, but when I finally got hold of the editor, we arranged to meet up for a drink near his home in Wilmslow. It was early summer by then, the Alex had just been promoted, I was in Alsager for a few weeks, and I had time on my hands. I prepared a dozen items for consideration, including a rather cringe worthy cartoon strip called Alex & Sandra! Huw was rather taken aback, certainly unprepared for my enthusiasm and overflowing copy. So we got together and completed issue #6 ready for the new season, with a splash of colour on the front to give the publication a little polish. I was always keen to give fans value for money, so we made sure that the number of pages increased to 32 and that the cover price remained at one pound.

The new look and increased size seemed to work. Sales doubled, there was loads of feedback, letters and emails, and before long we could comfortably add more pages. It really grabbed supporters' attention, other contributors came on board and, out of the blue, we were invited for lunch with the Alex chairman. The club even threw in some match tickets so that we could watch the game later in the, ahem, comfort of the wooden seats in the main stand. I'd been in there once years earlier, and it wasn't the most luxurious spot in the ground. Cramped, hard and rickety is probably the best description of the seating back then, but it was a freebie from the chairman, so we accepted gratefully.

When we sat down to lunch with John Bowler, the chairman was honest about his intentions. He didn't know what to make of the fanzine, and wondered if it was a rival to the matchday programme. It wasn't, as any readers of the rag will confirm. It was a bunch of supporters having their say, spouting hot air about the club, the players and experiences on their travels. We also poked fun at our rivals, printed daft cartoons, photos with captions and spoof articles similar to *Private Eye* material. Basically, it did everything that the programme could not. I think a few other people associated with the club had voiced their concerns, and the chairman was keen to check us out. We were on best behaviour, clean shirts and all. He had no worries, and effectively gave us his blessing. It was the continuation of a decent relationship with John Bowler, especially after our dissertation dialogue a couple of years earlier, but one that would, over time, be tested more and more.

A few issues into the season, it became clear that Huw didn't have the time. He had work, college stuff and a young family to consider. That was fine and I was delighted to take it on alone, but with his departure went some of the production skills. There was no way I'd let the rag die, and I was very lucky that my mate Jonesy stepped in. He was something of a wordsmith, a clever writer and real pedantic old sod. That's just what *Super Dario Land* needed. I owe him a lot. Not only did he ensure that a tip-top standard was maintained, he often reined me in when I came up with ludicrous ideas for features and articles. I was a bit of a maverick, while Jonesy was without doubt a steadying influence. He also took most of the photos and, essentially, stood flogging the magazine home and away for years. Without him there's no doubt it would have withered, especially in the latter days when I was usually chatting in the pub until 2.55pm rather than buckling down to drumming up a few sales along Gresty Road.

Selling at away grounds was always a challenge, as many of the travellers had invariably seen the latest issue the previous week at home. Still, there were always fifty plus who welcomed the second and third opportunities to pick up a copy. We also sold plenty to opposition fans, especially as *SDL* built up a decent reputation across the leagues. Away days, however, also had their problems. Fans were usually on the beer for a few hours leading up to kick-off, and with the alcohol came increased levels of abuse. Anyone with a different viewpoint would become very vocal, fans that didn't rate the publication delighted in hurling insults as they passed our point of sale. The club loyalists who thought that nobody should challenge the official line of the programme tut-tutted as they walked by, noses in the air, trying to avoid even a brief glance at our often controversial covers.

Blackpool was the scene of one confrontation. Not everyone approved of the fanzine and some just didn't understand it. There was also jealousy. One lad, who I never quite saw eye to eye with, bowled over one afternoon when we travelled to the seaside, armed with our latest edition. With his mates beside him, full of ale, he started a rant about wannabe journalists, accusing me of using the club for my own means and boldly predicted that I'd be gone in a few years, leaving the Alex trailing behind as I moved on to bigger and better things. I didn't bother replying, as my words would have made little difference. He'd made his mind up about me. I was a charlatan, a user, someone who was piggybacking the Alex, building a reputation and then escaping to make my fortune.

'Hope you don't sell any, you w*nker,' was his parting shot as he tried to knock the copies from my hands.

If only he knew how hard it was to break even! Some issues took three or four matches to cover costs, and when we did make a few quid those associated with its production were treated to beers and a curry.

There were also some great moments brought on by the fanzine. On that trip to Blackpool we tried to buy some Crewe Alexandra rock. We couldn't find it anywhere, and one seafront vendor compounded matters when he said that they only made it for the bigger clubs. That kind of attitude always strengthened my resolve to stand by the Alex no matter what. Big clubs, indeed!

So we thought we'd do something about the situation, and introduced a whiff of Blackpool to Crewe with issue #17 of *Super Dario Land*. It came out just before Christmas 1996, coincidently when the Seasiders were the visitors. It cost a few hundred quid, but we had a thousand sticks of rock specially made with Crewe Alexandra running down the middle. The wrapper around the centre even had a jolly red Alex Santa! So we handed out free sticks of rock to anyone and everyone, not just the people who bought the fanzine. It raised many a smile, especially from the visiting Blackpool supporters. And that was the whole point of the fanzine - to entertain, lift spirits and distract from the more formal and tedious aspects of football.

Now I've never taken myself too seriously, and I have been happy to take criticism when it's deserved. One afternoon, however, stood by my bus stop pitch in a fine drizzle, I was rather taken aback. A long-standing supporter of many years, someone well respected, came up to me and expressed his dismay at our latest publication.

'I think that's shocking what you wrote,' he told me, 'about Mark Rivers. It's a disgrace. I won't be buying the fanzine again,' he added with a shake of his head.

Okay, so we carried a few risqué articles and heaped plenty of flack upon those who deserved it, be it players, club staff or people from the wider game. We spoke our minds, but usually in a constructive manner. I didn't write the piece about Rivo, which was a rather scathing assessment of his recent efforts on behalf of the Alex, but as editor I accepted full responsibility for printing the article.

'Why don't you reply in the next issue,' I suggested, 'put your point of view across, challenge the writer and make the readers think a bit?'

His reply saddened me, because he felt that his words wouldn't stand up to scrutiny.

'I can't write fancy words,' he told me, 'I wouldn't know how to express myself like you do.'

Now I'm no ogre, and I think I'm very approachable. That he felt intimidated to contribute a piece of written material made me feel bad. So I suggested that he penned a few words that I could edit, and then I'd run it past him and submit the piece as normal. He wouldn't do it, concerned that others would ridicule him. And then he was gone. So I wrote a piece myself, trying to balance the original article. When it was published, the following month, I made a point of handing a copy to the guy, free of charge, to show that his comments had bothered me, and that I wanted to involve all Alex supporters if possible. He took the issue in good faith, and I repeated the exercise the following month, although he told me that he didn't expect any preferential treatment. I knew that, but I wanted him to realise that I valued his opinion, that the cost of the fanzine was never my concern. Even when he refused to buy a copy we still chatted in the bar, also at away matches, and his views were always noted. He made a point of buying the next issue, thanking me for taking the time to win him over and address his concerns. As far as I know he picked up a copy each month until we put the fanzine to bed, many years later. Things like that made the whole process worthwhile.

Others incidents got me in serious trouble. The girlfriend from London, the one that saw red when I disappeared to Brighton, came up to Crewe once and foolishly agreed to help sell the latest issue. She was a cracking salesperson, good enough to operate in some of the most competitive London dealing rooms. So I had no qualms letting her loose on the streets of Crewe to sell a few magazines. A group of Huddersfield fans had other ideas. She was drumming up business outside the Royal when they came off the station. They cracked a few jokes, asked me if she was game for a laugh and then winked at me. Seconds later they carried her away down Nantwich Road. She had a tongue that could kill at forty paces, so I expected her to give them a severe verbal lashing. She didn't, as she was terrified, I later discovered. They whisked her into the Brunswick and nobody saw her for fifteen minutes. Eventually, I thought that I should see if she was okay. She was fine, now the centre of attention at the bar, drink in hand, and her pile of fanzines gone. She had sold all thirty copies. To punish me, for letting them kidnap her, she bought them all a drink! On the up side, she didn't speak to me for the rest of the afternoon!

It never was about the money, and if a young kid had 80p change in his pocket but wanted a copy of *SDL* then he got it. If there were copies left over after two or three games on sale, they were given out free of charge. When fans waved me away, the kind who refused to engage with sales people of any kind, I simply slipped one in their hand and asked them to enjoy it, to give it a try. That wasn't a cunning sales tactic, I just wanted the whole Alex community to embrace what the fanzine set out to achieve.

We didn't reach everyone, but I think we made our mark and provided an alternative voice for about a decade. I also met Andy, Jim, Richie and Mike, lads associated with other fanzines who became great friends over the years.

I was always proud of the publication, but I also found that being associated with the magazine linked me with the club I loved. *Super Dario Land* wasn't just a fanzine; it was Crewe Alexandra's fanzine. I was part of that, and I felt part of the whole Alex experience more than I ever had. It also opened many doors, but I'm pleased to say that my nemesis from that day at Blackpool has been forced to eat his words over the years… I'm still here, churning out nonsense about the Alex!

BATTLE OF BRIZZLE

Making the same mistake twice isn't to be recommended, so after promotion at Chester I was cautious about making rash predictions. What ended in tears back in 1991 was not something I wanted to repeat. Just staying up was the priority. But keeping a lid on things was easier said than done when the squad was possibly the strongest I'd seen in years. The players coming through ensured that we were raring to go for another exciting season. In fact, the mid-90s saw a real purple patch, a wave of talented players – homegrown and bought in – that not only entertained, they did so with an artistic flourish and scored plenty of goals. So when the side was fine-tuned over the summer of 1994, it became apparent that the Alex looked a decent each-way bet for promotion – yet again!

There was a solid core, a squad that really was good enough to rise to the First Division, effectively the second tier following the formation of the moneybags Premier League. It sounded great, the First Division.

It just needed Martyn Booty, Shaun Smith, Gus Wilson, Steve Macauley and Gareth Whalley to deliver consistently. They were the dependable types, workmen that went about their business with no fuss. I always imagined that the manager relished coaching such professionals, men he could rely upon to carry out his carefully prepared tactics. The rest were flair players that the fans loved, the showmen who scored the goals, looked the part and talked a good game.

A couple of them stood head and shoulders above the rest. Ashley Ward was an elegant player, a true talisman striker who probably modelled for the *Roy of the Rovers* comic strip in his spare time. There was no explosive burst of pace, but with the ball at his feet his strength saw him glide past helpless defenders. He was also courteous off the pitch and regularly fed us snippets for the fanzine.

Darren Rowbotham was another who knew how to get supporters on board, happy to face his critics if he turned in a below par performance. He operated out wide, but always seemed to appear on the score sheet. He was a maverick, and although he caused no problems at Crewe in his first season, I got the feeling he'd had a few disputes at other clubs.

One player was easily my favourite during the 90s, a period when I let nothing get in the way of time spent with Mistress Alexandra. Neil Lennon was a tough and determined midfielder from day one. He was a fans' favourite as soon as he turned out for the Alex at the start of the decade. A Man City trainee that didn't make it at the top level, he found his feet under Dario Gradi's coaching. He was a no-nonsense player and made the centre of the park his own, with uncompromising tackling, a sure pass and the occasional thunderbolt shot. But he was so much more than that. He was a leader, an inspiration to the players around him and the fans on the terraces. His passion drove supporters like me, and when you considered missing a game it was his face that popped into your head. He'd not accept that. He was a tough taskmaster and we had to match his passion and commitment.

Another kid starting to make his mark was Danny Murphy, a wise old man in a youth's body. There was nothing Murphy wouldn't try, from audacious free-kicks to inch-perfect passes over seventy yards. Older players respected him; the fans worshipped him. He had it all, and the pound signs lit up the chairman's eyes each time the youngster scampered onto the pitch.

So in the 1994-95 season he was a regular, a class act alongside the fiery Irishman Neil Lennon and the calm figure of Gareth Whalley. We had a midfield to match any side in the division. Murphy seemed to appear on the score sheet as often as the strikers, and the precocious scallywag from Chester must have made the experienced heads green with envy. Against Birmingham, at Gresty Road, he converted the sweetest free-kick, curled effortlessly around a five-man wall to leave the 'keeper rooted to the spot as the ball tucked inside the top corner of the goal. He was a big game player who rarely fluffed his lines.

As the last of the cold winter Saturdays gave way to spring, most agreed that we'd had an impressive campaign back in the Second Division. I was content to build upon the progress of recent seasons and see the club as a whole develop on and off the pitch. The players had other ideas and kick-started a ten-match unbeaten sequence that propelled us into the play-off places, narrowly missing out on the second automatic spot. We knew all about the end-of-season games, and blocking our route to Wembley was a double-header against Bristol Rovers. They had failed to beat us in the league that season, so confidence was high. A stopover in Somerset, not Avon, was essential.

***

Bristol Rovers encountered financial difficulties during the 1980s and were forced out of their Eastville Stadium in the heart of the city. For nearly a decade they played games at Bath City's Twerton Park ground. Not ideal for their supporters, but great for visiting fans who fancied a weekend away.

Bath was picture postcard beautiful when Jonesy and I arrived by train, quaint and yet bustling, clean and tidy, elegant and vibrant. The properties in one estate agent showed plenty of seven figure price tags, and the windows of bespoke shops carried items that were not bought with loose change, businesses where it's best if you don't ask the price. If you had to enquire, you probably couldn't afford it. The pubs and bars were packed - with locals, tourists, drinkers and diners from Bristol enjoying the delights of a nearby gem. There were also plenty of Alex fans, many wearing their colours with pride. We did our best to blend in, as footy tops don't go down well around the up-market bits of certain cities. We played it safe, as we fancied seeing it all.

Then, having spent an amazing evening enjoying the stunning Georgian architecture, supping ale by the river and eating posh pizza with a knife and fork, the following lunchtime we hopped on a bus that took us to Twerton Park. It's a suburb of Bath, a big housing estate, a few shops, businesses and pubs. To be honest, it all looked a tad run down, the bit most residents from the centre would rather brush under the carpet. There was no warm and fuzzy reception for us, nothing like the sparkling hospitality enjoyed the previous night. As we arrived, a few hundred yards from the ground, several locals glared and one stuck his finger up. Nice. I wasn't wearing any colours, but Jonesy was now wearing one of his red Alex tops. It was obvious that we followed Crewe. They took an instant dislike to us.

Undeterred, so we tried the nearest pub, not the most welcoming place but a watering hole all the same. We didn't even get to the bar, as it was already rammed with Rovers fans. As most of them probably lived several miles away in Bristol, they also set out early on match days. A few parted to allow us through, but then a human wall formed and one middle-aged fella with a huge beer gut stepped forward to halt our progress.

'Piss off,' he said, 'you're not welcome in here.'

One look at the barman, perhaps the manager of the dingy establishment, left us in no doubt that we were not getting served. The guy behind the bar turned away and left the obnoxious customer to run his own door policy. It was apparent that we would get a kicking if we hung around too long. A few other lads moved forward, making it perfectly obvious that they were ready if we fancied a crack at them. We just wanted a beer. I looked over to the window and saw an Alex fan, no colours, keeping quiet in the corner. We didn't want to blow his cover, so we backed off and made our way out of the door.

Across the road there was a gaggle of Bristol youths, probably fifteen or sixteen years old. They'd latched onto two other Alex fans walking down the road towards the ground. They were pushing and shoving them, trying to provoke a reaction. Then one of the group lashed out and kicked one of the Crewe lads on the back of the legs. His mates laughed, but an older fella stepped forward and remonstrated with them, calling them idiots and urging them to back off. He was a decent, brave man, as similar situations have ended very differently. The lads dropped their heads and shuffled away, probably looking for other victims away from prying eyes.

We finally got into a pub after a five-minute walk the other way. It was a mixed crowd, Alex and Rovers fans just about getting along. The usual pub taunts and chanting was in full swing, and as we made it to the bar a crash to the left signalled the first ruck. An older Alex supporter had shoved a Bristol lad and both were grappling on the floor, glasses and bottles already sent scattering from the table beside them. Within seconds there was a melee, about fifteen involved, but two massive doormen stepped in and stopped it escalating into an all-out pub brawl. A crowd gathered outside wanting to get in, but the doors were slammed shut. It had the makings of another Beehive, but thankfully it was over no sooner than it had started.

We got served when everything calmed down, and chatted to a couple of Bristol lads who were shaking their heads. Two of their idiot hardcore had started the trouble, and they were genuinely embarrassed. We'd seen it all before, but it was always heartening that the bulk of fans were decent and just wanted to engage in friendly banter. We headed to the ground soon after, as there was still a nasty vibe about the place. In the streets that led to the small stadium, people looked nervous, constantly peering over their shoulders. Some parts of Bristol are notoriously rough, and it looked as though plenty of the city's inhabitants had taken a day trip to Twerton Park.

Then a roar went up. About one hundred Alex faces emerged from a side street, all heading towards the ground. A group of Rovers fans rushed over and bounced about in the road, fired up, arms waving, gesturing to the Alex mob to have a go at them. It was the usual posturing, but there was no chance it was going to escalate. Three police horses swept past us, closely followed by two vans. The local constabulary was clued up and ready for any trouble. The incident blew over quicker than it started and a cordon was formed to encourage the Alex boys into the ground, the right end of the ground!

Inside, the away enclosure was basic, to say the least. Residents of Bristol zoo would have complained. It was a non-league ground with a few trims, upgraded to pass the Football League requirements. A few days later the Rovers fans would be housed in similar conditions at the Gresty Road End, no roof, but big fences and poor facilities. That was the football experience for most fans when they travelled away from home. There was no red carpet, but we were there for the football, and at least the sun was shining.

The Alex following swelled the crowd to over 8,000 and there was a cracking atmosphere leading up to kick-off. I went to the front of the small terrace, up against the steel fencing directly behind the net. I wanted to see some goals. We'd enjoyed a fantastic run-in, unbeaten since late March, so confidence was high that this would be another successful season, our second appearance at Wembley and promotion to the second tier of English football. We were invincible.

There was no reason to doubt this, as we had the makings of a superb team. There was experience, aggression, youth and pace in the side. Dele Adebola was one of the latest academy products, a man-mountain in attack. Records show that he was born in Lagos, Nigeria, but a moment in his presence and the unmistakable Scouse accent suggested that he'd spent most of his life somewhere near the River Mersey. Adebola was a happy-go-lucky kid in a giant's body. Perhaps my favourite early memory was during a pre-season match at Gresty Road two years earlier. The opponents were Bristol City, sporting a wacky new away kit of purple and green. They looked like Wimbledon ball boys. The game played out in true friendly fashion, end-to-end, few serious tackles and a hatful of goals. The Alex had a comfortable lead and Dario Gradi decided to bring on a substitute.

So our secret weapon lumbered on, an enormous figure that filled his over-sized kit. He chased about, bumped into a couple of City players like a runaway dodgem car, and then raced into the goal mouth like a man on a mission. There was a scramble, Adebola surged forward, and several defenders and the 'keeper tried in vain to smother the ball and player. It was a hopeless task, like watching the heaviest rugby prop bulldoze over the line. In the dying seconds of that meaningless pre-season encounter a new star was born. Adebola fell into the net and somehow took the ball with him. It was the scrappiest goal I'd seen, but he was a destroyer that would make defenders' lives hell. Dele Adebola was a monster.

The best-laid plans have a habit of going pear-shaped, and with stalemate at half-time a few fans were getting worried. Even Adebola failed to threaten the Rovers' goal. The two-leg format meant that an away goal was essential, so anything to give us an edge would have been perfect. A scuffed goal from Neil Lennon, a header from Steve Macauley, or a box-to-box dropkick from 'keeper Mark Gayle would have done the job.

Sadly, it didn't happen. Rovers didn't pose too many threats, but the Alex just couldn't break the deadlock. Gareth Whalley couldn't find that killer pass, Francis Tierney seemed off his game and even Wayne Collins couldn't produce anything to give us that vital lead ahead of the Tuesday night return. The final seconds ticked away, a few coins landed in the away end courtesy of some generous Rovers idiots in the paddock to our left, and then the referee blew his whistle. We had the home game to come, but there was real concern on the faces of the Crewe fans around me.

Then the fun started. The first Rovers fans hopped over the fencing immediately, testing the police and stewards. Like any other sporting event, once a few make it onto the pitch there's little point trying to stem the flow. Just prevent any serious disorder, stop the two factions meeting up. That's exactly what they did, and the police horses that had divided fans outside the ground galloped onto the pitch and formed a line in front of the away end fencing. Stewards joined them and tackled a few enthusiastic Rovers lads that thought they were at the rugby, very keen to jump into our end.

I climbed onto the barrier and hung on to the metal fencing, looking across the pitch at the hundreds of Rovers fans now heading in our direction. I wasn't causing any trouble, just amazed at the sight unfolding before me. Jonesy took a photo that captured the moments before significant numbers advanced towards our enclosure. A human wall of stewards had formed but a few of the more determined and aggressive home supporters broke through and gestured at Crewe lads to join them. The police responded immediately, with officers and horses racing into position to restore order. A few fists flew, but the barrier did its job. The Bristol masses were ushered away from the visitors, and I received a baton to my knuckles to encourage me to get down from the fence. That was fair enough. They were doing their job.

That wasn't the end of it though. The walk away from the ground, to buses, cars and the train station was messy. Playing at the compact Twerton Park stadium suggested that Rovers were a small outfit, but they are still a well-supported club. They had significant numbers, with plenty prepared to cause trouble after the match. It wasn't complete chaos, but the police struggled to prevent a number of incidents that took place away from the main group of Alex fans escorted from the ground. One lad, in his late teens, took a blow to the back of the head from an unseen assailant. We watched the cowardly culprit run away before police or the Crewe supporter in question could react. It's the most pathetic kind of assault, and potentially fatal. Idiots like this have forever given football supporters a bad name.

***

Three days later, a hefty number of Rovers fans descended on Crewe. Pre-match was uneasy, raucous Bristolians making the build up to kick-off rather uncomfortable in the pubs around Nantwich Road. It's a strange dynamic the whole midweek thing. When you're at home you tend to be working until 5.30, maybe 6pm. Then it's a brief stop-off at home, a shower, change and a bite to eat. So you don't get down to the ground until 7pm. As a result, home fans can be thin on the ground in and around the pubs at tea time.

Away fans have a different agenda. If you're catching the train from Bristol then you need to set off early, avoid cutting it too fine before the match starts. So invariably you take a half-day and get to your destination around four or five o'clock. Then you have time for some food and, of course, a few beers to loosen up ahead of the game. It's always been the same for me, sometimes taking the day off to ensure that the travel goes smoothly. I also like getting to a town and taking a look around, not just sitting inside the pubs.

The Rovers lads in blue and white were not interested in sightseeing, and were getting louder and louder in the Crewe boozers that were happy to accept their custom. Sometimes, when you're stood alongside a hundred boisterous away fans, there comes a point when you can't take it any more. So we headed to the ground a little earlier than usual and took up our positions on the Popside.

It was a strange feeling that evening, knowing that over the summer the stand would be transformed into an all-seater area. There would be no more jostling and slamming like punks on the dance floor, nor surging forward like lunatics at the January sales, or bouncing up and down, shoulder-to-shoulder when the Alex scored. Similar was about to happen to the Gresty Road End, but for the three Alex fans stood on the roof of a terraced house behind the stand, clinging to the chimney stack for dear life, they were glad it hadn't happened yet. Theirs was a stunning, unrestricted view, and just ninety minutes remained, a football match that would take us to Wembley or leave us in tatters once again.

Long before kick-off, there was relentless chanting that echoed around the stands. Everyone wanted to be part of it, so if the Popside subsided, the Paddock took over, and then the 'D' stand boys from the seats also joined in. It was a constant hum, banging on the metal panels at the back, slamming seats and stamping feet. It was our war cry to the players, our call to arms for the club's big guns to deliver the knockout blow.

Finally, the gladiators emerged. The Alex were up for it, ready to battle. They needed to be, as it was a full-on contest from the start, incredibly tense with so much hanging on the outcome.

Danny Murphy was unplayable, and slipped passes to Dele Adebola and Francis Tierney. Billy Barr crashed a volley against the crossbar and Wayne Collins drove countless shots on target. But we were denied, time after time, as Rovers blocked, tackled and threw bodies and the kitchen sink in front of goal.

How the first half ended goalless remains a mystery, but similar happened after the break. A few token attacks from the visitors was never enough, but the Alex couldn't find a way through Rovers' stubborn defence. The players were running on empty; we were pulling our hair out.

Then a stroke of genius by the gaffer, introducing Darren Rowbotham during the first period of extra time. He was straight into the action, hooking a loose ball from a corner into the roof of the net. GOAL. One-nil to the Railwaymen. Job done. Thank you very much. Start the queue for Wembley tickets.

My abiding memory is of the final minutes, deep into the second period, perhaps 115 minutes of the battle over, and we were winning.

Then the roof fell in. The clock in the corner of the Railway end stopped and the lads on the terraced roof almost lost their footing. Rovers scored. The lucky gits. It was 1-1 with just seconds remaining. There was uncertainty. No, there was absolute confusion. Did the away goal count immediately, or would there be some more time added, penalties or a golden goal maybe?

The answer came with two short blasts from the referee's whistle. Neil Lennon dropped to the floor and cried into the turf. Mark Smith ran from his goal and tried to lift him to his feet, but Lennon was a dead weight, the life drained from his limbs in a moment. Others sat down, totally distraught, unable to make sense of what had happened. Four games, two in the league and two in the play-offs, and Rovers had failed to beat us once that season. But they were going to Wembley. They'd stolen our scarlet ribbon and painted it blue. It wasn't fair. Football had kicked us in the bollocks once again.

The Bristol players ran to their goal scorer and the first of their supporters poured over the Gresty Road End fencing. That was an additional smack in the teeth. There's something incredibly insulting about opposition fans invading the pitch - our pitch! But there was nothing we could do. A few Crewe fans considered the situation, looking around for back-up. But heads were down, despondency already setting in as the blue and whites covered the penalty area, celebrating with their players, the sods that didn't even win the game.

Nobody stepped forward to defend our patch, see off the invaders. Bodies filed out of the Popside, disappearing from view as they headed down Gresty Road. There was much sorrow drowning to be done, anything to forget what he had just seen.

Out on the floodlit pitch they carried flags above their heads, horns sounded, and a few heartless Rovers fans taunted the Alex supporters still scattered around the ground. This is where it ended for a couple of months. It was time to go home, with just one final glimpse of the ground where we spent so many Saturday afternoons and Tuesday nights. Some didn't want to leave. They needed a few more moments, as if paying their respects to the season that had just fallen. I left my spot by the second pillar, the place where I often stood. That was the last time I'd be there, before the plastic seats arrived to stop the ebb and flow of bodies up and down that terrace. There would be no more swapping ends, no chasing the Alex goals and no more trumpet. The football authorities wanted us to grow up and watch games in an orderly manner. It was the end of an era, a chunk of my supporting life chopped off in its prime.

FROZEN PIPES!

Supporters always want more, whether that's better players, a higher league position or success in a cup competition that has previously seen disappointment. So during the 1995-96 season there were few complaints. New faces were recruited, the old guard matured like a fine wine, and a bunch of academy products gave credibility to Dario Gradi's desire to secure the club's future by investing in youth. It was certainly paying dividends. The cup exploits were also impressive, and in the first few months there was excitement on three fronts, although the elements tried hard to hamper our progress.

Defenders Lee Unsworth and Ashley Westwood were brought in, and kids like Danny Murphy and Mark Rivers made an increasingly significant contribution. Murphy in particular looked a class act. He was a perky midfielder who was comfortable on the ball, had superb awareness and a keen eye for goal. He looked a yob with his close-cropped hair, but an intelligent football brain lurked beneath the spiky façade. Mature beyond his years, there was little doubt that he was destined for greater things. It was always a case of how long would we enjoy his services.

Seeing the youngsters break through lifted supporters, especially when results went our way. It endorsed what the manager was trying to achieve, and we had no reason to doubt him. It was the club ethos, to give them opportunities before resorting to journeymen players from elsewhere. The likes of Murphy suggested a very rosy future for the club. For once, everyone was happy, and any murmurs about lacking ambition were dismissed as complete nonsense.

The cup story began after we thrashed Darlington 4-0 in round one of the League Cup, a stunning first leg at Gresty Road that really set the season rocking. It was part of an unbeaten run of ten games, twenty two matches without defeat if you added the final months of the previous season. There was an air of invincibility about the side and this rubbed off on the fans. Rob Edwards, Dele Adebola and Rob Savage were in full flow, with Steve Garvey, Mark Rivers and even central defender Steve Macauley all on the score sheet in the opening weeks. Everyone met up for games with a smile on their face, enjoying one of the best spells in the club's history.

The return leg at Feethams was a formality, and a 1-1 draw did the job without asking the players to run themselves ragged. In previous years the League Cup had jeopardised consistency and progress in the league, and early exits were dismissed as part of the overall plan to gain promotion. Now there was a real hunger for more. Victory over Darlington set up a tasty encounter with Sheffield Wednesday from the Premier League, and it was no surprise to see Gresty Road almost full for the fist time since the Popside terrace was converted to seating during the summer.

With most areas of the ground packed, it made for an impressive spectacle under floodlights. The Alex players believed in themselves, and so did we. The only concern was the noise. Most of us wondered if the switch to seating would ruin the atmosphere, but as the game progressed it was obvious that the Popside was still capable of raising the roof. Groups of supporters had coordinated efforts at the start of the season, and vocal pockets were dotted along the stand. If one area started, the rest soon followed. It didn't feel the same, but we soon settled in, yours truly sat in block R02, row D, seat number 069.

Something else happened this season. Each time the Alex attacked there was a ripple effect as fans left their seats. It was an automatic reaction, supporters standing if the person in front or to the side got to their feet. So a strange situation developed inside the ground, especially on the Popside. The stewards had new orders, to constantly approach the offenders, issue polite warnings, and get everyone seated during the game. This soon became tiresome, and I think most of the stewards found it a real pain.

It was around this time that Tim, another Alsager fan who joined our group, started a protest. It was peaceful, just designed to highlight the stupidity of the football authorities, the boring bunch of grey suits that were trying to take the passion, energy and fun out of the game. Flyers were handed out and safe standing was called for. That was the start of an ongoing campaign, and regular friction with some stewards. It didn't help that Mexican Waves also became a regular feature, just another way to stick two fingers up at the establishment.

Against Sheffield Wednesday there were numerous reasons to stand, as it was an incident packed match. At half-time we trailed 2-1, with a cracker from Rob Edwards keeping us in touch. What surprised me was the passion and excitement on show in the away end. Taking that lead into the break was a big deal to the visiting fans. They knew they were in a cup-tie. Beating Crewe was no longer a foregone conclusion; they needed to lift the Wednesday players.

The second period was equally frantic, end-to-end, with more goals threatened as both teams attacked relentlessly. It was a proper, ding-dong cup game. Then, after fifty requests aimed at enforcing the new all-seater regulations, Rob Edwards doubled his tally and gave us a deserved equaliser. We all stood and applauded our hero, much to the annoyance of the stewards who had just got the Popside in order. That became an ongoing game, just another bit of matchday fun as far as we were concerned.

Then the final whistle gave us legitimate reason to stand and acknowledge the team's success. We held Sheffield Wednesday that night. It felt immensely satisfying, not quite the scalp we'd dreamt about before the match, but enough to give us a good chance at Hillsborough in the second leg. The feel-good factor continued and there was a surge of interest in the League Cup campaign.

Over in Yorkshire the story gets interesting. A sizeable Alex contingent made the trip, and there were fans dotted around the city during the afternoon ahead of the official coaches arriving. Before the game we took a look around the centre and then headed to the stadium, still an hour to kill before the game. So four of us wandered into a dingy bar not far from the ground and everything but the jukebox fell silent.

'You're not welcome in here,' said the barman, fresh from a course to improve his customer service skills.

That was unsettling, especially with fifty pairs of close-set eyes locked on and ready for the signal to attack. But we had a secret weapon, Mike, our mate who lived in the city.

'What? I live here,' he said in his broadest Yorkshire drawl.

That did the trick and the barman grudgingly delivered four cold lagers. They soon realised that we'd come from Crewe, but the fact that one Sheffield resident was present seemed to placate them. Just in case, we kept our jackets buttoned up to conceal the varied Alex tops beneath, to avoid attracting any more attention from the local morons. That didn't stop a few choice remarks, most from bitter Wednesday fans aggrieved that we'd deprived them of a win back in Crewe. They confidently predicted a romp for their side, delivered with a smug grin.

The match wasn't one-sided, but the home team always had their noses in front. It was a grim night, a wet fog sticking to our clothes as we shivered in the first of the cold weather. Rob Edwards grabbed one for Crewe, another strike that made him the focus of watching scouts once more. And Neil Lennon added a rare goal that showed that he was a true all-round player. Wednesday led 3-2 at half-time, but we still believed that the Alex could get back on level terms, and we never discounted the win. That optimism spoke volumes. It was also incredibly satisfying watching our best players match the supposedly superior Wednesday team, but it was also disheartening knowing that they would soon be gone.

The fog held off and the home side stepped up the pace after the break. We couldn't match them during the fourth quarter of the battle, and to be honest their class was too much for us. We lost 5-2 that night but scored a moral victory and got one over the knuckle-draggers from that backwards Sheffield bar. They didn't maul us, and only a handful of other sides scored twice at Hillsborough that season.

***

A brief distraction soon after the League Cup exit came courtesy of an incredible 8-0 demolition of Hartlepool United in the Auto Windscreen Shield. The game set a number of records, and was a rare match that saw eight different names on the score sheet. It didn't mean much, and few gave a second glance to such minor competitions. But any such win can only boost confidence, and the Alex also progressed in the league.

Still, it's always been the FA Cup that engenders so many emotions, fuels dreams and fires passions in supporters. The Alex began against non-league Altrincham in November 1995, a fixture that started my love affair with the competition in the late 70s. Thankfully, it didn't end in defeat. It also evoked great memories, and going into a game expecting to win made me appreciate the transformation of Crewe Alexandra under the man from Milan.

The modest 2-0 scoreline suggested a spirited performance from Alty, but the Alex always had their name in the draw for round two. That's what mattered, and the prize was a home game against Mansfield Town. The manager spoke out as his players prepared for this game, keen to emphasise that he appreciated what the FA Cup meant to Crewe supporters. He wanted victory just as much as the fans, but tried hard to keep expectations under control. He was a level-headed man, enjoying good support from the chairman and board. They had given him a ten-year contract several years earlier, something unheard of in football circles. Not for the first time, the club I loved stood out from the crowd.

The pre-match rhetoric wasn't misplaced, and another 2-0 win in the second round meant that the Alex went into the much-anticipated third round draw. I was in London when news of our next opponents trickled through on the radio. Hardly a headline tie for the sports channels, but I was ecstatic. Southampton away popped out of the hat, England legend Matt Le Tissier and all. I phoned a few of the lads based in the capital and planned for another cracking football day out.

The journey to the south coast, albeit on a very chilly Saturday morning in January, was straightforward. A number of southern-based Alex Exiles joined our train en route to Southampton, and everyone was optimistic ahead of the game. Those other exiles put my longing to return to Cheshire in perspective; they missed it just the same. The work was fine, I was earning good money, but I yearned to be closer to the football. I wanted to take things to the next level, and living so far away made that ultimate commitment to the Alex impossible.

Still, with others who shared similar frustrations by my side, we made an early start, one that meant breakfast on the train so that we arrived in perfect time for the pubs to open. It must sound as though my football days out revolve around drinking, and they often do. But it's more than that, a real social occasion, a chance to meet friends you only see once or twice a month, sometimes only a couple of times across an entire season. The alcohol certainly loosens the tongue, and many a heated debate has been had around a pub table or stood at the bar. More often than not it's the most trivial subject matter. But that's all part of the great football experience, and something that I've always loved.

When we arrived, Southampton town centre was strangely quiet, even mid-morning when shoppers usually busy themselves before disappearing home to watch sport on TV, or get ready to head out to the local ground. It was cold, for sure, ice still visible on surfaces in the shade.

Then the first rumours started, that the match was in doubt. We looked at the grassy patches around benches and areas of public open space. The surface was perfect, firm but definitely playable. Other Alex fans arrived, some after a long journey by train, others on coaches having set out at 5am from Crewe. There was disbelief that the game was in danger of being cancelled, hundreds of pounds wasted by some supporters. We grabbed a beer while we waited for further news. Some fans headed to the ground, hoping to make sense of the confused situation.

Then it was confirmed, a snippet on the radio as we sat in the boozer enjoying another cheeky pint. The call came through from one of the lads at The Dell. The game was off. The pitch was fine, apparently, but the toilet pipes had frozen, cracked and filled the changing rooms with water. Unbelievable, but that was the reason given. I felt sorry for the travellers from South Cheshire, I really did. Some were staying over until Sunday, a wasted journey and a big hole in their pockets. Others were told that their coach had disappeared to fulfil other jobs, not returning until 5pm when the game was scheduled to finish. They were gutted. We drank up and headed back to London.

We were disappointed about the cancellation, but there was still time to catch a game. So we headed to south east London to watch Millwall take on Portsmouth. That finished 1-1, but it was the crowd that fascinated me that chilly afternoon. I watched a 10-year-old standing behind the goal, fired up and animated, shouting non-stop abuse at the Pompey 'keeper who was stood a few metres away. It was nasty stuff, expletives you'd expect from a foul-mouthed adult. Then a bloke stood up and slapped him on the shoulder.

'Good lad,' he said, just a few feet from us.

It was his dad, who then continued the barrage of filthy language. It was a different world, certainly something I'd never seen at a Crewe game. It was just another day that I was proud to be an Alex fan.

They rearranged the Alex cup match for early February, a midweek slot that made it a nightmare for fans who had to shuffle work and family commitments. I didn't have a problem, but I got a call from the *Crewe Guardian* paper asking if I'd file a match report for them. They didn't have anyone available to cover the game, but were keen to carry an eyewitness account in that week's edition. I was flattered, something else that came about because of the fanzine. Another bonus was that it saved me a few quid, as I got a match ticket for my troubles. The last thing I wanted was to convey the match action through beer goggles, so it was a more subdued pre-match for me when I sat with friends in a Southampton pub ahead of the game.

The Dell was amazing. It's a shame that many of the old grounds have disappeared, all supposedly in the name of progress. Southampton's compact stadium meant that supporters were almost on the pitch, just yards from the players, like a theatre's gallery. We generated some fantastic noise that night, belting out song after song as we tried to push the Alex lads to victory. I had to check myself a few times, stop losing myself in the moment and scribble a few notes about the game. It was everything we hoped for, plenty of good movement and a genuine desire to win the game, not simply contain our illustrious opponents.

The Alex players certainly didn't look out of place alongside the Premiership stars, but Southampton's talisman midfield playmaker Matt Le Tissier was the difference. He delighted and disappointed the travelling fans with a typical moment of genius. We'd seen his goals on TV, but when he converted that night it was in pain and not awe that we watched the ball nearly rip the net from the posts. So the Saints went into the break with a single goal cushion, but like the Sheffield Wednesday League Cup match before it not a single Alex fan gave up hope.

The Alex played football, passed the ball just as effectively as Southampton, and made it perfectly obvious that they had no intentions of rolling over and making it an easy night for the hosts.

Then mild-mannered Gareth Whalley equalised, out of the blue. We'd pressurised but a goal hadn't looked likely. He didn't know what to do in the moments after he scored. I dropped my pen and notepad in the jubilant celebrations that followed, forgetting my newspaper duties in an instant. We didn't stop singing after that, and I had to find a few quiet minutes to complete my notes when the final whistle sounded.

With my scratchy match report filed from a Southampton phone booth, I watched other Alex fans head to their coaches. I walked to the train station with a handful of other London-based fans. We had a couple of hours on the train, probably home by midnight. I didn't envy the Crewe lads who had four hours or more on the motorway ahead of them.

Our turn came the following Tuesday night, when an aged Mini Metro huffed and puffed up the motorway. I was in the back with two large fellas from London, two more up front, all of us desperate to see the replay no matter what conditions we had to endure.

I can't explain it, but I went to the replay expecting to lose. Maybe the journey affected me, and perhaps I was finally growing weary of London life and the associated hassles it added to my football passion. I was tired and watched the game in a trance, largely unmoved, just proud that the Alex came close once again. I'd done my bit and had a night off, disappointed that I had to travel hundreds of miles when the match finished.

We lost 3-2, with another stirring performance, but I was at peace. The defeat washed over me like a cool evening breeze. The Alex gained plaudits from across the country as millions saw the gallant effort on television. I watched the game again on video, in the early hours when we returned home. I say home but it wasn't, it was just another place to lay my Alex hat. That time alone, watching the evening's match again, took me closer to what I wanted to call home. It was another precious moment with my football club that few could possibly understand. I now knew what I wanted from life.

SHE WORE A SCARLET RIBBON

Sometimes you just have a feeling that luck is on your side, and that everything is going to work out fine. For me, hacked off with a nomadic lifestyle, in 1997 the sun, stars and various planets must have been perfectly aligned. It was a peach of a year, and I finally moved to Crewe in the spring.

It wasn't the parents, a girlfriend or even work that finally saw me return to Cheshire. No, it was Mistress Alexandra. She had been nagging me for some time, and as always she got her way. I'd spoken with my mate Alan about it on numerous occasions, and he was also hankering to quit his teaching job in the south. So in another of those ridiculously rash moments, we agreed to meet the following week.

For a few months while we tried to find a decent place to rent, his dad's house in Wells Green - halfway between Crewe and Nantwich - became our home. For the first time since becoming a Crewe fan, some twenty years earlier, I was finally based in the town that I had visited every other week. It was temporary, but it felt like home. There was no early start getting to those remaining fixtures at Gresty Road, and meeting familiar faces at Crewe station ahead of away day travel became the norm.

The season was peppered with juicy incidents, from an embarrassing 5-1 thumping away at Port Vale, to Wimbledon's Vinnie Jones winding up the Popside in the third round of the FA Cup. However, all eyes were on the league form, as another crack at the play-offs was on the cards. We won a surprising number of games by a single goal, and there was a stubborn resilience about the squad that suggested something special was brewing. Sadly, in the final phase, 1-0 defeats against eventual division winners Bury, and soon-to-be promoted Stockport, proved that we didn't quite have enough to deserve automatic promotion.

It was away at Edgeley Park that something bizarre happened. I joined Mike and Andy on the train and arrived late morning, hoping to watch a lunchtime kick-off on TV, and invariably down a few pints. Stockport station has one of those grim under passes, always poorly lit and dripping with water. As you emerge on the far side there's a steep service road that takes you up and away from the back end of the station. The three of us ambled towards the top and then heard a roar, a war cry from a bunch of lads who had just appeared at the bottom of the ramp. We looked round and saw this mob of about ten charging towards us. So we legged it. The chase lasted about fifty yards until Andy gave up, completely knackered. So we stopped as well, ready for the worst. Then I clocked one of the lads. I'd seen him many times at the Alex. Either he'd transferred allegiance to Stockport or they'd mistaken us for County fans. He recognised me at the same time and called off his dogs. Panic over. He was one of the old school hoolies, only attending the high-profile games against our rivals. It was just another day out causing trouble, and he had a bunch of youths under his wing. We shrugged it off and headed to Castle Street, a calming beer the only medicine for beating hearts.

We lost that day, and with just a handful of games remaining it looked as though a play-off spot was the only option. Ultimately, we claimed the last available place and booked a double header with Luton Town. That didn't bode well, as the Hatters held us 0-0 at Gresty Road and embarrassed us 6-0 at Kenilworth Road just before Christmas.

In fact, on that cold December afternoon, it wasn't a great day for Andy and me. Far too many lagers pre-match lit the fuse, and the referee enraged us with two Alex dismissals. That was unheard of. Crewe Alexandra loved the Fair Play award. We decided to defend the club's honour, stood behind the goal and remonstrated with the referee and his assistant. Then we had a pop at the Luton players who had tricked the officials. Through a haze of pre-match alcohol this probably didn't sound too good. At one point we were practically on the pitch, banging the advertising boards to attract maximum attention. Mistress Alexandra had been wronged! A number of stewards warned us to pipe down, then an officer of the law issued one final caution. How we stayed in the ground is beyond me. Our protests made no odds; the Alex got a proper mauling that afternoon.

So it was with great trepidation that we prepared for the semi-final. Beating Luton in the home leg wasn't critical, but it proved to be a valuable cushion.

Luton took a deserved lead in the first half and Gresty Road quivered. There were too many mistakes, big Dele Adebola couldn't find his touch and stood on the ball countless times as he tried too hard. Steve Macauley looked a little slow at the back, and the Luton pressure promised more goals. I wondered if the players would choke, whether they would cope with the pressure that we felt on the sidelines.

They answered any doubters out on the pitch with a determined display. Mark Rivers was a shining light that afternoon, and he drilled a quality equaliser to set up a superb finale. Colin Little nicked it for us, collecting Adebola's scraps to lob the Luton 'keeper and give us a precious lead ahead of the second leg.

That night at Kenilworth Road, just three days later, was a heady mix of anticipation, apprehension and expectation. Emotions were running high and a ticket to Wembley awaited the winners. Bizza drove down, collecting me, Richie, Mike and Andy along the way. The events that played out in their compact stadium that night will forever stay fresh in my mind.

For starters, Luton took a two-goal lead. That was horrendous, and another season washed away before our eyes. I saw Alex fans slump to the ground, totally dejected and inconsolable. Luton didn't control the first half, but after David Oldfield slammed the second goal past Jason Kearton even the most optimistic supporters seemed to give up hope. Some had moaned before and during the game, wondering why on earth livewire Robbie Savage had been omitted from the play-off games. Rumours about a big fall out with boss Dario Gradi dominated conversations, and it split the fan base. If he was fit, then he should have played.

Then, no more than a minute after Luton had extended their lead, Colin Little popped up with perhaps his most significant contribution in an Alex shirt. GOAL. Suddenly, there was a glimmer of hope. We still had a chance. We pushed and probed for what seemed like hours. And then, as we all stood in unison to watch the ball leave Shaun Smith's boot, it happened.

The equaliser came midway through the second half. Smithy, increasingly the man of the moment, added another goal to his growing collection and sent the travelling Alex contingent crazy. We had the vital away goals, more than Luton managed at Gresty Road. We just needed to hang on. It was a ding-dong final period, but the Alex players rose to the occasion. They were immense. Andy and I ran to the barriers at Kenilworth Road once again, but this time to grab some precious moments with our ecstatic players. It was a magical few minutes. We'd won, and we were off to Wembley again!

Then something very peculiar happened. It was the last game of the season for Luton's considerable support, and dipping out of the play-offs was no reason to postpone the annual pitch invasion. This time, with several thousand Crewe fans celebrating at the far end, the final game tradition took on a much greater significance. As the first home fans piled onto the pitch there was a flurry of activity from the men and women in orange and yellow jackets. It looked as though the night could turn ugly. Then a trickle became a torrent as several thousand Luton supporters raced up the pitch beyond the halfway line. Police dogs arrived on the edge of the playing surface, and more officers pushed through the gates along the bottom of our enclosure. There was genuine concern amongst the Alex fans stood around us. Was an all-out battle about to commence? Losing was bad, but did it have to end like this?

The wave of supporters stopped just shy of the penalty area. A line of stewards and police were already in place, but they were not needed. The Luton fans started to applaud. It was aimed at us, not their players. There was a moment of disbelief, but then everyone started to clap. They gave us a magnificent send off, and we thanked them. They were amazing scenes, and very touching.

As we drove out of Luton, Bizza couldn't help himself. We stopped at a junction, he wound down the window, and asked a passer-by if they knew the way to Wembley. The poor bloke hadn't a clue what he was talking about. Perhaps a good job that it wasn't a Luton fan. We disappeared, every one of us doubled up with laughter. The schoolboy humour never ceases to be amusing.

***

Any football supporter's life is peppered with song, be it melodic or derogatory, sung on the terrace, from the sterile seats or in the bath during a pre-match ritual before a game against your fiercest rivals. The positive songs always make me smile the most, and in particular the ones that talk of triumph and progress. My favourite is one usually reserved for FA Cup days, when the road to Wembley stretches out before you. However, *She Wore A Scarlet Ribbon* also became a preferred anthem that night at Luton as that twin towers dream became reality for a second time.

It wasn't the cup, but two weeks later in the early hours of Sunday, 25 May as we whistled down the motorway on a Mikro coach from Crewe, we were on the way to Wembley for a play-off final showdown with Brentford. Hearing fifty passionate supporters singing at the top of their voices sent shivers down my spine. So this book could only ever have one title, and with no apology I give you the lyrics to the song that always makes me smile, no matter where in the world I happen to be...

She wore, she wore,
She wore a scarlet ribbon,
She wore a scarlet ribbon in the merry month of May
And when, I asked
Her why she wore that ribbon,
She said it's for the Alex and we're going to Wem-ber-ley,
Wem-ber-ley, Wem-ber-ley,
We're the famous Alexandra
And we're going to Wem-ber-ley

Okay, now tell me that you read those simple words. You didn't, I know you didn't. It might have been muffled, a little reserved, but you had to sing. I did, and countless times across the unforgettable day in London that changed Crewe Alexandra forever.

It should have been a carefree experience, something to enjoy, every moment savoured and stashed away to be recounted to kids and grandchildren years later. But that's not how football fans work. We'd been there before and had the emotional battle scars of a penalty shootout fresh in our minds. We needed a 7-0 half-time lead before we could relax. It was no joke. The afternoon was just beginning but most wanted the final whistle to sound, so that we knew where we stood, whether it was First Division football or the same old mediocrity for another year. That's not fair, as those exciting seasons of play-off ups and downs were never average. We just wanted so much more.

The clock seemed to stop leading up to kick-off. It taunted and forced us to contemplate umpteen potential outcomes as we paced about, awkwardly trying to prepare ourselves for the game. We gave up on the packed pubs near the ground, so alcoholic anaesthetic was out of the question. The police nudged us along when we considered a detour, so we aimlessly wandered towards the hustle and bustle around the stadium perimeter.

I bought a tatty wraparound flag to kill time and show my allegiance, despite already wearing the latest Adidas replica top. One cocky Crewe fan even had next season's shirt, something to do with his dad knowing the MD of the manufacturer. We chatted to friends, acknowledged old faces and shook hands with strangers. It was a marvellous atmosphere, but I wanted the action to start. Jonesy took photos, air horns accompanied sporadic outbursts of singing, and fans muscled in as radio and TV interviews took place by the steps that lead up to the seating. As everyone slowly moved into the main arena, the splash of red and white that opened up was phenomenal. Brentford had greater numbers than us, but the massed ranks of Crewe fans made a spectacular sight.

So finally, after ten long months of toil, the match started. I tried to think of the positives, like Shaun Smith scoring from the Alex half at Griffin Park just a month earlier, a 2-0 win that played a significant part in us making it to Wembley. So the omens were good. Surely it was our day?

The Alex excited, frustrated, enthralled and amazed in equal measures over the season. At Wembley they looked really special, knocking the ball across the expansive bowling-green pitch. Dario Gradi's teams were designed to play on such sumptuous surfaces. And yet the tension mounted as attacks came to nothing, and Brentford dug deep to foil each promising move. But we dominated, easily 60-40 as the half progressed. To be frank, Brentford never showed up. Either that or the Alex were quite simply a cut above. They pumped a few long balls forward to exert some early pressure, but there was no finesse, no suggestion that they would unpick our defence with anything other than a lucky punt. But we didn't make our superiority count. It was torture for over thirty minutes. It was one of those games when you wonder if you'll ever score.

Then, cometh the hour, cometh the man… well, it was 35 minutes into that knife-edge first half to be exact. Shaun Smith, a thorn in Brentford's side if ever there was one, smashed his third goal of the season past the hapless Bees' goalkeeper. Danny Murphy whipped in the cross, Steve Macauley nodded the ball into Smithy's path, and the gritty Yorkshire man did the rest. The Crewe half of Wembley leapt from their seats and danced for joy. Our moment had come and 'One nil to the Railwaymen' echoed around those famous stands for several minutes.

The whole team deserves a mention for the incredible build-up to the goal. Murphy's passing was exquisite, Colin Little was a mischievous imp darting in and out, Mark Rivers too fast for the Brentford back four, and Dele Adebola at his bulldozing best. Gareth Whalley was steady, nudging balls wide to Murphy, while Phil Charnock was the perfect stopper who sat deep to allow the creative lads to express themselves. At the back Macauley was a rock alongside Ashley Westwood, both a threat from corners and free-kicks, while Lee Unsworth shut everything out down the right. Smithy, well, he could have put his feet up and enjoyed a cuppa for all we cared. He was the man. He had delivered when it mattered most. Jason Kearton worked hard between the sticks, but there was no way that he'd fluff his lines on such a massive occasion. The whole team was magnificent.

So we were winning, but that slender one-goal lead was a scoreline that merely added to our worry over the [expensive] half-time refreshments. Was it enough to see us through? That's when the self-doubt creeps in. Questions are asked about staying power and our ability to go the distance. Could we survive the expected Brentford onslaught in the second half?

We shouldn't have worried. We hammered them 1-0 that day. It should have been five, maybe six. But that is immaterial when years later the statistic that counts is the single goal that sent us up to the First Division. The three substitutes got their moment in the sun as the final minutes played out, Seth Johnson, Chris Lightfoot and Steve Garvey doing what was necessary to run down the clock. Then that sweet, high-pitched shrill saw Brentford heads drop and Alex fans soar. Players fell to their knees, Dario Gradi, Neil Baker, Steve Holland and John Fleet hugged and then sprinted onto the pitch, unable to contain their joy.

We slapped backs, embraced, sobbed tears of joy and kissed each other, punching the air and revelling in Heather Small's silky tones as M People's *Movin' On Up* was blasted from the Wembley speakers. The trophy was collected and ten thousand voices roared their approval. Medals for each Alex champion were carefully hung around weary necks, and then it was time for the players to shoot jets of champagne at each other on the pitch. Looking down from our lofty spot, it was a sea of red and white flags. It was wonderful, and Wembley '93 was a distant memory already. The reds were going up!

The team had the obligatory group hug, and the sponsors' photo was taken, then Murphy grabbed the gleaming silver cup and hoisted it high above his head. We roared again. He looked justifiably proud. But I didn't see him initially. The reflection was Mistress Alexandra. She looked divine, her beguiling smile illuminating the stadium as thousands of her followers watched on, mesmerised by her beauty. We were all madly, hopelessly in love with her. She had taken us to the Promised Land.

***

Back in Crewe, after a journey that seemed to take about fifteen minutes such was the delirium on the coach on the way home, the atmosphere in the pokey Alexandra Suite was like never before. Radio Stoke's Graham McGarry carried the trophy from the official coach, reporters grabbed quotes from croaky-voiced fans, and the beers flowed all night. That compact bar was very special back then, and from 8pm that evening it was rammed, wall-to-wall beaming smiles. The intimate atmosphere became a sweaty crush as more and more ecstatic supporters piled into the rooms. The bar staff buckled and club officials had to pitch in, with chairman John Bowler also pulling pints. It was one big, happy family.

People slowly drifted out into the street, some gasping for air, others wanting to watch the carnival unfolding down Nantwich Road. I'd never witnessed anything like it. Cars crawled past, a steady procession of colourful flags draped across bonnets, horns blaring and passengers hanging from the windows. Even people who'd stayed at home during the day were out on the streets celebrating. The pubs were overflowing, punters drinking on the pavements and shaking hands with the usual Saturday night crowd that looked on with envy. We posed for photos by the Gresty Road sign, a memento of the evening. Jonesy stood behind the lens, while I took my place alongside Alan, Tim, Gant and several others by that iconic sign. The flash popped and that magic moment was captured forever. Opposite the Brunswick a huge Alex flag was draped from the building opposite. The whole street was in party mood. We ducked into the *Passage To India* for a curry, beers and a chance to relive the most fantastic day with friends.

TELLING STORIES

My love of writing blossomed the year before our play-off triumph, when I left London and went to work in Leeds. I know, yet another city ticked off a very long list of places that I have briefly called home! It was a temporary transfer that lasted a matter of months, before I finally made a permanent move to Crewe with my friend Alan.

As ever, it was a convoluted tale. I was still in the murky world of recruitment with one of the national agencies. The switch up north involved a woman, a lucrative pay rise and growing tired of London (and, therefore, if you believe the quotation attributed to Samuel Johnson, tired of life). They were all bad decisions. It also meant an awkward matchday trek on the TransPennine service for Alex games. That meant a change at Manchester Piccadilly to get back to Crewe, often hanging around the station waiting for a connection. The only bonus was occasionally sharing the journey with my good friend Mike, then based Leeds. At least that meant a few hours of Alex chat and the occasional beer when we changed trains.

My time with the agency didn't last long. The Leeds office was a bunch of chancers hoping that a lad who had operated in the cutthroat environment of the capital would transform them over night. I wasn't in the mood to tolerate false promises, or having to take on twice the work originally advertised. I decided to take another chance, so the next day I ditched the job, there and then, no messing about. The girlfriend - one of the daft reasons I went up to Leeds - wasn't impressed. She suggested that I should grow up, start taking my responsibilities seriously and forget about football. It was advice that went in one ear and out the other side.

Instead, I dropped into the offices of a football agency that produced audio and Internet updates for clubs up and down the country. I'd used their service a few times over the years, and decided that there was nothing to lose by sticking my name in the hat. They were expanding, the editor liked me and welcomed my enthusiasm, and without further ado I was thrust into a small booth to make a sample recording. I suppose my decent knowledge of all things footy, plus the strange but clear north-south accent made me a decent fit. They liked what they heard. As they didn't have anyone to properly cover Crewe Alexandra, Port Vale or Stoke, I got a contract, freelance stuff, meaning that I could base myself anywhere as long as I made it into the office three days each week, or when required.

So I was up and running, writing football copy and recording breaking Crewe Alex stories, and sometimes updating the Stoke and Vale phone lines. And they paid me for the privilege! I also added a few snippets for Tranmere, even Stockport, because the editor realised that I could cover most northwest sides in depth. It was great at first, and I suppose this was the turning point for me as a football supporter, realising how some of the information I regularly read was manufactured.

We all read newspaper articles and wonder which match the journalist has been watching. Incorrect players are regularly attributed with passes and goals. They have a good understanding of the game, but often little real knowledge of individual teams - especially the lower division clubs. So I thought that I offered something authentic.

At the agency there was a great mix of lads (yes, no ladies) and they supported clubs from all divisions. They had the facts, they went to matches and they often spoke to players and other club officials. So it was solid information that was recorded ready for supporters to lap up when they phoned in.

The growing football addiction, however, didn't gel with the girlfriend. I was working a few days at the agency, putting the *Super Dario Land* fanzine together and travelling to most Alex games. I thought that it was a well-rounded football diet. She didn't, and without thinking her actions through she made the classic schoolgirl error. It was ultimatum time. Shame, as we had enjoyed each other's company for over a year. It coincided with that offer from Alan, to move home to Cheshire. So things rather fell into place. I was gone the following week.

The agency work continued and I was back in Crewe, well, Nantwich, courtesy of a decent little rented house that Alan sorted. It was on the junction with Barony Road, just along from the *Hobson's Choice* shop on the corner. We looked out onto the council football pitches spread across the Barony, and *The Rifleman* pub was a three-minute walk into the estate behind the house. I set up a mini office in the spare room, the fanzine operation blossomed and I travelled to Leeds when required.

What started to trouble me about the agency and some of the other journalists was that they doubled up and wrote about multiple teams, often from details gathered from TV reports and newspaper coverage. There was no first hand knowledge in some cases. The same applied to me, especially when the editor asked me to cover other clubs. I did it, because I loved writing about football. But I asked myself if I'd be happy paying for a similar service elsewhere, if I knew that the information was rehashed, second hand details spruced up and resold?

Everything in life, I have found, is based on numbers, targets and profit. The agency was no different and had a very competitive edge, much like the wider world of football I suppose. If I'm honest, it was increasingly sales focused. They wanted callers to stay on the line for as long as possible, at the premium rate. My Crewe statistics were decent, and it was good quality information that I recorded. But you know what, I felt like a fake.

Eventually, much as I revelled in that intense football environment, alongside like-minded fools that ate, drank and slept the game, I concluded that it was all a sham. Maybe that's a little harsh, but it wasn't the kind of journalism that I wanted to be part of. It took advantage of fans that were desperate to know even the most obscure snippet of information.

My time came too soon, as the Internet side of the business was only just finding its feet. If that had been in full flow, allowing me to focus on the written word while revenues were driven by online adverts, perhaps I would have been more comfortable. Instead, it was all about the two and three-minute recordings, strung out to ensure that the caller was kept on the line until the final seconds. These were premium rate numbers, meaning hefty bills for the unfortunate addicts at the other end.

Don't get me wrong; it was a decent service that did provide a good central point of information, up to date and available whenever you wanted to call. It was just very expensive, and as a supporter I felt that it was playing on emotions, drawing fans to a service that would hook them and bleed them dry. So it was added to the long list of jobs I walked away from. I stopped making the arduous trips to Leeds and spent my time in Crewe. On the downside, I had to earn some cash elsewhere.

Thankfully, salvation came with a letter from a guy at the *Sunday Express.* They'd seen the fanzine and wondered if I'd be interested in supplying matchday copy at Alex home games. It meant scribbling a few notes, bashing a story together and phoning it through a few minutes after the final whistle, to be used in the Sunday paper. It was all tied in with the Alex gaining promotion. Apparently, playing higher-profile Division One teams meant that more people would want to hear about Crewe

Alexandra. That sounded great, writing about the Alex in an official capacity, reporting on a subject I knew plenty about.

So I called them, sorted out a few details, then nearly fell off my seat. They were going to pay me, handsomely, for just a few column inches. I was at every game anyway, so this was a piece of cake. I didn't even accept the press passes, as I chose to stay in my season ticket seat on the Popside. That was probably for the best, as journalists are meant to be impartial. Bouncing up and down in the press box, berating the referee and singing *Blue Moon* wouldn't have looked good sat next to the stiff reporter from the *Sunday Times*!

The writing wasn't an official club role, but I could give my opinion. The Alex were playing some of the best teams in the country and I was living in Cheshire. I'd never felt closer to Mistress Alexandra in my life.

AWKWARD THREESOME

'You'd forget your own birthday if I didn't remind you,' the missus once told me.

It's true, remembering dates and anniversaries has never been my strong point, unless football was involved. So recalling the night I met the future wife has always been simple. It was the eve of our first home game in Division One. West Bromwich Albion, Saturday 16th August 1997. We lost, 3-2, mainly due to that scruffy git Lee Hughes. I'll never forget his smug grin when he scored the winner, peeling off to taunt us before he celebrated with the jubilant Baggies.

So knock a day off and I'm sorted, that's when we met, love, how could I ever forget? If only the wedding anniversary was tied in with an Alex match I'd have remembered to buy her a present every year!

In fact, our first meeting was inextricably linked to the Alex. I was settled in the rented house in Nantwich, but we hadn't properly celebrated finally arriving in Cheshire. So we decided to throw a housewarming party, with mainly Alex-related friends invited. The first *SDL* issue of the new season came out in late July, so I asked Karen, one of the matchday sellers, if she fancied coming along. She did, as long as she could bring a friend. That helped to balance the male-female numbers, so everyone was happy. Her friend, of course, was the wife to be.

That all sounds quite dramatic, as though we sped off in the night to Gretna Green or hopped on a plane to Vegas. We didn't, and Elvis did not read the wedding vows in one of the Gresty Road goalmouths that night. If I'd been forced to repeat after him, I would almost certainly have forgotten my lines, unless they'd asked me to honour and obey Mistress Alexandra.

I suppose any other blossoming romance would have continued the next day, with a walk in the park, a lunchtime meal or maybe a trip to the cinema. Unfortunately, I had to disappoint her immediately. There would be no follow-on date that Saturday. There was a match, the biggest game in our history as far as I was concerned. Gresty Road was about to welcome the First Division's finest. There was nothing else on my mind. The party had run deep into the early hours and bodies were scattered around the house - in the lounge, kitchen and on the stairs. My only concern was turfing this bird out, politely of course. I wanted to see her again, but I had a million and one pre-match rituals to complete. It was Saturday morning. There were only five hours to kick-off!

'Shall we go for some breakfast,' she very sensibly suggested. 'That nice café on Pepper Street?'

It was a lovely spot to eat, no doubt about that. But this was matchday morning. The lads would be arriving in Crewe around 11.30am. A sausage, egg and bacon bap from the greasiest spoon on Nantwich Road was the order of the day, followed by an early start in the Royal.

'Er, sorry, love to, really I would, but the lads will be here soon. I need to crack on. I'll ring you, maybe on Monday if that's okay?'

So she knew where she stood from day one. I think Karen gave her a pep talk later, explaining my nasty habit, the addiction that would make me beg, borrow, steal and cheat to see an Alex game. She should bail out immediately or suffer the consequences. I didn't have the best track record; a journeyman lover if ever there was one. A series of car crash romances that had broken hearts around the country, including my own. I don't think Karen did a very good job of putting her off. She was a footy chick and probably saw nothing wrong with my errant behaviour.

So amazingly, following the briefest fling over cocktail sausages, egg sandwiches and a few beers at our housewarming party, she came back for more. What did surprise me was her knowledge of football, a refreshing and slightly disturbing trait in a woman. So when she joined me at a few games there were raised eyebrows from the boys, but no major concerns. It would blow over; she'd soon tire of the football banter, long journeys and excessive drinking. The lack of shopping on Saturdays would eventually frustrate her, so everything would sort itself out. It usually did. Besides, there was no way our matchday schedule was being changed – not even for Miss World. Well, unless they introduced a replica top round, and she wore an Alex shirt.

So the girlfriend started tagging along during the glory days, a period that appealed to even the most miserable Crewe resident. The conspiracy theorists that believed Dario Gradi and the board didn't want promotion were shot down in flames. The ground was always busy, and talk about building a bigger main stand was rife.

The only problem was Mistress Alexandra. She was miffed. It was an awkward threesome, and I was sharing our precious time with someone else, time that had always been hers. With another woman! I can't be sure, but when wife-to-be stumbled at the top of the Popside one day, fought to maintain her balance and was only saved from a nasty fall down the steps when an alert steward grabbed her arm, I have a good idea who was responsible. The old girl always was a little jealous.

Things took a turn for the worse in early December. The lads called an emergency meeting and insisted that the girlfriend was despatched home. Everyone was tetchy, as we'd just been hammered 5-2. It was a miserable afternoon all round. The Alex were reeling, and scapegoats were sought. Our band of eight brothers needed a serious word, post-match in the Brunswick. It was Stoke away the following Saturday, a match for dedicated, time-served connoisseurs only. An all-dayer was on the cards, in and around the Stoke pubs, likely to get messy at the ground. Derby days were sacrosanct. She was not invited. I didn't have a problem with this, as the other lads rarely brought their ladies along. It cramped everyone's style. Girlfriends, wives and partners were allowed out for seaside matches, League Cup encounters (but no further than round three) and low-key league games. Local derbies were a no-no, as was the first round of the FA Cup. They were simple rules that we all adhered to. I just had to break it to her gently.

'But I've done my Christmas shopping,' she told me as I tried option number one.

It was my trump card, every woman enjoys shopping – especially at Christmas. She was far too organised. So I tried another angle.

'I don't need to see my sisters. We're getting together next week, then on Boxing Day as well,' came the reply that killed off option number two.

I had one last rabbit in the hat. It was one of the lads' annual rituals, a Saturday match before Christmas when we all shopped for girlfriends and wives. She'd ruin the surprise if she came along. Surely she understood and could allow me some time with the boys?

'That's sweet. You all shop together and give each other advice,' she gushed, 'maybe you're not a hopeless bunch of losers after all.'

Job done, hopeless loser or not! A white lie and the football day was safe, no need to quote the lads. All I needed to do was remember her present. And a decent one at that.

Apart from missing the pre-Christmas encounter with Stoke, which was a stunning 2-0 win and covered in the next chapter, she didn't take the hint. I liked her, a lot, but she wanted to muscle in on the footy scene that had been mine for years. I'm not a greedy man, jealous or particularly protective of my time and possessions, but the football is different. It involves others, people I have trusted for years. She was still on probation. A long probation!

Eventually, it was something else that finally quelled her desire to accompany the lads and me to all but a handful of Alex matches beyond that first season. Enter Welsh Ade, who was rather unique. She was never keen on him, on account of his rudeness, loudness and general obnoxious behaviour. He wasn't one of the Cardiff crew from Liege, oh no. He was a Swansea boy, working in Crewe and also playing for our Sunday League team, the Union Vaults in Nantwich. He was a good laugh, admittedly a little raucous and a real handful when he'd had a few lagers. He was our secret weapon on the Barony pitches; a bustling striker that made defenders' lives hell. He was often too much for the referees who could hardly understand his strong south Wales accent. So he took more early showers than most.

The girlfriend tolerated the ruffling of hair, the bad language and even giving him a lift home one night. Wolves away, however, tipped her over the edge. Ade was bouncing off the ceiling by 11am that day, especially after an hour in the Stafford Arms pub by the station. It was an ill-advised stop but the real ale emporium was hard to resist. By the time we arrived in Wolverhampton town centre he was rocking, chatting to random strangers and generally making a nuisance of himself. He was one of our away-day regulars, unless he could get to see Swansea play. So we knew what to expect and generally made allowances. At Wolves he was a monster. In the final pre-match pub he took things too far, tipping a sachet of sugar into the girlfriend's drink. I thought she was going to explode, combust on the spot. Her massed ringlets of curly hair stood on end and her eyes bulged. I closed mine, half expecting to see Ade spread out on the floor. But she bit her tongue, and blanked him for the rest of the day. The other lads made sure he kept his distance. I was glad to see the back of that trip, especially as we lost 1-0. That was her last Alex away day, and Mistress Alexandra shed crocodile tears.

BRAGGING RIGHTS

They barely had chance to polish the Play-off final trophy before Alex fans were banging on the club doors asking for ticket details. It was a First Division feeding frenzy and nobody wanted to miss out. Season tickets were soon sorted, but all eyes were on the Football League HQ and the much-anticipated release of the new fixtures.

It's like having a second Christmas when they finally arrive in June, carefully unwrapping the outer layers and teasing yourself for a few minutes longer. You know what teams are coming, but you don't know what order or when you'll be playing them. For us, two fixtures stood out from the rest – Stoke City, home and away. Port Vale was old hat, but Stoke and their shiny new ground was the main event. Some famous old football names made up the list, but we hadn't seen a full-bloodied derby with the Potters for over seven years.

The first get-together of old foes was scheduled for December, so it was important that we built up a decent head of steam. It was a mixed start, challenging to say the least, but slowly but surely we picked off a few stragglers and got points on the board. We beat Norwich, Portsmouth and Tranmere, then drew with Middlesbrough and threw away a three-goal lead at Reading to take just a point. As if that wasn't bad enough, Morris Dancers accosted us outside Reading station.

Then things went pear-shaped, we started losing games, and at one point it looked as though the New Year would see us relegated. Even Stockport turned us over at Gresty Road, followed by a worrying and embarrassing 5-2 thrashing by Huddersfield Town.

Incredibly, there were calls for Dario Gradi's head; such was the desire to see the Alex keep improving. He'd worked hard for fifteen years, but after four tough months a few numpty supporters wanted a change. We were second bottom, just Pompey beneath us in the table, but they had games in hand.

As if we needed any more bad news, one of my favourite players tripped me up and then stamped on my crown jewels. He didn't literally, but that's how it felt when Dele Adebola handed in a transfer request. I was distraught. Why would he want to go anywhere else?

Next up was Stoke, two weeks before Christmas, at their fancy council-funded stadium perched alongside an incinerator (something that amused our tiny minds for years). It was a complete sell-out, the game we'd all wanted to see, but now wished wasn't happening under such challenging circumstances. The Stokies turned up keen to see their annoying little neighbours mauled, while Crewe fans wondered if the season could get any worse.

It didn't, and the hero of countless high-profile matches stepped up, assessed his options from thirty yards out, and then drilled an unstoppable free-kick past the Stoke 'keeper. Shaun Smith was the man.

'One-nil to the Railwaymen,' we sang, secretly wishing that we could emulate the Arsenal of old that would score and then shut up shop, boring the opposition into submission. In true Alex fashion, we carried on playing and left ourselves wide open. It was fortunate that Stoke were woeful that winter afternoon, as they didn't look likely to score had we played until midnight. So when Colin Little added a second fifteen minutes from time, the Red Santa hats flew into the air as though Christmas had come early.

Soon after the artful dodger's goal, a Stoke supporter ran onto the pitch in disgust, a one-man protest to berate the manager. The stewards tried to grab him but he was a fan on a mission. He made it to the home dugout, bouncing about and foaming at the mouth. His side was losing; no, it was much worse than that. A rival that hadn't previously registered on the radar was outplaying them. We annoyed Stoke that day. Big time. Now, with their season already in tatters, he wanted to vent his anger.

With cameras clicking and police bearing down, he dipped into his pocket and produced a season ticket, ripped it in half and tossed it to the ground in front of the startled coaching staff sat on the icy cold bench. It was a sad, miserable sight, but pure comedy for the watching Alex fans still delirious after the second goal.

On the final whistle boos rang out around the Britannia stands, but not in the away end. The Stoke fans were livid, and scuffles broke out as some tried to pile onto the pitch. They even fought amongst themselves, some calling for the manager's head, others wanting chairman Peter Coates to bite the bullet, most just distraught that they'd lost to Crewe - the chip eaters as they loved to call us.

It was surreal, caught between celebrating our win and enjoying their misery. The stands had emptied well before the referee stopped the fight, Stoke battered and bruised, shaken and surprised by our spirit. It was all the more remarkable as so many pundits had predicted a romp for the home side, little Crewe likely to be torn. How wrong they were.

The mood darkened as the police let us out onto the car park, some heading to cars and buses, others hoping to get to the train station. A bit of trouble was always likely, but with one result we seemed to have engendered increased hatred. The Potters' wrath arrived in the form of a few coins, then chunks of gravel collected from the waste ground surrounding the parking areas, and then came the bricks. Panic spread across the faces of police officers and stewards, ready for trouble but never expecting such ferocity. People knew each other, Stoke fans from Crewe, kids like me from Alsager who had grown up with Stokies, including some of the Naughty 40 lads that were in my school year. Now they snarled and surged forward, hoping to land a punch. Thankfully, it was just a reaction to the defeat and their slide down the division. There wasn't sufficient hatred to warrant all-out war. They disappeared, slowly but surely, tails between their legs, still trying to comprehend what had just happened.

Back in Crewe the partying started immediately. It wasn't quite May '97, but car horns sounded as the first fans arrived on Nantwich Road. People waved at the coaches as they swept down Gresty Road, some with damaged windows. Then, much later, like an army returning from battle, the lads who'd braved Stoke town centre and the train station slipped into the pubs, many sporting cuts and bruises from post-match bust-ups.

The evening's *Green Un* was the most coveted publication, and I joined the queue outside the garage by the *Passage To India* curry house. We knew the score, we knew what time the goals had gone in, and we knew that the victory had given us hope, a chance to get clear of the drop zone. But seeing it in print, being able to wave that paper around in the pub, confirming our superiority, taunting any Stokies daft enough to venture out and recounting the match to Man City, United, Everton and Liverpool fans who had probably sat in the pubs all afternoon, well, it didn't get much better than that.

The headline read 'HUMILIATED' in huge inky letters. It was our day, a chance to mock the big-club devotees who rarely saw their teams in the flesh, but turned their backs on the Alex many years ago, perhaps during the dark days of the seventies and early 1980s.

Some of them will have made the return fixture on Easter Monday, jumped on the bandwagon and seen us beat Stoke at Gresty Road. I don't begrudge anyone coming back after a few years away. Enduring season after season of misery was enough to drive even the toughest fans crazy, so seeing some old faces back to help fill the ground was good enough for me.

Beating Stoke though - TWICE - must rate highly with any Alex fan when talk turns to favourite seasons and most notable achievements. I think some would have accepted relegation at a push, providing we'd been guaranteed those sweet victories that announced our intention to break free from our small club shackles. It was, after all, our first year in the higher division, and many thought that it would be a one-off experience, a brief dalliance in unknown waters. But when the final weekend arrived, just three weeks after we'd beaten the Potters at Gresty Road, Crewe fans were in dreamland while Stoke and Manchester City were scrapping it out (quite literally) to stay in the division. It meant nothing in real money, but we had the bragging rights for at least the next twelve months.

***

To say that Crewe Alexandra was the dominant local club around this time would be stretching the truth, but in terms of league position the record books do not lie. We were better than Stoke and Vale. That was a black and white fact. At the end of that summer we had something else to shout about – our record transfer fee was smashed AGAIN, and it dwarfed the cash that had been splashed down the A500.

First, I should wind back the clock a few months. Dave Walton was signed from Shrewsbury in October 1997, to help stop the rot that set in during that blustery autumn. The fee was £500,000 (half a million quid) and would rise depending upon appearances. Talk about raising the bar, our previous record was £100,000 for Marcus Bignot at the start of our First Division adventure.

Walton was just the player we needed, a real monster, a man mountain. He was impressive wearing an Alex shirt and a tad intimidating off the pitch. I discovered this to my cost during a night out in Nantwich. I'd joined the Sunday League footy team, drinking in the Union Vaults with Welsh Ade. It was a Saturday night out, enjoying a few beers, having a laugh and a joke. Then a group of Alex players appeared, also looking to wind down after a tough match. I can't remember the opposition that day, but I think we'd lost. So I couldn't resist throwing a few questions at the players, enquiring why things had gone wrong, and what they thought about the situation.

I ended up with Shaun Smith, a very quiet fella who stood at the back of the group listening in. I'd had a few by now, so I suppose that I was quite loud and vocal. I put a few questions to our left back, asking him why he didn't shout more, talk to the other players and improve communications out on the pitch. I thought his body language was all wrong, and that hunched shoulders sent out the wrong message to the fans on the sidelines. He became animated when I suggested that he needed to look like he was bothered. He wasn't shouting, but I suppose for Smithy he looked a bit agitated.

The discussion and ensuing heated debate attracted big Dave Walton. I discovered that he's a 'steam in and ask questions later' kind of fella, certainly when I was lifted off the floor and pinned to the wall. It was a surreal moment, looking down at one of the club's newest players, him glaring back, his over-sized hand wrapped around my throat. It happened in a flash and I was in no position to negotiate.

'It's all right, Dave, we're just talking,' said Smithy.

Thankfully, that was enough, and I slid down the wall as the big fella loosened his grip. The bouncers came running over but the commotion was over. No harm done, me in my place. Smithy walked off and we never did finish that chat, although we talked much more a few years later when his testimonial season cropped up.

The mere half-million we spent on basher Walton was eclipsed when Rodney Jack signed from Torquay United for £650,000 at the tail end of July '98. It was a statement of intent from the club. The figure was astronomical, the kind of money once spent running the entire club for a season! Alex fans were riding the crest of a wave, albeit one from the south coast rather than Hawaii. Most wondered if the gaffer had lost his marbles spending such cash on one player. The crafty English Riviera club had seen him coming, we thought, although plenty raved about the young lad from St. Vincent. So when he didn't start the season we began to worry.

When Jack eventually took to the field against Oldham Athletic, in the second leg of the League Cup first round, we all dropped to the manager's feet and worshipped. The lightning fast striker was an instant hit amongst the fans, making a block-busting start on that glorious August evening. I was stood on the Paddock for some reason, probably with Alan who had always preferred that side of the ground. The mood was relaxed and all talk was about the league. The match was floundering at 0-0, and we were losing 3-2 after the first leg at Boundary Park.

Enter Mr Jack. He twisted and turned, just a couple of yards from our position on the terrace, slipped past static defenders and then unleashed a ferocious net-busting 25-yard drive that flew into the roof of the Oldham goal. Wow! The gaffer knew his onions. If only he read the stock market like he did up-and-coming players, we'd all be millionaires.

So we bedded in, spent big and made Stoke look small fry. These were the halcyon days, the time that older fans will never forget. The support grew steadily, but it was always apparent which fans had just joined the fold. They were the overly critical ones; supporters that expected promotion to the Premier League to follow instantly. Others, those who had been around for a few years, knew that it was time to savour the moment and just enjoy the ride. The roller-coaster was only just getting started.

A QUESTION OF PRIORITIES

Two years into our fantastic First Division journey, 1999 to be exact, and straddled across two incredibly turbulent seasons, my world was turned upside down. Life was busy enough on the football front, but I've never been one to keep things simple. In the space of nine months, I got married, signed on the dotted line for Rolls-Royce and Bentley Motors, bought a new house and had our first baby - roughly in that order. To think that a couple of years earlier I had vowed to become a bachelor!

So what do I remember most? Was it my first day at work, getting married by the beach in Jamaica, collecting the keys to the house, carrying the wife over the threshold or the first screams of a trainee Alex fan? No, it was missing the final home game of the 1998-99 campaign, when fans said goodbye to the tatty wooden main stand and our new space age mega-stand started to rise up like something from *Close Encounters,* just without the fancy lights and beepy sounds.

That's a disgrace, an awful admission. Those other highlights were amazing, but I wanted my Alex experiences to continue uninterrupted alongside them. And I missed a historic moment in Crewe Alexandra's history.

I can't blame the wife, though; it was Bizza's fault. He also married this year. His stag do took place in early May, a drunken orgy around the historic streets of Edinburgh. I almost had to disappoint him, not happy about missing the Portsmouth match that marked the end of an era for the Paddock and wooden seating areas. But I couldn't do that, and he wanted to know the score as much as I did.

There was an additional complication that weekend, namely filing copy for the *Sunday Express*. I forgot to tell them I'd be away, only realising my gaff on the afternoon of the game. I was sat on a patch of grass, supping a can of cider and looking like Rab C. Nesbitt after a rather testing Friday night session with Bizza's entourage. Enjoying the glorious May sunshine, we were happy to watch the world go by as our bodies slowly recovered ahead of the next session.

'Shit, I need to do a match report,' I yelled at Bizza when I realised that I hadn't passed the assignment to another freelancer.

'Give one of the lads a call,' he suggested, thinking surprisingly clearly for a man with a heavy alcohol-to-blood ratio, and someone about to tie the knot.

So I did, and Andy saved the day. A series of five or six phone calls sufficed, a few supplementary text messages and I was sorted. All the facts gathered, a few fancy words wrapped around the players involved, and I phoned it through.

'Sounds like a party at Crewe today,' suggested the copy taker at the other end of the line.

It was, just a stag party about 250 miles from the ground. Then I had a brief panic. Had the lads at Gresty Road stitched me up, pulled a fast one and fed me some duff data? Now that would be hilarious, reporting goals and incidents that didn't happen! I dismissed the notion and rattled off the 400 words they had requested, keen to return to the drinking games. The Alex beat Pompey 3-1 that afternoon to round off another very satisfactory season. My dodgy copy appeared in the paper the following morning, and we all got very drunk in Scotland. Again.

Back in Crewe, a few days later, I couldn't resist taking one last peep at the old girl. Safety barriers were in place, netting and boarding sparing her blushes as the first bulldozers moved in. It was a sad moment, a slice of Alex history disappearing before my eyes. The enormous steel framework that was taking shape in the background was spectacular, but it looked vast and soulless. They call it progress, and the future was emerging as I stood gawping at daredevil workers high up on the metal girders. Crewe Alexandra was ready for the 21st century, I'm just not sure that some of its supporters were.

The new stand was, however, very necessary, the only way that we could compete with the city clubs that dominated the division. The structure boasted 6,000 seats and took the overall ground capacity to a handful over 10,000 people. Most of the big guns, like Wolves, Stoke, Bolton and Middlesbrough boasted 20,000 capacities. It was a significant step forwards, but we remained one of the minnows in a deep pond full of greedy predators. Gresty Road was now covered on four sides, a professional sporting arena. So we gave ourselves a fighting chance, but the club lost a little something, that small club mystique that often placed doubt in Goliath's mind.

One player who would not play in the new-look Alex stadium was Seth Johnson. The tough-tackling midfielder earned a well-deserved move to Derby County after the final match, a deal put on ice earlier in the season because of spectacular loyalty and a request by the player himself to fight the Alex cause, that of survival in the First Division. It was a gesture that will never be forgotten, although I bet the directors didn't see it that way. I half expected to see him covered in cotton wool as he ran onto the pitch during those final weeks, with chairman John Bowler camped in the technical area, begging the referee to look after the club's prize asset.

Seth was a blood-and-thunder fans' favourite. We didn't want him to leave, but like Danny Murphy, Dele Adebola and others before them, Johnson was ready for the bigger stage. The money wasn't bad either, the £3.4m price tag a handsome figure that allowed expansion in many areas, not just the recruitment of new players.

In fact, Dario Gradi always said that the cash from Seth's move paid for the stand. It was already planned some twelve months earlier, but I suspect that without that sizeable windfall the club would have been saddled with debt for many seasons. It's just a huge chunk of brick, steel and plastic, but for services rendered, dedication and value added to the club, I often wonder if it should be named the Seth Johnson stand. Many Alex fans would agree, but I suspect that honour is being kept in reserve, possibly for the man who found the player one hot summer during a pre-season tour of Devon.

***

When the new facility opened, it was with a heavy heart that we vacated our seats on the Popside, somewhere that had real meaning to Crewe fans young and old. We stood there as children, then as men, and later sat obediently for two wonderful seasons of First Division football, occasionally frustrating those poor stewards tasked with enforcing the 'no standing' policy. It was a proper old stand, nothing fancy but the scene of so many memories. We bundled them up, good and bad, and waved goodbye for the last time.

Switching sides was exciting, like moving house but having someone else sort the gas, electric and new kitchen. Everything was shiny and new, the toilets had seats and the hot water taps worked! We didn't really have a choice, as the Popside was given to the away supporters, with the Railway End also theirs if they needed to spill over. Plenty of the big clubs required the extra space, giving them a decent allocation of about 2,300 seats. At the time, none of our lads fancied the Gresty Road End either, so we decided to perch ourselves at the top of 'B' block, opposite our old seats on the Popside. It was nosebleed territory, about a mile from the pitch, but an amazing perspective on the games that played out below. I was transported back in time, to my younger days at Old Trafford. Now the Alex players looked like matchstick men, but they wore fancy footwear instead of hobnail boots.

There were many new faces alongside us up in the gods, and that meant greater revenues for Crewe Alexandra, extra cash to pay the players that demanded ever more to wear the shirt. Alex fans were in new territory and just wanted the squad to compete, so even our wage structure was smashed. The football world we had known for years was evolving, very quickly, with posh TV screens on the concourse walls and a new bar that served warm beer at half-time. We had arrived.

As things changed at the Alex, I knew that my supporting life would also follow a different path. I struggled organising my time before, and with so many changes afoot I conceded some ground. The worst element of any obsession, addiction or a routine that you can't break is the impact on those around you. For those early seasons in the First Division I was a nightmare. Hardly a game missed, too much time in the pubs before and after kick-off, hours on road and rail depriving the wife of any quality time. I peaked in the late 90s, which coincided with a hectic year on the domestic front. It was a good thing, I often tell myself, as I was on the way to all-out football addiction. The point of no return, when no amount of medication can save you. I didn't want to hit the emergency stop, go cold turkey and spend weeks locked in the spare room. I needed something akin to a nicotine patch, bring me down slowly but drip-feed the football buzz without too many nasty after effects.

So as a fully paid up member of the married clan I considered my options. There was a little nudge from the wife, suggesting that more Saturdays should be spent feathering the nest in readiness for our new arrival. That gave me palpitations, and I had visions of weekly shopping expeditions, endless hours trawling the baby shops. So I bought a season ticket, but promised to cut back on the expensive away days. That, I convinced myself, was a substantial compromise. I had hoped that marriage would bring additional perks, along the lines of a tax break, but there was no discount for anyone recently hitched when I handed over the cash in the club shop. Now that would be a good selling point, something to encourage under-the-thumb husbands to renew their Alex vows.

So I plodded on, no longer a regular member of the away day club, more an occasional day-tripper. Those train trips, beers and food, plus a hefty admission fee soon added up, and it was the sensible option to cut back. But I missed them. I was excluded from my extended family. It wasn't the same sat at home cuddling the radio, or watching corporate faces recounting match facts at 4.50pm on the television. Money was tight, more so when we bought the new house just one month before our first lad was born. Suddenly I had serious financial obligations and a list of priorities longer than the half-time queue for over-price pies. The onus was on me to make the right life decisions.

Over the years I juggled my money, nearly always jeopardising something, paying Peter with cash borrowed from Paul. I'd buy match tickets when credit cards needed to be cleared, talk flatmates out of investing in a new fridge and then buy the latest Alex shirt.

Thankfully, as the money got tighter I never put the mortgage payments at risk, although I know some who did and lived to regret it. Trips to see the Alex away at Portsmouth, Middlesbrough and Cardiff were swapped for new carpets, a cot and the first pushchair. Seeing that pregnancy bump become a screaming bundle of joy, a little person that kept me awake all night and thanked me with sticky lumps of green poo, well, how could I trade that for a Tuesday night in Bury?

HE SHOOTS TOO SOON

The fanzine was going well, the *Express* paid for matchday copy, I started updating the Alex section of the *From The Terraces* website and the *Evening Sentinel* even asked me to do a column. I was hooked, couldn't get enough football information, and I couldn't pump enough written material out to the eager masses that wanted to read my nonsense.

On the domestic front my oldest lad was teething and I was doing my best to teach him how to say Da-Da-Dario. So I suppose there should have been more pressing matters. Still, a junkie needs his fix, and writing a book about something I loved seemed the perfect addition to my football stable. I'm not sure that the missus agreed, but she had her hands full. Literally!

So one sleepless night, the kind when you can't drop off no matter what you try, I crept downstairs and scribbled a few notes. I'd taken enough sleeping tablets to stun a medium-sized elephant, but there was too much swirling around my head. I wanted to write about the incredible achievements of the previous few years, and reflect upon the successful first seasons in Division One. But that didn't feel quite right. There was much more than a promotion and a few high-profile players to talk about.

Suddenly, it dawned upon me. Several people had contributed to the phenomenal improvements around the club, but there was one man who seemed to do more than most. Dario Gradi was the catalyst, the man who had dragged us from the basement and saved us from endless jokes. It tied in almost to the year with my ever-increasing obsession, circa 1983, when a 17-year-old was starting to see every home and away match, digesting every snippet he could get his hands on. This was THE era, the best times the club had ever known.

So *The Gradi Years* was born, the book I just had to write, my offering to the messiah and a place amongst the literary elite (well, a place on the second shelf at Crewe Library at the very least). It started as a pile of scattered notes, personal memories and accounts from individuals that agreed to be interviewed. It was always going to be a chronological plod through the years, but I really wanted to bring it to life with first-hand accounts from players, directors and of course the supporters who had lived the dream. So I had a mountain to climb, but if the Alex could make it to the First Division it was the least I could do. I worked that night, and then ploughed on at a frenetic pace for the next three or four months. The wife wasn't impressed, but she knew what she'd bought into the day she met me. That's what I told myself, but I changed a few nappies to keep the peace, ordered takeaways to save her cooking and bought her a lovely new iron to keep on top of the baby's clothes.

I wasn't that bad, honestly, but she was far too tolerant and I should have been returned to the dark ages. I knew this, and guiltily added her name next to dad's on the acknowledgements page for tolerating my obsession.

Apart from the wife wanting to kill me, everyone else was very accommodating as I put the book together. Former chairman Norman Rowlinson really surprised me, as he was a lovely guy. Before our meeting, I had visions of a harsh, abrasive man, someone who had run countless successful businesses and also been ruthless enough to chop several underperforming managers at Crewe Alexandra. So when I sat waiting in his timber firm's offices at Willaston (now a housing estate) I was a little apprehensive.

I shouldn't have been, as he strolled in with two cups of tea, a packet of custard creams and a beaming smile. His outstretched hand met mine and he ushered me to a huddle of comfy chairs. Like your favourite uncle who always gave you a quid to spend on sweets, he was a friendly face to start the interviews rolling. He was honoured that I wanted his input as I compiled the book, which amused me no end. After all, this was the man who started the Dario Gradi story.

He was warm and receptive, fascinated about my project, and very frank with his answers. He likened his 24 years as chairman to a prison sentence, which tickled me from the start.

First we talked about the decision to recruit Dario Gradi way back in 1983. Rowlinson had been very stubborn, and he told me that he couldn't understand why a southerner would want to move to Crewe, running a northern club in the heart of an industrial town. He was eventually won over by Gradi's determination, plus the fact that he caught the train to Crewe and demanded an interview. Rowlinson liked that perseverance, but he was no fool, as he'd seen turbulent times at Gresty Road. After Peter Morris had left the club he knew that he had to get it right, choose a manager who would make a difference. So after an evening chatting about football, business and possibilities for the future, he was convinced that Gradi was the man. He stood out a mile from the other candidates and the astute Alex chairman offered him a contract on the spot.

I also asked about the Tony Waddington era. He paused for a moment, and then explained what happened. It was a tough decision sacking any manager, but in that case he felt that he made the right one. Spending was out of control and the players coming into the club were not bringing about sufficient change to warrant their inflated salaries. He liked Waddington but didn't think he could produce the required results on Crewe Alexandra's budget.

So he acted decisively. That's what chairmen are paid to do, although he never took a penny from the Alex. The club was almost on its knees financially, and he had been paying the players' wages out of his own pocket. He just didn't shout about it. That wasn't his style. He took flak from supporters and endured the 'Rowlinson Out' campaign as best he could. Being a despised figurehead was the low point in his time at Gresty Road, but he carried on in the background, making sure that the club didn't go under. I didn't mention the apple hitting him on the head away at Bury back in 1980. He would have probably laughed it off, but I was getting some good stuff and thought I'd leave that unsavoury incident in the past. I'm sure that he had survived worse.

One hour in Rowlinson's company was enough to convince me how passionate he was about the Alex. I thought back to my youth, running onto the pitch and joining chants for the chairman's head. I consoled myself that I didn't know any better, and that I wouldn't repeat my foolish actions now that I knew so much more about the man. As we continued talking about the club's renaissance under Dario Gradi he was brimming with pride. The appointment was a good choice, and he knew it. The club was now in safe hands, especially with John Bowler also providing an aura of calm from the boardroom. It was a stable team and he was the godfather figure.

From the influential chairman who recruited one of the country's longest serving managers, I switched to the maestro himself. I needed a few sessions with the manager and grabbed the first up at Reaseheath, one wet afternoon when training had nearly finished. John Fleet and a few of the academy staff made me feel very welcome, gave me a brew and installed me in the players' lounge while I waited. Academy starlets came in and out, pacing up and down, hoping to be offered a place on the bench that weekend. Gradi was still out with some trainees, working in the driving rain, trying to improve even the tiniest facet of the youngsters' games.

About thirty minutes after the normal finishing time he walked into the building, dripping wet but ready to fulfil his next obligation. I could hardly moan that he'd kept me waiting, as he was out there coaching the kids of the future. As it happened, the likes of David Wright, Dean Ashton, David Vaughan and Stephen Foster were put through their paces that day, the next batch ready for first team duties. It was another few minutes before I saw him, drying off in the kit room and making a few notes about tactics that needed to be improved. But you don't tell Dario Gradi to work on his punctuality. When he arrived it was straight down to business.

'So why are you writing this book,' he asked me, as though I was some kind of lunatic. 'Why now? I'm still here. Why not wait until I've gone?' he added accusingly.

He was just as sharp off the training pitch. It was a fair point, and maybe I should have waited a few more years. I'd collected the ball, done a cheeky sidestep and whacked it over the stand. I'd shot too soon, when I should have looked for support, bided my time and kept possession by the corner flag. So he was right about the timeline, but the club was riding on the crest of a wave. I wanted the book to end on a high, but there was no way I could suggest that relegation was on the cards. So I considered my answer, trying hard to keep my mouth shut as I gazed in awe at the man. I wore the expression of a stalker-cum-groupie, and kept my hand firmly on the notepad and pencil that vibrated in sympathy with my nerves. There was a growing urge to hug him, and I considered offering to clean his boots. Thankfully, I found my tongue.

'Okay, it's about you... but you've transformed the club more so than anyone else,' I told him, dancing around the tough defence that he set out before me. 'We're in the First Division, and even you know we're punching above our weight. I want to write it now.'

I wondered if he was going to punch my lights out, react badly to my suggestion that he could take the club no further up the leagues. But that wasn't this issue. It was more about modesty.

'Don't go writing that,' he told me, 'I've only pulled a few things together. Plenty of other people work hard behind the scenes.'

Nice one Hornbrook. One minute in his company and I had annoyed the man already. The Crewe Alexandra manager has been accused of many things, but thankfully patience is one of his better qualities. He tolerated me and we sparred for a while, testing each other over ninety minutes. Fleety brought us another cup of tea to help keep the chat flowing, giving me more valuable time to peep into the mind of a genius. He could do no wrong in my eyes back then.

Gradi answered every line of enquiry in depth and threw plenty back at me. He's a very intelligent man. He made it hard, probably trying to get the best from me. He was defensive of his players, staff and methods, and incredibly honest and realistic about the club's prospects. He had ambitious plans for the future, all within budget of course.

I asked some pretty stupid questions that afternoon, but he didn't complain. I'd made a list, rehearsed a few lines, but when you sit before the man who had dragged the football club I loved from laughing stock to role model organisation, well, it all went a bit wonky for the man with the Dictaphone. He wanted to get off for his evening meal and I wanted to know about his pre-match preparations, half-time pep talks and how he dealt with athlete's foot. He smiled, shook my hand, and then slipped away. It was just another distraction for the man trying to run a football club. For me it had been one of the best few hours of my life, sat opposite the man who had made dreams come true for so many devotees.

Over the next few months I survived further sessions with the gaffer and managed to remain professional. I even avoided asking for his autograph! Then I met with John Bowler, Gill Palin and other key figures from around the club to really flesh out the story and put Gradi's achievements in context. I had a bagful of quotations, some great interviews on tape and plenty of ideas. The structure of the book was in place, but I needed to check dates, fill in the gaps and bring the whole story to life with anecdotes from supporters.

Perhaps the greatest assistance outside the club came from 'The Railwayman' (aka Andy Scoffin), a fan of umpteen years, message board contributor and occasional letter writer to the local papers. I'd seen him on the terraces many times, but had never met him properly until he responded to an advert for information about the early Gradi years. He had the most extensive collection of clippings, photos, signed footballs, programmes and replica shirts I'd ever seen. It put my collection to shame. Mine was a few scribbles on the back of a postcard to his veritable cave of Alex delights. It was wall-to-wall red and white, collected from the late 1960s. I was an amateur in his company.

With his help and a few references to my friend Marco's statistical epic of 1997, the book was put to bed over the summer of 2000 and despatched to the printer. I'd hoped to involve a local firm, but nobody could touch the guy who produced the fanzine for price, speed and delivery.

So the copies arrived in the back of a white van driven up from south Wales. I dashed outside and almost ripped the doors off, desperate to get a glimpse of my creation. Paul, the printer who had delivered countless editions of *Super Dario Land* on time, could see my excitement. He had a loose copy to hand, to save me ripping open a box and unsettling his careful packing. I sat down and flipped through the pages as though I had no idea what the book contained. It was a magical feeling, seeing my own words in print, so different to the pieces that appeared in the newspapers or the fanzine.

'You sitting there all day, or you going to give me a hand unloading,' asked Paul, finally rousing me from my daydream.

He had a home to get back to. It was just another book to him, just another football club. To me it was nearly a year of my life. Now I had to sell a few copies to pay the invoice, and hope that Mistress Alexandra liked what I'd written.

TRUE GENTLEMEN STEP ASIDE

Shaun Smith gave me a wry smile as I walked into the *Hawk Inn*, a cosy pub on the main road through Haslington. I was there as part of a committee to kick-start his and Steve Macauley's testimonial season. We hadn't spoken since Dave Walton defended his honour and pinned me to the wall by my throat. Smithy obviously found it amusing several years later. I liked the guy, although he still looked a miserable old sod at times. His left foot, though, I wanted to hack it off and take it to the local taxidermist, mount it on the wall alongside the plasma TV and picture of the family. Now that would be a trophy to start guests talking, but I hate to think what Mr Walton would do if he ever tracked me down.

Both Macca and Smithy joined us in the 1991-92 season, back in the old Fourth Division. We required a few older, journeymen types to help us on the road to promotion. So the two gritty defenders were the perfect foundation, solid players to mop up behind the fancy flicks and slick passing that sometimes caught us napping. They arrived as non-league warriors, both prepared to roll their sleeves up and get dirty. Neither player shied away from a tackle, both scored goals and their team mates respected them. They were trusty, long-serving professionals that testimonial seasons are designed for, a way that supporters and parent clubs can say thank you with a golden handshake to see them safely on their way.

They certainly deserved it. Well over 700 games between them, they'd been instrumental in two promotions, helped younger players develop around them, and not once did we hear either complaining about contracts or team selections. I suppose fans on the sidelines could relate to the pair. Macca and Smithy were real players, no make-up and no rehearsed interview techniques. In fact, after Wembley '97, both were awful on camera. Two men caught up in the moment, speaking their minds just as the supporters would have done. They mumbled, looked to friends and family in the crowd and rolled out the worse football clichés. They had just done their job and wondered what all of the fuss was about.

For the testimonial finale, the plan was to stage a high-profile match in the summer of 2002, when both players had served a full ten years at the club. Their contracts were up and, with the clock ticking, Father Time was not on their side. They accepted this and prepared to move on. No fuss, no complaining, no moaning about life and football treating them badly. That, I suppose, is what made them stand out for me.

Other events were planned, like golfing days, a big-screen race night and a cricket match. So when Peter Hallett from the organising committee called me one evening, asking if I'd like to compile the souvenir brochure, it was an easy decision. I'd survived Smithy's hitman, and Macca was our leader. How could I possibly say no?

Over many years I had been lucky enough to chat with Macca on numerous occasions. Intelligent and thoughtful, I always remember him talking about his mates from home. They sat behind desks, grafted in factories and worked outside in all elements. He knew he'd been lucky, earning a decent salary doing something he loved.

Smithy, well, we'd had our moments, and even in the fanzine we occasionally ran critical pieces. He was a quiet, private man. He had his say, could lead the team with the right words when required, otherwise he'd sit back, out of the limelight. Few knew enough about the man to properly judge him, me included. But face to face, in that function room at the *Hawk Inn*, I saw him as a bloke outside of the football environment, but a man who served Mistress Alexandra, just as I followed her.

Players come and go, some quicker than others. I would, however, include both men in my all-time Alex XI, but not for their ability alone. Being brutally honest, neither were the most talented, certainly alongside some of the younger Alex players, and I suspect that both players would agree. But if the judging panel were to assess enthusiasm, effort, determination and guts, well, they'd score off the chart. They gave 100% when they wore the red of Crewe Alexandra.

That was certainly true during their final season as the testimonial committee's work played out to a depressing backdrop of Alex results. Smithy played on, but it was unusual to see Macca leave the pitch without a cut, bruise or bandage, and he spent much of 2001-02 on the sidelines.

Consequently, he was able to join the fundraising team in planning the various events and sporting days out. What struck me was his concern for the supporters. The committee was hell-bent on raising maximum funds, but Macca was adamant that ticket prices and entry fees should be kept to a minimum. If individuals wanted to bid more, then that was fine, especially at the sportsman's dinner when all manner of paraphernalia was up for grabs. I must have supped too much lager, as I ended the night winning the auction for a Shaun Smith match-worn shirt. We both found it amusing, but the wallet winced as I paid up later.

It wasn't the best way to end ten years with Crewe Alexandra, with Macca substituted during his final match that ended in defeat at Wimbledon (the relocated Milton Keynes version), as the manager tried to snatch something from the game. Smithy saw out the season, but defeat at Birmingham and a draw at Nottingham Forest sealed our fate. He played as we beat Rotherham 2-0 on the last day, although we needed about thirteen to scrape through on goal difference. I placed the bet, of course, refusing to give in. I even spoke on a Radio Stoke phone-in, skirting around the snide comments and flying the flag of resistance until the end. The Alex, including Smithy, gave everything that day, but it wasn't enough and we slipped down on goal difference. Such is life, it's a cruel game, and it was a disappointing end to a couple of wonderful Alex careers. But that's football at its fickle best.

***

Sadly, due to complications securing suitable dates with a number of clubs, the testimonial committee agreed with the players that it would be easier to postpone the grand finale game for twelve months. It was like a year extension, but Macca and Smithy wouldn't be playing for the Alex during the season. All a tad bizarre, but we ran out of options! Celtic had been mentioned as potential opponents, but they and others demanded expenses that would have wiped out the fundraising efforts. That was a huge disappointment to everyone, especially for me, as the souvenir programme was geared towards the lads finishing their Alex careers that summer. So it was all a bit of an anticlimax. However, the additional time created opportunities, and Dario Gradi's contacts came up trumps. Instead of one, the committee was able to plan a Merseyside double-header to send the Alex stalwarts off in style. They were, quite aptly, made up.

So putting everything on hold turned out to be a good thing. When the games finally happened during the summer of 2003, against Liverpool and Everton, they were sell-out events. Not because of the opposition alone, it was a mark of respect, a collective thank you from thousands of Alex supporters who wanted to see their heroes one last time. Jamie Carragher, Dietmar Hamann, David Unsworth and Kevin Campbell were on show, but all eyes were on the departing duo. They looked a little star struck, but who could blame them. When they were kicking around the non-league scene, over ten years earlier, I doubt they ever thought that they'd line up against some of the best in the Premier League. So they stepped out alongside lads they'd known for years, but faced internationals.

After the Liverpool match I bumped into another favourite player of mine, but one that left me with bad memories. There were plenty of calls for photos of Macca and Smithy, posing with various guests, friends, players and, in particular, Danny Murphy. The former Alex man was the perfect link, a kid that the older players had protected when he burst onto the scene as a 16-year-old. The three even combined at Wembley to score THE goal that took us to the First Division. Our long-serving duo was delighted to see him back at the club having made it into the Liverpool senior team. We stood in the Railway End, almost by the advertising hoardings, with celebrations ongoing behind the glass of the modest hospitality suite above us. Snappers from local and regional papers wanted 'that shot' with the trio together, and when the commotion subsided I stepped up and took a few pictures of my own.

From the edge of the pitch, a couple of young Liverpool lads called over. They had been waiting patiently, then took their chance and shouted to Murphy for his autograph. He did look over, for a second, but dismissed the pair with a wave of his arm and a mumbled excuse. He was late, apparently, and needed to catch a train. There were brief protests, the lads almost pleading for his signature. They had, after all, come to the game specially and waited for him after the final whistle. It cut no ice and they disappeared. I wanted to say something, ask him to reconsider, just spend a moment with these eager Liverpudlians. But he was gone, up the stairs to the testimonial reception, too busy and seemingly too important to hang around any longer than required once the formalities were done and dusted.

I was one of those kids once, in awe of such players, desperate to be noticed and afforded a little time. I don't know what those lads thought, whether they forgave him or struck him from their most wanted autographs list. I thought it was poor form. A tiny blot on his copybook, but I was left with a sour lasting memory. Shame.

I've seen Murphy signing autographs since, visiting the Alex, doing charity work and more. So he's no bad egg, and perhaps that night was a one-off. For some time, however, I've thought that players should be prepared to do more, to really appreciate what some supporters endure in their quest to follow their team. Of course the players get abuse, bad press and more. That's wrong, and in many ways it's asking a lot for relatively young men to be model professionals, always getting things right. But a couple of kids, come on. Macca and Smithy signed autographs, chatted and posed for photos until the last guests had gone. That's my memory of them.

The lads did well from the testimonial events, upwards of £100,000 to share between them. For ten years' service to the Alex, from two genuine fellas, few could moan about that. It's a drop in the ocean compared to the salaries of players these days. I know they donated some to charity, and as a parting gesture they took everyone associated with the fundraising committee (plus partners) out for a wonderful meal at the *Broughton Arms* in Balterley. It wasn't the delicious food or fine wine that flowed during the evening that made it all so special, it was their company, the fact they really appreciated what we'd done. Macca's wife came over to me later and thanked me for the kind words I'd written in the testimonial brochure. As I told her, it was merely a reflection of what Alex fans thought of her husband, and his team mate Smithy. It was a pleasure taking part in the organisation of the many events, and gaining a further insight into their lives as I compiled the programme. I can count on the fingers of one hand the other players for whom I'd be willing to do similar.

Smithy appeared at Gresty Road during the 2010-11 season to see his old club in action. Immaculately turned out in a well-tailored suit, he was in perfect shape. A few supporters joked that he could still do a job for the Alex, and I'm sure that I almost caught him smiling. He'd become a fireman since I last saw him, and he loved his new job. He was an honest, hard-working guy, enjoying a career path that he would surely have followed if Dario Gradi hadn't given him a chance when he was still hoofing the ball down the left wing for Halifax Town.

The same is true of Macca, who became a physiotherapist and later teamed up with one of his former clubs, Fleetwood Town, as first team coach. Both men deserve all the luck in the world, as they gave us immense pleasure over the years. Clubs have to move on and recruit fresh blood, but the Alex lost two dedicated professionals when they handed back their kit for the last time. A couple of true gentlemen stepped aside for the next generation. Those young kids had big boots to fill.

THERE'S ONLY ONE DEANO!

Anyone who has accused Dario Gradi of producing only midfield dwarfs need look no further than Dean Ashton. He was a kid from Holmes Chapel, only in a man's body. There were rumours that Arsène Wenger offered £5m to take him to Arsenal before we'd even seen him at Gresty Road. He was unique, a one-off. I sometimes wondered if he'd been crafted in a disused railway workshop, a Frankenstein's monster but with dashing good looks, a fearsome beast all the same who didn't know his own strength. He was a strapping six foot two, built like a heavyweight champion, but a player with great skill, finesse, a thunderous shot and a forehead that could stop a train. His country needed him, and to numerous observers of the beautiful game he was the archetypal English centre forward.

Unlike other young teenage debutants, like Michael Owen, Wayne Rooney and, most recently, players like Jack Wilshere, Ashton's early first-team career wasn't a screaming success. He had to work hard. The lad looked hefty, sometimes unwilling to run, and a few unsavoury comments resounded around the harsh stands before he won everyone over.

He emerged from the youth shadows with massive expectation weighing heavy on his young shoulders, and in 2000-01 he was used sparingly, many times from the bench, but still scored an impressive eight times. One of the goals, at home to Gillingham in April, saw him receive a pass without breaking his stride, and then trick two defenders by running the wrong way, swivel, move inside and rasp the ball into the top corner.

It was unbelievable technique that left opposition players shaking their heads. He upped his contribution to ten strikes the following year, but it ended in heartache for him and the club as we finally bowed out of the First Division after five seasons.

That must have been a culture shock to the players, but relegation also brought significant changes to our matchday schedule. For starters, we'd ditched the Royal as a pre-match drinking hole a few months earlier. The turning point was the Man City home game, an almighty invasion that left most pubs awash with drunken monsters that pissed in the street. Takeaways were trashed, and *Blue Moon* was sung relentlessly leading up to kick-off. They stole our song, so yes it narks me. We could hardly hear ourselves think in the Royal, our regular boozer, let alone discuss the merits of our emerging striker. So when they started dancing on the tables we called it a day and headed to the Brunswick.

That move was probably a good thing, as it marked the start of a new era for us. The Brunnie became our preferred pub and it was packed on matchday, with a great mix of supporters who always provided some top banter. Our group now numbered around ten, starting just after midday and holding our spot in the corner by the front window until 2.55pm most Saturdays.

We also decided to join the noisy boys in the Gresty Road End, a chance to sing and escape the sterile main stand. A couple of drummers appeared, a funny young lad called 'Spud' sat in front of us with his dad, the Alexandra Suite was available at half-time, and the atmosphere was incredible. We also got a few freebie pies from a lass we knew in the catering hut tucked away in the corner, but don't tell the club.

Ashton was often the hot topic, and everyone wondered if he would live up to expectations. Despite his obvious ability, he had some serious competition as we started our assault on Division Two. Rodney Jack looked a class above in the lower division, flame-haired waif Steve Jones was a bolt of lightning down the right wing, and another local lad, Rob Hulse, was determined to make the centre-forward spot his own.

It wasn't until November that Ashton made the score sheet but, like a juggernaut that struggles to the brow of a hill, with momentum on his side the big striker was unplayable. He banged sixteen goals during that promotion-winning season, with a hat-trick in our historic 8-0 Football League Trophy mauling of Doncaster Rovers. He had arrived, and the scouts came flocking to Gresty Road like flies to shit, all hopeful they could pull a fast one and grab a bargain. He certainly looked the part, with a streak of blonde added to his neatly-coiffed hair that soon caught the eye as he ran out onto the pitch, resplendent in white boots and red socks rolled up above the knees. It was his trademark, his dash of Eric Cantona flair. He was a superstar in the making, but remarkably humble and down to earth when we chatted to him after games. So we liked him. I wanted to be ten years old again, so I could stick his poster above my bed. I wasn't, and the wife would have asked serious questions if I'd dared suggest it.

Just one season in the Second Division was quite enough, and it was fantastic renewing old acquaintances in the higher division. I'd caught the fever again and slipped into that habit of attending almost every game, despite promising the wife that some weekends would be reserved for family time. My youngest was born by now, another inconvenience to a supporter that wanted to devote maximum time to his club. My boy was gorgeous, but it unsettled the routine I'd developed over the last couple of years. I felt constantly guilty, but couldn't shake the desire to resume my football obsession. The snip was the only way to prevent further disruptions in later years, so a trip to Leighton Hospital was arranged before there were any silly ideas about expanding the family further. How selfish was that?

Still, with another youngster demanding the wife's time and energy it was only right that I helped out. So I started taking the big fella to a few games. He'd been to some already, but as a baby he usually slept through most of the action. So at four years old he was ready to be indoctrinated, and I grabbed the first opportunity to introduce him to Ashton.

It was late November, and the Alex had struggled to find any consistency over the early part of the season. Sunderland arrived at Gresty Road hoping to take three points en route to the Premiership. We turned them over in front of a massive crowd just shy of capacity, winning three-nil, with two goals for Steve Jones and a screamer from Ashton, all three in the space of ten frantic minutes. He signed the eldest's shirt after the match, a regular ritual for proud fathers wanting their kids baptised into the Alex faith. So when he got home and asked his mum to wash the messy pen scribble off his shirt, I was gutted. I grabbed it before she could commit the heinous crime and stashed it away upstairs. To this day it's still in a precious box of memories up in the loft.

One major highlight of the Ashton era also involved a father-son moment, away at Wigan's then JJB Stadium. It was a last-minute decision, a chance to disappear for the day and use the family railcard. So we headed to Lancashire on the train with a few hundred Crewies. My lad had his mini Alex scarf wrapped around his neck, the latest replica shirt and one of my old badges pinned to his cute denim jacket lapel. I was proud as punch as we walked through Wigan town centre, bought him a pie and headed to the stadium hand in hand.

Wigan were all over us, and it was a typically robust and hard-working Paul Jewell side if ever I saw one. But they struggled to contain Ashton, Jones and Craig Hignett who all invited challenges from the Scouser's henchmen. The referee missed nothing, and Ashton almost burst the net with two unstoppable penalty kicks within six minutes to leave Wigan on the ropes. They hit back, that was expected. So at 2-2, deep into injury time, we hoped to escape with a point.

Ashton thought otherwise, ignored calls to keep possession and camp out by the corner flag, danced past kamikaze defenders and drilled the ball low and hard past a horrified Wigan 'keeper. If I could bottle that feeling of elation, absolute unbridled joy as I lifted my lad high into the air and saluted the goalscorer, well, I'd surely convince the *Dragon's Den* millionaires to back my venture. But that mattered little. As I looked to my eldest he was singing 'Deano, Deano, Deano...' with one thousand delirious Alex fans. I didn't stop smiling all day.

The big man completed the season with twenty goals to his name, and he finished on a high, scoring five in the last six games. We lost 3-1 to Norwich on that final day, but Ashton scored, of course, and then most of the 9,800 crowd danced on the pitch after the final whistle. I have never seen anything like it, with red, white, yellow and green mixing without a hint of trouble. He waved as the team saluted the crowd, and his departure during the summer looked inevitable. Norwich had shown an interest already, and we wondered if discussions took place after the ground had emptied, Delia Smith trying to swing the deal with a basket of delicious home baking no doubt.

So during the close season all the talk was about Ashton: would he stay or would he go? That he started in the first game against Cardiff was a massive relief. He was our talisman figure by now, a guaranteed goal machine on top of his game. When he received the ball the Gresty Road End stood, hopeful, expectant and increasingly reliant upon his potent strikes. He scored on that opening fixture, and it was the start of a purple patch that would last until the New Year.

That Christmas was particularly sweet for us, and especially Ashton. He scored most games, and away at Wolves he gave us a cracker of a present. The team was purring, and other academy graduates were also well established in the first team. David Vaughan looked a capable midfielder, Steve Foster a towering defender and Kenny Lunt one of the best tactical players since Danny Murphy. Even Mark Rivers had returned to the party for a final fling. Everything was clicking, defenders couldn't live with Ashton, and he lifted the crowd each time he touched the ball. It was more a case of when, not if he'd hit the net, and then how he'd deliver the killer punch. He was comfortable heading, volleying, driving from distance and just being in the right place at the right time, to tap in the simple ones. He was Dele Adebola with added panache.

We didn't know it, but the New Year's Day fixture would be one of his last. In Leeds we met up with Mike and headed to his local. It was rammed with home fans, which was no surprise, many of them acquaintances that our good friend introduced to us. However, they were not a very nice bunch. Typical snarling city types, full of themselves, not really interested in hearing about the Alex, just wanting to shout about Leeds. They gave us stick for two solid hours, taking the Mickey and predicting a goal blitz for their team. To be fair to them, they walked down to the stadium with us and jokingly wished us all the best as we headed to the away end.

They probably wished that they hadn't. Ashton did the business after fifteen minutes, showing his class in front of goal. The Alex section went berserk and the noisy celebrations reverberated around the stunned stadium. Just hearing a few choruses of 'Deano, there's only one Deano...' sent shivers down my spine. For a few seconds the Leeds vocal hardcore fell silent, shocked to see their team trailing to little old Crewe. It was an incredible feeling, a real high point for Alex fans, taking the lead at one of the so-called glory clubs.

The utter disbelief on the faces of arrogant opposition fans was a picture, and plenty of Alex lads dished out what had been thrown at us in the pub earlier. They didn't like it, and the infamous Leeds roar soon returned, urging their side to fight back. They did, wave after wave, but they couldn't score. Ashton was immense, retaining the ball and taking a battering from several tough defenders. He rarely reacted badly - no matter how much close attention he received. If he was scythed down, he'd leap to his feet and look for the ball. He was hungry to score and just accepted that less talented players would resort to dirty tricks.

A second for Ashton would have been fully justified, but it was a Crewe lad from the mid-90s who secured the points. Mark Rivers, a love him/hate him Marmite kind of player, was enjoying his second spell with the Alex. Most were happy that he'd retuned to give something back to the club that produced him. So seeing him celebrate with his fellow players was a special moment, one of his last strikes in a Crewe shirt, and I suspect the highlight of his penultimate season at the Alex.

None of the Crewe fans moved on the final whistle. They stood as one, applauding and punching the air as the players ran over to acknowledge our support. I wish that I'd had a radio with me that night, to listen to the post-match phone-in that must have been a feisty affair.

Instead, Mike took us back to his favourite boozer. We couldn't resist it, seeing the blokes who had spouted off just a couple of hours earlier. We entered cautiously, as the situation could have gone one of several ways. Our concern was unwarranted. The Leeds lads were full of praise for the Alex, more perplexed by their underachieving players. Well, all except for one guy, called 'Lurch', for obvious reasons, and he refused to look anyone in the eye, or join the conversation. Even his mates called him a miserable sod. We didn't care, as we'd won, the Alex moved into 9th position in the Championship table, and we had one of the country's best marksmen within our ranks.

One thing I have learned as a Crewe fan is that you should never count your chickens. Two weeks later Deano was wearing a Norwich shirt. It was a decent move, and I'm sure he made a few quid from the transfer. He had certainly earned it over the five seasons he wore our colours. And yet most people wondered why one of the bigger clubs didn't take a chance on him, especially on an English striker with all the attributes to become one of the game's greats.

For us, the departure happened far too quickly. He left the club on 12th January 2005, when the Alex were just two places from a spot in the play-offs. That's right, close enough for a stab at the Premiership. It was heart-wrenching, losing our main man, and yet it was no surprise. Including Leeds away, Ashton scored in eight of the previous ten games, twice in two of those matches. Countless scouts had watched him, and it was just a question of time before someone took a chance on the lad.

We always knew he'd be sold, but not when the club was flying high, in its best ever position. It felt as though the board had no regard for the fans, happy to cash in whatever the cost. I know that's not the case, and listening to Dario Gradi countless times over subsequent years it was apparent that the money was needed to keep the club running smoothly, debt free and able to continue operating a top academy. After all, that's what delivered Ashton to the fans.

Back at Gresty Road, everything went pear-shaped the day his peg in the changing room became available. At the time there was consternation, but nobody predicted the storm that followed. It soon became apparent that Ashton scored more than a few goals. Although he was a striker, the team revolved around him. He was a target man, so the defence could hit the ball long and he'd hold it up, relieving the pressure on the rest of the side. We went nineteen unbearable games without a win, only surviving on the last day of the season with a 2-1 victory over Coventry City. It was the beginning of the end as far as our days in the Championship were concerned.

***

As a footnote to the Ashton chapter, it was very sad to see him retire from football so young. He was only 26 years of age. A badly timed tackle during an England training session left him severely injured, and he never properly recovered. Apparently, the player responsible didn't even contact him, not even a good luck message as he bravely tried to return to full fitness. In interviews some time after announcing that he would not be playing again, Ashton wasn't bitter. That was a mark of the man. He spoke eloquently about his career and said that he'd been privileged to make it as a professional. Some of his friends from his Crewe Alexandra days were not so fortunate. He did play for England, once, and scored in an FA Cup final for West Ham. We were lucky to enjoy some of his best years. One day, my grandchildren will ask me who my favourite player was. I won't have to think twice.

THE PEOPLE'S GAME

Tim Jervis from the *Crewe Chronicle* arranged the photo, a group of sixteen Alex fans wearing cheesy smiles, replica shirts and waving their arms in the air as though they had just won the cup final. A few kids sat in the foreground holding a placard. My youngest was perched precariously on my shoulders, and a mix of male and female supporters all added to the family feel that readers love. The club shop and the towering main stand were the backdrop, the ideal picture composition for the weekly rag. We sold our souls and played along for the camera, but the publicity was necessary to get things moving.

That was the start of the Crewe Alexandra Supporters' Initiative (CASi), a new fans' group to revitalise links between the club and the fans. The post-Ashton collapse of 2005 onwards brought things to a head, when the club's fortunes nosedived and we avoided relegation on the final day. We felt far removed from the important decisions that dictated where the club was heading. We needed a voice.

I'd toyed with the idea of a new group over several seasons, but a message-board frenzy finally started the ball rolling. Several other people were keen, a few with knowledge about committees and the formal stuff that goes hand in hand with establishing such not-for-profit organisations. The general consensus was that in Crewe we'd been cast adrift from the people's game, that a privileged few pulled the strings and expected its puppets to bob up and down obediently like *Thunderbirds*.

Ultimately, getting a few supporters alongside the board of directors or, going the whole hog, assuming overall control of the club we loved was the long-term objective. The latter idea was a tad pie in the sky, but the inaugural meetings attracted around two hundred fans who were keen to stake our claim, and show the club how much it all meant to us. A hostile takeover was never planned, nor was it practical. But it was time to raise the stakes, test the water and see if the Alex would take us seriously. I never harboured ambitions to become formally involved with the club, but the idea of facilitating greater supporter involvement really excited me.

The concept of supporters owning and running matters on and off the pitch is a cracking idea. Unfortunately, making such dreams become a reality is easier said than done. It's been attempted across the country at many clubs, but most schemes have eventually failed. Results on the pitch ultimately drive the fans. That, sadly, invariably involves money, something the average working class supporter does not have in abundance. The cut-throat businessmen, the risk takers who accumulate sufficient wealth to buy in to clubs, are the ones who can offer the resources necessary to effect significant change. Few, however, give over their riches for nothing, and unless they can assume control and make the key decisions they are rarely interested. So we wondered if it was possible to mix old and new, create a unique working relationship with the people already in power at the Alex.

We had a massive task on our hands where the board was concerned. Like the long-serving manager and steady chairman, the guys in the background had pontificated over Gresty Road matters for donkey's years. Their hearts were in the right place but many felt that decisions were now being made for the wrong reasons. It was all about fuelling Dario Gradi's ambitions at Reaseheath, creating the perfect academy. Players were being sold too quickly, and although facilities at the ground were decent there was nothing special for the fans. Even the new main stand seemed to be geared up solely to generate revenue, not offer Alex supporters somewhere to meet and call home.

So it was a tough nut to crack. We needed fans on board, able and willing to step forward to demand better. We needed the club to listen. We wanted to make everyone proud to be associated with Crewe Alexandra.

So to meet resistance at the first hurdle was disappointing. The old supporters' association still existed, albeit in name only. A few of their members offered encouragement, but others cast scorn on what we hoped to achieve. Even at the first meetings, when the group's name was decided, there was dissention. CASi sounded like khazi (a rough and ready outdoor toilet), according to one. It did, if you wanted to be petty and childish. So before we'd properly started there was squabbling. It was then that I realised how divided the club's support had become, and that winning over hearts and minds was going to be very difficult.

We pushed on, and after a few early events there was a real buzz. We made it clear that the group would try to increase communications with the club, and hopefully improve the matchday experience for the fans. Many still asked questions and wondered what on earth could be achieved, but money was raised and a few key changes were implemented before the end of the summer.

For starters, we managed to get a big screen and projector in the Alexandra Suite. Too many supporters headed to the pubs before games, mainly because you could watch the early afternoon Premier League games with a pint. There was some reasonable dialogue with the club, but on matchday bar pricing we hit the buffers. That was one of the key issues, giving Alex fans a good deal and still boosting the club's coffers. We knew that we had a battle on our hands.

The 2005-06 season started well, with Billy Jones, Luke Varney and David Vaughan all picking up goals. That always puts supporters at ease, and for a brief spell the sale of key asset Dean Ashton was forgotten.

Then everything changed. The previous campaign's miserable form returned, and we endured one of the worst spells I'd know as a supporter. The problem was goals, or the lack of them. Either the opposition defences tightened up, or our lads lost their shooting boots. From late August through to the end of March, the Alex won just five of thirty-six Championship games. We were awful, and fired blanks in ten of those matches. Bottom of the Championship, we had just six games to save ourselves.

Most dramatic was the reaction towards the fans' group. Like supporters leaving seats empty when times are bad, the same happened to CASi. The numbers involved dropped off, and some pointed the finger suggesting that it was all a waste of time. Only the hardcore remained, mostly the faces who had stepped forward in the early months of the initiative.

Perhaps the main aim of CASi was inclusion, to unite and galvanise the support. This extended to away games, a pursuit that many Gresty Road regulars rarely enjoy. When they do, it's often done alone and the many associated matchday pleasures are not fully enjoyed. So we encouraged people to come along. We needed a lift after the dire performances on the pitch, so the group organised a trip to London, to coincide with QPR away in early April. It was a great chance to see the capital, squeeze in some sightseeing and meet up with the Alex Exiles who had been happy to support the new group.

Unfortunately, what began as an innocent day trip became another infamous outing. The morning and early afternoon were spent around the tourist hot spots, with a few beers enjoyed en route to a mass get-together in a Wetherspoon pub not far from Shepherd's Bush. It was fantastic seeing people like Big Simes, Wilko, Matty and many more, all exiled fans who struggled getting to games, something I knew all about from previous years in the wilderness. The ale flowed far too easily, as usual, and we only just made it to the ground after a last-ditch scramble to grab several taxis big enough to accommodate our large group.

The match was a blur, but the perfect antidote to our nightmare season. Kenny Lunt and David Vaughan ran proceedings from midfield and also popped up to hit two deserved goals. QPR's was a consolation effort and took little shine from the important 2-1 result. The Alex players ran over to us, visibly delighted and relieved to have grabbed three precious points.

The win dragged us to within touching distance of safety and set up a mouth watering game with Sheffield Wednesday the following Saturday. They sat one place above the drop zone, and post-match chat that was all about our chances of pulling off another miraculous escape. It was a great day out for the fans' group.

For some, however, there was too much drinking and not enough chat. As others started to drift away, catching the six and seven o'clock trains back home, I carried on in a West London bar, encouraged and ably assisted by my neighbour Dave. We had an hour until the last train, so plenty of time to grab another one. We did, and then shot across towards Euston station. Of course we missed the last train to Crewe, sidetracked in yet another bar, this time on the station itself, chatting nonsensically to similarly lubricated footy fans from clubs of every colour.

We needed a plan. Dave had never failed to get home after a night out, an unblemished record of nearly twenty years. This, however, was his first major excursion with me, an experienced delinquent with a record of unreliability as long as an orangutan's arm. So we hopped on the next train north, to Birmingham, thinking we'd be able to grab a local connection from New Street station.

How wrong we were. Several delays, an argument with the inspector about the validity of our London-Crewe tickets, and needing to grab a pee when we arrived in Birmingham derailed any lingering hopes of catching a train to Crewe that night. We were stuck and Dave was mortified. We checked the joint kitty and found about £30, and that included the loose change. So a taxi was not an option. We headed into town for a beer to drown our sorrows.

Now Birmingham is the UK's second city, so you'd expect pubs and clubs to stay open into the early hours. That was the plan, to linger as long as possible and then grab the next train home as first light broke. We did the obligatory 80s bars, a few proper Brummie boozers and then headed to the clubs.

That's when the problems started. Dave had trainers on and we both looked like typical football supporters, hardly the best-dressed on the nightclub circuit. Three clubs turned us down, the door staff shaking their heads in utter disbelief that we'd tried to blag our way into their establishments looking more tramp than Travolta.

Birmingham winger Jermain Pennant was our last hope. He arrived in a flash motor as we loitered by yet another club. The Brummies had held high-flying Chelsea to a 0-0 draw and he loved the attention, a girl on each arm and a gaggle trailing in his wake. I caught his eye, mentioned how impressive he'd been playing of late, and asked if he'd seen Gary that night. I have no idea why I said Gary, it was just a name, a desperate attempt to form a bond, trick him into thinking that we had a friend in common. He didn't stop. He didn't even look back. The bouncers growled and we moved on before they pounced, to an all-nighter café that was full of drunks, prostitutes and a few kids that should have been at home. To add insult to injury, the owner decided to close around 4am, as business was slow and the place was full of people who had nowhere to go, like us!

So we hit rock bottom that night and spent three uncomfortable and very cold hours trying to get some sleep in the Birmingham Bullring. Dave's missus was not impressed and hung up the phone when he tried to explain the situation. My wife just rolled her eyes the following morning. She'd seen it all before.

Although chaotic and not the best way to win over your mate's good lady, days out like QPR were the highlight of the first year with CASi. The football was awful that season, so most of the trips away and the fundraising events provided some much-needed light relief.

On the pitch, it didn't even go down to the wire that season. The Alex won one, drew two and then lost away to Leeds. It was all over, nothing to play for but pride on the final Saturday. We beat Millwall 4-2 but it counted for nothing. There was little confidence in the squad, and self-doubt ripped through CASi. That awful relegation brought changes to the playing personnel and the supporters' initiative.

The fans' group was, at its best, a superb collective, with great camaraderie. Unfortunately, although new faces drifted in and out, the main events were driven and supported by the same people. I started the journey with incredible optimism, but from the outset I saw doubt on the faces of older fans, men and women who had tried before. My enthusiasm seemed to annoy some of the old guard; they still loved the Alex, but they had become bitter towards the club's hierarchy. It was sad, and I couldn't understand why they'd given up hope of operating on a par with the wise old men sat around the club's top table.

It took a meeting with the chairman to tip me over the edge. We'd had a few get-togethers, which was good progress, although it always felt as though the dates agreed suited them and not the supporters. Still, getting around the table with John Bowler, the marketing manager, accountants and the stadium manager was a start. We could get our points across, represent the group members and make suggestions that would assist the wider fan base. One night, however, talk turned to money and the perilous financial balancing act that kept the chairman awake at nights. He talked purposefully about keeping the club afloat and the complex pricing structures necessary to make any business viable.

Then he dropped a clanger, for me at least. He suggested that Crewe Alexandra needed to operate along the successful lines of Manchester United. I hadn't heard anything so ridiculous in my life. There was no comparison. The United model was built on pre-war working class heroes, thousands of workers looking for a distraction from their day-to-day toil, the Busby Babes, Munich, lifting the European Cup and seemingly hundreds of trophies won under Alex Ferguson, not to mention the branding phenomena like George Best, Eric Cantona and David Beckham. It was ridiculous to suggest that any similarities existed apart from us also being a football club. The chairman's argument was that we should 'sweat the asset' and squeeze every possible penny from the supporters who came to Gresty Road. That's what they did at Old Trafford, he told us. I almost walked out of the meeting that second.

Football, for most clubs, is not a business, at least not in the true sense of the word. Daft rich fans pump money in, supplementing the meagre incomes that have no chance of covering the spiralling running costs. Man United are in a league of their own, perhaps thirty divisions above Crewe Alexandra, although it's only three on paper. Clubs like the Alex are driven by the supporters, people from the local community, not day-trippers from all over the country desperate to spend hundreds of pounds in the club shop on the rare occasions they can get match tickets. Suddenly, I realised that the club wasn't listening. They were on a different wavelength. They meant well, I think, but didn't get the overall picture.

So, after less than a year, I decided to step back, allow someone else to take the helm at CASi, someone with hope and belief that we, the fans, could actually make a difference. I didn't say it, but I felt that the barriers between the club and its supporters would never be broken down. But the last thing I wanted to do was dishearten the others further. So I moved aside, mouth shut.

To me, it seemed like a 'take it or leave it' kind of deal. If we played along and the club's hierarchy was feeling charitable then we'd get to peep over the top of the fence, but climbing over was forbidden. That was as good as things would get, in my opinion. The desire to create a genuine and regular two-way communication channel between the supporters and the football club had not, in my opinion, materialised. That had not necessarily been a failure on the part of the fans, more that some within the club didn't want such unwelcome 'interference', for want of a better word.

At no point did we meet all of the board members, or Dario Gradi, as part of those early meetings. What did happen, however, was a step in the right direction. The occasional, haphazard meetings soon became regular fans' forums. Real question and answer sessions when directors faced supporters up close and personal, often with pie and peas, not just shareholders at the stuffy, Annual General Meetings. The minions were finally allowed to sneak a look at the king.

Dario Gradi was always the focal point at the Q&A evenings. He was the perfect spokesman, someone who could field questions on any topic and relieve pressure on the other members of the panel. I love the man, really I do, but he operates from inside a protective bubble. Everything in his world is perfectly fine, and you could almost sense the board's surprise that those fans around them could find fault in what Gradi and the club were trying to create.

For me, there was a complete lack of transparency. The club met with us, talked and listened, although I suspect that most of our input went in one ear and out the other. The idea of club officials meeting, greeting and chatting to the masses is great. In practice, I've decided that it's a charade, an exercise in paying lip service

The only way to have a genuine voice was to install a fan on the board, just as many other supporters' groups had campaigned for over the years. But it needed to be more than that, and from day one I always thought that we should have set up a Supporters' Trust, a vehicle that could establish a financial stake, maybe attract new revenues that could be invested into the club - but with caveats such that the fans' voices were heard. John Bowler was not keen on this idea in the early days, especially during that first year of the new group. Whether he was unsure, uneasy or just not convinced, I don't know. His shake of the head, and a nonchalant wave of the hand stopped any discussions dead in their tracks. He'd change his tune a few years later, but that's another story. It was my last involvement with CASi at committee level, and I moved on, ducked calls to reconsider or assume other roles. I had to get out while I still had my sanity.

I accept that many supporters don't understand the intricacies of football finance, as it's an incredibly murky subject. However, I don't like being treated like an idiot. Football is a business, and yet it's so much more than that. Supporters are flesh and blood. Too often Gradi and the board members that were prepared to face the Crewe public were dismissive, reluctant to accept that we, those on the other side of the fence, had anything sensible to say, especially where money was concerned.

During one of the last nights when I was still wholeheartedly involved with CASi, I looked Gradi in the eyes as he answered another critical question, one of those desperate 'why' pleas from the heart. I don't doubt that he told us the truth, and that he believed in the club and those around him 100%. His look, however, suggested that he understood the reason for the question, but that he had to deliver the agreed line. After all, he was also a director. Maybe I read too much into such meetings, but across the many forums that had been staged I got the feeling that those posing the questions always left the building knowing little more about the club, its people and how it all worked than when they arrived. There were more questions that night, but I was all washed out.

I supped up, acknowledged those around me that also had that sinking feeling, then slipped away knowing that the answers given would be unlikely to yield anything worth knowing. The cynics had said before the meeting that we were wasting our time. I was starting to agree with them. It felt as though my supporting boots were slipping into concrete. Did I fight my way out or accept the inevitable? Mistress Alexandra wasn't giving me any guidance, and for the first time in years I was losing my grip on the club I loved.

SORCERER'S APPRENTICE

Steve Holland was a dead man walking. He stepped up to the plate over the summer of 2007. It was hardly a disastrous season that led to the handover, but with expectations so high amongst supporters even one of the country's most experienced managers looked weary under pressure to succeed. I think Dario Gradi wanted a quieter life, still hands-on but out of the firing line. The fan base was slowly dividing, the media constantly nibbling away and suggesting that it was time for change, so Holland was given the call and installed as cannon fodder.

The club's directors were in a state of shock, as the Alex were set up to play at the higher level. The wage bill was uncomfortable, the facilities top notch but the crowds were on the slide. The books hadn't balanced in years, and those oh-so essential player sales had dried up somewhat. They needed an escape clause, something to appease supporters and breath life into the club. The answer was to promote from within, and the worst kept secret in football became a reality as Gradi shuffled aside to assume a technical director's role, while his academy coach of many years took centre stage. So there was no hunt for a new manager, more a clever sleight of hand that left most - including the national media - scratching their heads. Who was actually in charge?

Nobody could fill Gradi's shoes, and yet Holland had to squeeze his size tens into the Italian maestro's petite hand-stitched, leather loafers. The seams were always likely to burst, and it was just a question of when not if he would fail.

Don't get me wrong; I wanted him to succeed. We all did. It was the natural progression, the sorcerer's apprentice finally getting to stir the pot, buy his own ingredients and cast the magic to keep Alex devotees pouring into Gresty Road. It just didn't work, and many of us are still baffled as to why it collapsed around his ears.

It wasn't the worst of starts, and most accepted that the new man needed space to breath. I didn't, it was a preposterous suggestion that Holland didn't understand the mechanics of the club, that he required time to stamp his own authority on proceedings, and that he needed to get to know his players. He'd been there for over a decade for goodness sake! He knew the club inside out. It was a cosmetic exercise, putting someone else pitch-side on match days. He even had Gradi and Neil Baker on the bench around him. Everything had changed, but once again nothing had really changed.

We limped through to Christmas with a miss-mash of results, just a win over Port Vale in Burslem to keep the majority off Holland's back. But a 4-0 thumping at home to Doncaster before the festivities was a real low point, and we signed off 2007 sat just above the relegation places. There was no urgency, and week after week the same limp excuses were rolled out. He needed time, the results would come, and we should keep the faith. That was getting increasingly hard. For the first time in years I wasn't enjoying the football. The matchday experience suffered, and I noticed our numbers falling, all of us trying to limit the damage.

By mid-March the situation was no better. Atrocious defending followed one decent performance, a rare win, but conceding too many sloppy goals became the norm. We picked up a few points and then lost to Bournemouth, on the penultimate weekend. It was a disaster waiting to happen. We crashed 4-1 at home to Oldham and the Gresty Road crowd turned to radios and mobile phones to check Bournemouth's result. The whoops of delight when we heard the other scores merely glossed over the underlying fractures that threatened to break the club. To those who could remember, it felt worse than the bad old days. The only saving grace was retaining our League One status - by the skin of our teeth!

At the start of Holland's second season, a combination of stress, increased pressure from supporters and a burning desire to succeed saw the rookie manager lash out. The chequebook went to his head. He splashed the cash, something that supporters are always calling for, but it was his targets that took everyone by surprise. My main gripe was that he seemed to move away from the youth players that he had crafted, developed and improved over ten years. That was a shocking message to send out, not only to the players hoping to break through but to the supporters who had stood by Gradi, the board and their determination to pursue a policy of developing our own to fill the first team and generate cash for the club.

Our matchday collective grumbled like old men, and we decided to return to the main stand where the professional moaners resided.

Singing and shouting behind the goal was a thing of the past. We had grown up; at least that's what we told ourselves.

The mass influx of new players actually installed some optimism, although it was such a seismic shift away from the club's comfort zone. Joel Grant, Clayton Donaldson and Calvin Zola were signed, their collective fees rumoured to have been around the half million pounds mark. It was a sign of desperation, but I was happy initially. The local papers reported the club's ambitious intentions and everyone rubbed their hands with glee when we beat Premier League Hull City during the pre-season. The wool was briefly pulled over our eyes.

There were, however, some niggling doubts as to whether the manager could handle some of the outspoken characters he had recruited. Anthony Elding, another incoming player that summer, was a classic case; a player that had scored goals at our level but obviously had issues with previous managers. He looked the part on the pitch and understood the need to lift the crowd. Unfortunately, he also knew how to wind up the management, and I suspect his dummy was thrown out of the pram on many occasions. Holland was the man tasked to deal with such players, and I wonder where Gradi and Baker were during his time of need? He'd spent years working with younger players; respectful teenagers who wanted to impress him. Bringing in rough and ready journeymen was a colossal mistake, but hindsight is a wonderful thing several years down the line. He was desperate, and the egg timer was running empty.

So Holland was on rocky ground as soon as the 2008-09 season started, incidentally with a home defeat to Brighton. A few cup successes deflected the early pressure, but just two league wins across August and September saw him backed into a corner. He was never going to last, especially with Gradi sat upstairs overseeing proceedings, watching the rumblings of discontent grow on a weekly basis. Interestingly, when questioned about the acquisition of certain players during the Steve Holland reign, Gradi later revealed that he and the board had been 100% behind the decisions taken. So they were complicit, but there was only ever going to be one man to take the blame.

I listened to Holland during radio interviews, the Monday cross-examinations that picked over the bones of the weekend defeat. It was painful, a man clutching at straws, slipping down a greasy pole with no sign of the bottom. Over the airwaves I heard the same, familiar dulcet tones, the same things that Gradi had always said but without the spark. Holland was like his mentor, but without the personality, which sounds harsh, and yet it was a sentiment echoed by many. He was a lovely fella, mild-mannered, thoughtful, intelligent and passionate about the game. Nobody would ever question that. But football is a results business and there is no room for pleasant passengers when you're spiralling down the leagues.

In *Dishers* pool bar, off South Street, before the Peterborough home game, a nasty late October fixture when the blustery conditions didn't help anyone, I was taken aback by the anti-Holland feelings amongst those present. This included long-standing supporters, pro-club men who had seen the worst of times many years before. There was hardly one vote of confidence for the manager. The chairman's calls for 'evolution not revolution' a few years earlier had fallen on deaf ears and it was about to be turned upside down.

'We want Holland Out, said we want Holland Out!' echoed around Gresty Road for several weeks before the inevitable departure. A couple of banners carried the demands, and the message boards and phone-in shows overflowed with Alex supporters demanding change. It was a very sad state of affairs, undignified and the last thing that anyone expected at Crewe.

Insults rained down from the stands, and if there was any mud slinging it was aimed at Holland. He was the Wally without the brolly during his time of need, and I didn't see anyone stepping forward to offer him shelter. The Alex supporters knew that his time was up; unfortunately, the board of directors did not. It was a slow and painful demise. They should have acted much sooner.

The chop came after a 2-0 home defeat to Orient. The jeers and boos were deafening on the final whistle, and few doubted what would follow. Holland won just nineteen league and cup games of the 72 he managed across sixteen turbulent months. Not the best statistics, or entry on your CV. But what did we know? The guy later moved on to Stoke and then Chelsea.

It was a messy and undignified exit from Crewe Alexandra, and yet there was no sacking. The chairman's statement said that the club would discuss other options with Holland. The experiment to emulate the Liverpool boot room of old failed and it was no surprise seeing Gradi step up to steady the ship once more. He didn't have a magic wand, and a 3-0 home defeat to Stockport suggested that the problem was one of quality, not Holland's management. I would have been very disappointed if the Alex players had suddenly upped their game, just because Gradi was back in charge. That would have been hugely disrespectful to Holland, unprofessional on their part that they had given less than 100% with him barking orders from the sidelines.

The squad wasn't good enough, simple as that. That was down to poor acquisitions made by Holland but signed off by the board. So we realised that the Alex were in a scrap, and that something radically different was required to halt the slide. Mistress Alexandra was wounded and ashamed. I didn't have any answers. I didn't know what to say to her. I felt totally disconnected from the club. Everything was slipping away, and not for the first time there was a feeling of hopelessness amongst the fan base.

CHEATED AND DESPONDENT

The moment you wake up and realise that your passionate support makes no difference, well, that's probably a good time to pull the plug. That happens at work and in personal relationships when you know that you've hit the end of the road, but not where football is concerned. For many there is no stop valve, you cannot simply withdraw your support. If a supermarket consistently sold me bad products, I'd take my business elsewhere. If the experience at the local cinema were overpriced and not enjoyable I'd stop going, or consider the theatre or renting a home movie. At football we trudge along regardless, as if it's a duty and we have a debt to repay over eternity. I was sick to the stomach after the Steve Holland experiment was hoisted upon us, with no apologies, no refunds, and no decent explanations about the decisions made by those in charge. I felt like a punch bag, used and abused, cheated and despondent. And yet I wanted to know how that torrid season ended, whether the new incumbent could reverse our fortunes.

We needed a miracle after Holland departed, something or someone to shake the club's very foundations. Complacency was rife, the steady-but-surely approach wasn't working and Crewe Alexandra were heading back to the basement division. It was unthinkable, but in that 2008 winter of discontent we were cast adrift at the bottom of the table.

The club waited a few weeks, until the end of the year, and then unveiled a Viking to lead the fight for survival. Gudjon Thordarson, *The Iceman*, a former Stoke City manager, was the most unlikely choice since the numerous mistakes of the 1970s and 80s. The appointment stank of desperation. Thordarson was all about motivation and direct football. It was like asking ballerinas to play rugby. And yet, any supporter offers a new manager a chance to impress, the opportunity to turn things around.

We queued up like lemmings to see the incredible transformation we hoped rather than expected would unfold.

When we settled down to watch the first home game under the new regime, it was something of a culture shock. Millwall beat us in an FA Cup replay, but we scored twice and the players really looked up for the match, more robust and, dare I say it, fitter after a few short weeks of training with the new man. We scored in every match that month and then, to confound all critics, Thordarson scooped manager of the month for February after four straight wins, to lift us out of the relegation places. It wasn't pretty, but it was effective.

Then the trouble started, on and off the pitch. It was expected, but rumours of training ground bust-ups, Thordarson locking others out of the changing room before kick-off and disputes about cash available for players took the shine off the brief revival. Who knows if that affected the players, but inconsistency during March and April left us on the ropes once again, this time with a bloody nose and no trainer to apply the magic sponge.

Everything hinged upon one game, and defeat at Stockport was unthinkable. During the week ahead of that pivotal game the implications played on my mind every minute of each day. I jest not. The wife telling me that it was only a game, and that the club would still be there next season just made things worse.

Ray drove to County, mainly because time was short but also so that we didn't get bundled down to the train station after the match. Rumours had been flying around the Internet message boards leading up to the game, and a heavy police presence was expected to prevent any trouble. So we did our best to avoid the post-match shenanigans and parked up on the other side of the ground, well away from the station. We found a spot alongside Alexandra Park, and that put a brief smile on our apprehensive faces. You always wonder if such things are a good omen, but sometimes you'll take anything as a positive sign.

We had an hour spare, so we headed to Castle Street. It was awash with Alex fans, a constant tide of red and white around the commercial area not far from County's Edgeley Park ground. It was a Friday night match, something of a nightmare for the police, especially when so much rested on the outcome. County were safe, but their hatred of Crewe was sufficient to want victory just to see us relegated. We'd have done the same - for them, Chester, Wrexham and especially Stoke and Vale. That's the nasty edge of football, and I suspect that it'll never change.

Around 1,500 Alex fans arrived, hoping for the best, and a massive queue formed outside the ground, everyone desperate to be part of a historic escape. Police horses pushed us in line as tensions rose, and we finally entered the away end, which was a real throwback to the 80s.

The match wasn't the best either, with errors from both sides creating numerous chances, but everyone from Crewe came for the result alone. So when the goals started flowing we sang, bounced about and then started to worry.

It was level at half-time, but when County raced into a 3-1 lead the singing stopped and it dawned upon those present what was about to happen. Dennis Lawrence pulled one back for Crewe, but County responded minutes later to restore the two-goal cushion. A consolation strike by Scott McManus, one of Thordarson's signings, gave the scoreline respectability at 4-3, but it counted for nothing. We were down, again, and the tears of a youngster to my right almost triggered my own waterworks. But I'd been there before, and no amount of crying would reverse the result.

The previous ten months had been wasted, the occasional high points forgotten as the referee blew full time. Despondency was etched across the faces of every Alex fan as they traipsed out of the County gates, a wall of police and stewards wearing worried expressions. They had good reason; as such disappointment invariably sparks a reaction - a very negative one. The home fans were already lining up hoping to add insult to relegation injury, and the vitriol was soon forthcoming.

We headed to Ray's car, heads dropped as we sloped off with no desire to drown our sorrows in the Stockport pubs. The rest headed for the station, and shouts and chants rang out into the night air as those from Crewe made their miserable way to the trains, barracked and abused as they went. Our season was dead and buried before the final match had kicked off. I took a call from another mate, news that it had kicked off outside the train station. It was a depressing night, and few words were spoken as we drove back to Crewe.

***

Midway through the Thordarson era, if that's what it can be called, something else happened that changed the way I viewed the football club. It was at one of the fans' forums, yet another one I couldn't resist, a meeting that doubled up with the release of the club's annual accounts. The same dutiful faces filled the Alex Suite, paying for over priced beers and hoping to hear that a Russian billionaire was taking over the club. I jest, because I wouldn't want to see that happen. A rich fan, maybe, someone who would do the right thing and not use the club as a plaything. Maybe then.

Instead, we faced the man with a controlling interest in Crewe Alexandra. Norman Hassall sat on the top table, John Bowler and Dario Gradi beside him, plus other directors like Jim Macmillan, David Rowlinson and Richard Clayton. Conspicuous by his absence was Daniel Potts, one of the directors who rarely appeared at the ground, or at supporters' meetings despite requests to do so. Perhaps it was a conscious decision to keep clear, or maybe the awkward commute from the Isle of Man made it tiresome. Whatever, it would have been good to hear his take on things.

Over the previous two seasons, rumours had been rife that a loan had been made to one Alex director, at least to a company that he was involved with. Moreover, an advert was placed in a national newspaper inviting offers for shares owned by two of the club's directors. It was a worrying move, but something the supporters knew little about. At the meeting, details were glossed over. As questions were thrown at the panel some of the directors became visibly shaken, ruffled and annoyed that they were being challenged, asked to explain their actions and future intentions.

Things came to a head when Mr Hassall was asked whether the loan would show up on the following year's accounts. He told us that it was sensitive commercial information, and none of our business. It was a matter for the accounts, nothing more.

He just didn't get it. Well, perhaps he did, and he knew that his position of power made him untouchable. I've always understood and despised the cut-throat commercial world that operates outside of the football bubble, but never accepted that such brutal rules applied at the Alex. Not at my Alex. It was painful hearing men suggest that our club was like any other business.

Mr Hassall made his excuses to leave, a little earlier than any of the other members of the panel who had started to field the usual array of football-related questions that dominate such evenings. I met him by the bar, and posed a question as he walked by. I asked if he had Crewe Alexandra's best interests at heart, and whether he would sell his shares if someone offered the right price. He wanted to brush it off, ignore my request for further information. But others were listening. He stopped and considered his answer. He smiled, the half-hearted kind of smile that rarely puts you at ease, then put his arm on my shoulder.

'I've always wanted what's best for the club, that's why I've been here so long,' he told me. 'But in business you can never say never.'

The second comment cut me like a knife. Football is not a business like any other, as too many emotional heartstrings are attached. He walked away satisfied that he'd dealt with another petty question, a minor annoyance as he tried to leave the room. I was left alone, a chill running down my spine. His words offered me no comfort whatsoever.

Many more details emerged over the next few months and subsequent year that left some supporters shaking in their boots. Other companies had been formed, to house different aspects of the core football business. The pitch is, we believe, now rented from Crewe Alexandra Developments Limited, a company that also carried the name of Mr Norman Hassall on its documents. A number of supporters tried to unravel what it all meant, but John Bowler assured us that it was to protect the longer term interests of the club. He could have told us anything. We are just football fans.

Nobody's been dishonest at the club; it's all been above board and legal as far as we can see. But there has not been sufficient transparency. I want to know stuff about the club, the day-to-day operations that affect what happens on the pitch, the initiatives running in the background, whether they work out or not. I don't want information second hand. I want to live and breathe the football club that I love so dearly, and feel that my involvement is worthwhile and appreciated. I am not just a customer.

***

Sadly, communications with the supporters didn't improve after the summer months. Sinking back to League Two (effectively the old Fourth Division) you would have thought that the club would have gone all-out to win over the support. There was nothing, just a ticket price freeze, although we'd be watching sub standard football. So it was a price hike. It was just another kick in the teeth as we lay squirming on the ground trying to make sense of the club's spectacular decline.

So I started my own stupid protest and decided against a season ticket. It wasn't being relegated or the money involved, it was the attitude of certain club officials and the arrogance shown towards the fans. It wasn't our club and they knew it.

I also refused to buy a membership card, something that drives me crazy. Every major supermarket, most airlines and some of the high street coffee shops have loyalty schemes, all designed to keep your custom and reward you for choosing their brand. They give you these free of charge. So at Crewe Alexandra you support the club most of your life and then have to pay for the privilege to become a member, discounts and all. Perhaps I'm missing something, being too critical, but I'm convinced that it could all be done so much better. As a 24-carat mug, I stubbornly started to pay on match days!

Increasingly, I was feeling like an outsider as we continued our journey with *The Iceman* at the helm of our club. The top table went quiet and there was no clarification about the new company structures. It was like looking through the frosted window of a Dickensian shop front. You can take a peep but whatever you do please don't touch. Oh, and you have to pay for that brief glimpse of the fancy goods. Like receiving a train set for Christmas, you tear away the wrapping, excitedly set everything up, and then you're told that you can only watch as the engine loops around the track. The good stuff, operating the controls, setting the signals and points, that's done by big brother. You can see the crash coming, an avoidable collision, but you have to sit quietly in the corner. That was my experience from high up in the main stand as the club crumbled around me.

Thordarson made it to early October 2009, but with one win in six he was never likely to be afforded the luxury of time. I heard the news of his dismissal and wasn't shocked, annoyed or worried. I felt empty. The club was becoming a laughing stock once again. All manner of crazy thoughts rushed through my mind. Was Steve Holland and, later, Thordarson set up to fail? I don't think so, but Gradi emerged from the whole sorry mess smelling of roses. Almost untouchable, he was the default setting, the drop-out clause if all else failed. Once again he assumed the role of first team coach. I couldn't help wondering if it was all manufactured to make us realise how lucky we'd been, that sticking with Gradi and the academy was the only way Crewe Alexandra Football Club would survive.

As a shareholder and director he sits on the board, supposedly an equal amongst other long-serving men, and yet he holds the trump cards. He built the club, at least in its current form. He has been hands-on at each and every level of its development, from tatty bottom feeder to respectable Championship outfit with decent facilities and a reputation second to none for developing and believing in its own players. Without him there would be nothing, and he has said as much during interviews with the local media and at fans' forums.

I don't think that the club ever wanted to change. They were scared of it. Switching managers was a convenient sideshow, something to appease supporters but maintain the equilibrium in the background. The most insulting aspect of the whole sorry mess was the way the national media continued to report our club. They hadn't watched our games, the calamitous defending, the powder puff midfield or the tippy-tappy forwards who looked good but failed to hit the back of the net enough to prevent the two relegations that plunged us back where we started all those pre-Gradi years ago. Those national hacks only see the good, continually applauding the club's ethos. They only see the glossy exterior, the much-heralded academy at Reaseheath, the Fair Play trophies and the apparent lack of debt. The relentless platitudes just wash over me now, as I have seen below the surface. All is not rosy in the Gresty Road garden, and no amount of pouting and smiling by Mistress Alexandra sat on her picture-perfect cottage garden fence will now convince me otherwise.

Maybe I got too close, and familiarity certainly breeds contempt. Sadly, having banged my head on the Gresty Road wall for so long, I now realise that a handful of supporters will never make a difference - certainly while there is no significant stake in the club spread across the fan base. I find the situation disheartening, unsatisfactory and incredibly frustrating.

So what would I change? Although I have joined calls for Gradi to move on gracefully, I have no idea who could step in and make a difference. His appointment in 1983 was unique and is unlikely to be replicated again. The bright lights of the Premiership soon dazzle most young, up-and-coming managers these days. There they have access to untold riches and resources. Gradi had offers but stuck with the Alex. He deserves immense praise for that, and I have no doubt that his intentions have always been in Crewe Alexandra's best interests.

However, he has become entwined in the very fabric of the club and it can't breath properly. If he sneezes the club catches a cold. We are totally dependent upon him. He picks the team, joins scouting missions, oversees operations at the academy and runs youth teams, holds press conferences and sits on the board. He certainly earns his corn. But at what price to the club in the long run? We can't live in the past forever!

BLUE FLAG FLYING HIGH

Getting emotional about my lads' choice of football team would be the easy option, a knee-jerk reaction if they picked anyone other than the Alex. It would be a soul-searching exercise in where I went wrong. But then I think back to my youth, what dad must have thought when I asked to watch the Alex and not Man United. Years later, mum told me that my defection had really upset him. Dad never said anything, as that wasn't his style. He bided his time and kept his own footballing faith. So in recent years it's been my turn to feel the pain.

'I support Man United,' my eldest lad told me when he was about eight years old.

Fair enough, I thought. No sleep lost there. As long as he attended the occasional Alex match I was more than happy to see him follow the other reds. In typical brotherly fashion, my youngest copied his sibling and also professed undying love for the team that started me on the rocky road of football fandom. Dad was delighted when I told him later that week, and my young boys had atoned for my errant ways.

So when my eldest's eleventh birthday came along last year I suggested something red, a United shirt, maybe a new school bag with the Red Devils' crest, or Wayne Rooney on the front.

'But I'm a Chelsea fan now,' he replied.

I nearly choked on my coffee. Had I failed as a father, set a bad example and driven him away from both Mistress Alexandra and United?

'But, you're a United fan...' I countered.

'Not any more, dad. I'm Chelsea now. I won't change again,' he said with the conviction of a man who had stood at Stamford Bridge's Shed End for several decades.

For a moment I half expected him to rattle off the *Blue Flag* lyrics for added authenticity.

I didn't know what to say. He'd committed the most heinous football crime, flitting from one big club to another. Sherlock Holmes was not required, however, as his switch came suspiciously soon after Chelsea lifted the Premier League title after three years of Manchester United dominance. He was now an impressionable youth, on the turn, just as I was back in 1976. Somehow, five seasons of Alex decline didn't do it for him. He had no intention of ditching United for Crewe; he'd chosen blue. Two minutes later, with my head firmly in my hands, the youngest appeared and confirmed the double transfer. They were both Chelsea fans!

The trouble is, kids seem increasingly fickle these days. There's too much choice on TV, in particular exposure to football. It gives them ideas and leads them astray. I'm sure we didn't chop and change teams when we were youngsters, apart from my one leap of faith from top-flight to basement in a single bound.

The wife came home and asked what was up, not through any genuine concern, more because I hadn't started the tea. I'd decided to starve the little buggers, withhold rations until they gave up the ludicrous attraction to a team more suited to soft southern tarts. I could have accepted Liverpool, Man City, Everton, even Stoke at a push, but Chelsea... what was that all about?

And yet I have found the whole experience refreshing and uplifting. The innocence of their choice, parental and geographic influences cast aside so that they can be part of something successful. During my lads' lifetimes, Chelsea had lifted the Premier League title, League and FA Cups. The west London club bought their success, just as Blackburn Rovers did under the enthusiastic and generous Jack Walker all those years ago, leaving Alex Ferguson redder faced than usual. But I can't tell my boys that. They don't fully understand the financial shenanigans of football transfers and mercenary players. To them football is fun, exciting and physical, and scoring goals and winning games is what it's all about.

My eldest lad has been to plenty of Alex games, a regular during our second stint in the Championship. He has about fifteen grounds under his belt, something that means little to him now, but I bet he drops the statistic into conversation as he goes through high school, when teenage lads start to brag about their football travels. I wonder if that will draw him in, when he reels off Pride Park, the Walkers Stadium, Turf Moor, Selhurst Park (plus pub quiz bonus point that it was Wimbledon playing that day) and the Britannia Stadium?

Then again, some of his experiences have been somewhat unsettling, enough to deter any up-and-coming supporter. The first was at Derby County, a chance to see the very impressive Pride Park. We met with friends off the train and found a kid-friendly pub for lunch and a few drinks. All went well until my eldest showed an interest in a game of pool being played in a side room. At four years old, and around three foot six tall, he just about peeped over the edge of the table. Then, as he watched a tense finish with both players on the black, the cue ball skipped off the baize and cannoned off his forehead. He had a lump the size of an egg within seconds. To make matters worse, we didn't realise how far the new ground was. His little legs were dropping off as we dashed to the game late, eventually taking our seats when the Alex were already leading 2-0. It was a fantastic match, ending 4-2 to the Railwaymen, but I had plenty of explaining to do when we got home.

Then there was Burnley, a last-minute decision, with my mate Darren driving to Turf Moor at breakneck speeds to ensure that we made kick-off. He was a regular at our house, often doing the BBQ thing with his girlfriend. So my eldest was pretty familiar with him, enjoyed a joke or two and regularly had a bit of rough and tumble in the garden – as kids do with friends of the family. Under the away stand, during the half-time interval, things went a little too far. Perhaps the game was too dour, or seeing the Alex slip 3-0 behind inside 20-odd minutes tipped him over the edge. Maybe we'll never know, but with no warning, as Darren took a sip of his piping hot coffee, the apple of my eye delivered a comedy punch to my mate's groin!

It got worse. Filled with crisps, chocolate and sweets, all with the intention of keeping the little bugger quiet so we could watch the football, as we sped back along the M6 after the game, there was a heave, a gag and a splutter as a gallon of stinking sick spewed from his little mouth. Darren had to pull over at the next service station. The car was brand, spanking new, the leather upholstery still smelt of cows grazing in the field, but the over-riding stench of sick was too much for him to take.

Later that same season, I lost my boy at the Walkers Stadium, home of Leicester City. It was pre-match, thousands of fans wandering around the perimeter of the vast new ground. He asked for a hotdog, so we walked over to one of the vendors. As I handed over the cash I realised that he'd left my side. He had moved away in a flash, distracted by a few balloons, and then been swept along by the crowds. I could see him about twenty yards away, but he couldn't see me. When I finally reached him, about thirty seconds later, he was crying, being consoled by a matchday steward. He was so upset that he couldn't speak. The steward refused to hand him over, unsure that I really was his dad. Then he spoke, and I melted as he jumped into my arms. We drew 1-1 but I felt guilty for ninety minutes.

Several years later I occasionally mention the incidents, worried that he's been psychologically scarred. Oh, and I forgot to mention that I dropped him between the seats at the Britannia Stadium when Steve Jones scored against Stoke. We celebrated for thirty seconds before anyone noticed him. We don't mention that to his mother.

He tells me that none of that bothered him. So then I consider the raucous singing, drunken shouting, aggressive crowds and the occasional outbreak of trouble, the stuff that enthralled and excited me as a growing boy. I have never hidden my lads from the ugly side, the rowdiness in pubs, the vulgar language on the terraces and the violence that comes with the local derby games. Like bullies at school, racists, cheats and liars, they exist in all walks of life. The sooner you can spot them and know how to face them the better. The lads know that some of the things they have seen at the Alex are not right. Crucially, they are aware of the dangers and know what signs to look out for. That's all I have ever wanted to teach them.

For now, I'm letting them find their own way. Both have been to a few games with me this season, but only when I've dragged them along. When they get there, see some of their mates from school and become consumed by the game, suddenly their eyes light up. I can tell that they have enjoyed the day. And yet the bug has yet to bite and properly take hold. The junior Alex shirts have been consigned to the back of the wardrobe, the scarves are no longer cool, and even the Alex alarm clock has been left without a battery high up on the top shelf, out of sight, out of mind.

To be honest, I don't know what I expect of them, whether I want them to follow my desperate Alex lead or stay true to the blue roots that, for this year at least, they are trying to cultivate. Despite exposing them to my daily intravenous drip of Alex nonsense they seem to be immune. The *Football League Show* highlights come on and they look away. I flick on the local radio sports bulletin and they switch off.

In their defence, wall-to-wall top-flight football has exposed them to the best, and I often find the pair glued to the Spanish *La Liga* games, extolling the virtues of Lionel Messi and Christiano Ronaldo ahead of Shaun Miller and Byron Moore. The almost daily fix of world class football is how they came across Frank Lampard, Ashley Cole, John Terry and Didier Drogba, as well as seeing their school mates flashing football cards of the Premiership's leading lights.

Sadly, David Artell and Lee Bell don't figure in those trading card collections. I can't stop that, and I wouldn't want to interfere with their development. They want to see skill, audacity, fancy tricks and, ultimately, a winning side. Who can blame them for that? I was the weird kid, wanting the intimate experience that came with basement football ahead of any results, league tables and superstars. Bob Scott and Geoff Hunter did it for me, but then look where I ended up!

Perhaps I'm secretly waiting for that weekly get-together to happen, when they fly the nest and become young men, meeting up on a

Saturday, them buying dad a beer and watching the footy at Gresty Road together? That's happened with my dad a few times since I left home, but not enough. I was always too wrapped up in my Alex bubble, rarely considerate enough to think about his football feelings. It's my turn to play the waiting game. So I live in hope.

LIFE'S NOT FAIR

One man who only ever had eyes for Crewe Alexandra, and was a constant over the years for many people associated with the club, was John Fleet. Known as the kit man in recent times, he was someone who knew the club inside out and performed umpteen roles.

He should be there now, busying himself in the players' lounge, sorting through the kits, reassuring those in need of a pep talk, popping the kettle on, chatting about the recent game and generally putting smiles on faces as he walked about the place.

Players come and go, but those behind the scenes at Gresty Road tend to stick around. He'd been there longer than most, and his passing on Tuesday, 10th May 2011 was very sad, completely unexpected and it affected many people.

Fleety took his lifelong allegiance further than most, starting his unofficial apprenticeship as a cheeky ball boy, clambering onto the corrugated roof of the old Gresty Road End to retrieve balls, long before the days of health and safety restrictions. That was in the 1960s when he was a child, a 'right mischievous young lad' he once told me. His playground was along Gresty Road, Bedford Street and Nantwich Road, the area surrounding the Alex ground, and on matchday mornings he'd nag players for autographs as they reported for duty ahead of the game. He was a fan long before the club paid him a wage, but even as a schoolboy he started earning a few pennies, collecting tea cups under the main stand, sweeping up and helping to push the heavy wicker kit baskets down to the train station when the first team played away.

In 2009, while I was writing a book called *Crewe and its People*, I decided that Fleety was an obvious character to include amongst forty other local faces. He was humble, and asked what was special enough to include him alongside former mayors, high-flying business people and sporting champions? I tried to explain how much he meant to people, especially the fans of Crewe Alexandra. But he didn't get it. A few weeks later, when I'd penned his chapter from the tapes recorded over several Friday mornings, he read it and smiled.

'Wow,' he said, 'you've managed to make me sound interesting.'

That summed him up - an unassuming guy who just got on with things, with no fuss, no pretence, and no airs or graces.

I learnt all about his days at Crewe during those 'formal' interviews, and yet they were simple chats, sat in the players' lounge under the main stand. There was always a cup of tea, a biscuit, and then a smile as he sat down, ready to talk football, the force that drove him every day.

From turning out for the Alex reserves and lining up against a young Brian Clough who played for Middlesbrough, to coaching kids before the arrival of Dario Gradi. That's something he deserves so much more credit for, trawling the Crewe area with Pat Slack, establishing the bones of a youth system and ensuring that a steady stream of reserves were developed to compliment the first team. This was long before the plush facilities at Reaseheath, when training games and fitness routines were completed on scrub land and borrowed pitches.

Then he slotted in as kit man, sorting out anything and everything that the squad required. He played practical jokes on the players, like Colin Cramb, Shaun Smith and Colin Little, but they always stitched him up later. He even dropped the Cheshire Senior Cup once, and had to Superglue the lid back together. Never a dull moment, his working life at Crewe Alexandra was hectic but fun.

One standout event for me was at Wembley in May 1997, a real high for all Alex supporters. On the whistle, when promotion to Division One was confirmed, I looked to the bench and saw fists raised in the air. That was the coaching staff. Fleety was nowhere to be seen, he was gone, already racing over to players to celebrate, a little boy lost in the moment, one of the lads rather than a more formal member of the club's staff. The Alex was everything to him.

I bumped into him hundreds of times over the years and I can't remember seeing him look miserable. Even when results were going against the Alex, he always had a few positive words of encouragement. He'd tell you that he'd seen real promise in some of the kids about to burst through; he knew about a striker that Neil Baker was scouting; or he had some good news about a player coming back from injury. It was always sometimes aimed at lifting your spirits.

Perhaps the best of Fleety was during the summer, on those balmy nights away from home, when we played pre-season friendlies against some obscure teams in Devon, the Midlands or even Dublin. There he was, trademark shorts and flip flops, shaggy grey Santa hair, leant against the barriers, swapping jokes with fans while the rest of the coaching staff looked on with serious frowns. He'd buy you a beer, feed snippets of gossip that supporters love to hear, and join in with the banter.

After my final interview session, piecing together sufficient threads to complete Fleety's section in the *Crewe and its People* book, I hopped on my bike and cycled down South Street. We'd wrapped things up early, as there was a situation developing at the club. Results had been poor, and then manager Gudjon Thordarson was under pressure. My phone rang, so I pulled over and looked at the caller ID. It was Fleety.

'You'll never guess what,' he panted down the phone, 'two minutes after you left, they came out of the boardroom and announced that Gudjon had been sacked.'

The comings and goings at Crewe Alexandra meant everything to Fleety, and he loved to serve up information to anyone who shared his passion. I don't think Thordarson had been one of his favourites, although he never had a bad word to say about the manager. After all, it was more about Crewe Alexandra - and the club always came first. He still went about his business, doing his best for everyone, keeping his personal opinions to himself. But there was always a mischievous glint in his eye, leaving you to fill in the gaps about what he really thought.

And that, sadly, was one of the last times we spoke properly. There was a brief hello before matches, then a few snatched words when Shaun Smith came to see a game in February 2011. Fleety greeted the former Alex left-back like a son, someone he'd really missed and was delighted to see back in the fold.

He had a thousand cracking stories, with many teasers about more tales to come when we finally sat down to discuss his biography. That was a project on the back burner; one of those books we both agreed should be written – one day, just not then. But the sands of time ran out, and I will forever have regrets that I did not meet with him again, supping tea, chatting nonsense about the Alex and chronicling his life.

The day after the sad news emerged, I was at Reaseheath. My eldest was playing in the Wilf Saunders Cup Final and the Alex kindly allowed the youngsters to stage their big match at the stunning facilities on the edge of Nantwich. Dario Gradi was there, looking a little lost, talking with several people from the club about the events that had just unfolded. In a way, it was probably what Fleety would have wanted; yet more young players emerging, and the day-to-day activities at Reaseheath still ticking over, but with one of its best-known characters missing.

Two weeks later, at the church on a drizzly mid-May morning, well wishers arrived over an hour before the service. It wasn't the kind of weather fit to send off one of Crewe Alexandra's finest, and yet it was the kind of conditions the man himself had trained in, helped to coach the up-and-coming players in the early 1980s, and busied about the stadium in his latter years, running errands and making sure that everything was just right. Fleety truly was a man for all seasons. Besides, a little rain couldn't put hardened football supporters off. If you could make it to a damp, miserable cup replay on a Tuesday night in the middle of winter, then you could make it to John Fleet's funeral. We all owed him that.

For me, it meant a 15-minute walk from work. Along Pyms Lane, across to Badger Avenue and then a sharp left up Ford Lane that rises to Coppenhall St. Michael's church, a magnificent structure that once looked over the town of old before the railway arrived. It was packed, quite literally, to the rafters. Like football matches of yesteryear, when Fleety's passion for the Alex took hold in the 1960s, it was apt that it was standing room only as latecomers filed down the aisles. There were many faces I hadn't seen at the Alex in years, and yet they came to pay their respects. They were there for him, because he WAS the Alex.

As the coffin came into view the church fell silent. Necks craned to catch sight of the bearers, the family and the man himself, now hidden from view in a beautiful casket, making his last journey. Alongside the many relatives and first-teamers from the football club, there were two familiar faces - Steve Macauley and Shaun Smith. They were favourites of Fleety, and I recalled countless photos that showed the three Alex stalwarts laughing, joking and playing practical jokes on each other.

Sat there in church, sombre, silent and saddened by the experience, I thought about god. I'm not a believer, but I've always respected others who do manage to keep the faith. I looked about the church, a sea of faces, young and old, and wondered why Fleety, such a decent man, had been taken so suddenly. If there is a god, how and why are such monumental decisions taken? Is there any rhyme or reason to it all? He was fit and active, he always wore a smile and he had many years ahead of him. Sometimes, life's not fair.

Unfortunately, for my close-knit circle of Alex friends, there was more sad news to follow...

STOP THE CLOCKS

With the play-offs, FA Cup and Champions League finals all done and dusted, I was still licking my Alex wounds in early June 2011. Another turbulent campaign was over but the spectre of player sales loomed large as the club joined others across the leagues in trying to trim the wage bill. It didn't bode well for the new season. The ever-decreasing circles of despair were threatening to take us still further down the English football pyramid, the next stop being non-league.

Such an awful outcome was unthinkable. That, however, was all I could contemplate as I chatted with friends about the perilous situation that faced the club. As with every summer break since my teenage years, the empty months saw me replaying games in my head and considering prospects for the future. I craved some football to take my mind off the statistical minutiae that most fans dwell upon. As an Alex fan, it always has been a case of what could have been!

Everything football was quickly put to one side, however, when I received a text advising me that my good friend and fellow Alex fan Mike Lazenby had lost his battle with cancer. It was from his dad, on Thursday 16th June 2011. I still have it on my phone, unable to delete it just yet. It was a short paragraph confirming the inevitable, but something I'd hoped wouldn't happen for some time. I knew it was coming, but it still smashed home like a hammer blow.

There's no point pretending that I fought back the tears, because I couldn't. The kids asked why I was crying and I did my best to explain. Then phone calls and text messages were swapped with the other lads. Just a few days earlier we had discussed meeting Mike at one of the pre-season games, and hopefully being able to get together for the opening fixture of the new season. Those plans were dashed. Mike was gone. Suddenly, the football didn't matter. It was one of those W.H. Auden moments, when the lines of the heart-wrenchingly beautiful *Funeral Blues* poem are so apt. I wanted to stop the clocks, maybe wind back time so that we could all enjoy a few more moments with Mike. That was selfish, but then life had been selfish to Mike.

I spent a few days reflecting on things, perhaps overly detached from everything and everyone around me. There was a sense of loss, bemusement, anger and disbelief, although I had been prepared for the news for several months. It took Mike's dad, Roger, to restore order with a simple and very dignified email. He asked if we, Mike's football friends, would attend the funeral and, if possible, supply Alex-related photos and stories that painted a picture of part of his son's relatively young life. Mike was just 31 years of age. It was the least we could do. It was an honour. So I headed to the loft, not to hide but to search through the mountains of Crewe Alexandra memorabilia that dominates the space. I needed to find a few photos, ones that captured Mike alongside our merry band on football days, and away on holidays together. I stayed up there for hours sifting through the most obscure programmes, photos of players that I had forgotten about, pin badges maybe worth a few quid, football shirts that fitted me in my youth, fixture list cards, scarves and mugs that have never been used to sup tea. Mike was involved in so many of the wonderful memories brought back to life that evening in the dusty confines of the loft. He was gone, but he was entwined in a past that will never be forgotten.

Mike first saw the Alex as a young lad, taken to a match courtesy of some hospitality from one of his dad's business contacts, McCorquodale printers on Frances Street, off Nantwich Road. It's another link to the late John Fleet who also worked at the printers around that time, before he assumed full-time duties at the Alex. That trip to Gresty Road was obviously enough for Mike and, just as I was many years before, he became hooked and made the Alex his team. His family lived in Leeds, so this was no easy football relationship for the youngster.

From day one he was grouped with the Alex Exiles, those who live away but still keep the club close to their hearts. As a 16-year-old he began making the train journey to Crewe, meeting up with Midlands and London-based fans, like myself. He also played the game, for the Exiles as I did during my London years. He was horribly athletic, the nippy wingman to my more central holding role. Okay, so I was never quite as fit as him. Whatever, he played the game with a smile, was the archetypal team player and always had something to say about the opposition. I remember playing a team of Arsenal fans, when the Alex visited one of the London sides later in the day. The Gooners had five substitutes, matching socks, shorts and personalised water bottles. We were a mish-mash band of ragamuffins in comparison.

'Soft southern tarts,' was Mike's typical observation, although they hammered us 15-0 that miserable, wet morning on Hyde Park.

Years later, when we recalled our days taking to the field for the Exiles and the Motley Crewe, he told me that I looked incredibly camp in my tight-fitting black shorts. He always did speak his mind, and he was right about the shorts. I looked like Kevin Keegan from the early eighties, just without the curly perm or talent. I wish Mike had told me earlier!

Simply watching and playing football wasn't enough for the opinionated Yorkshireman, and before long he was editing a new fanzine about the Alex. *We Are Crewe* hit the pre-match streets alongside our established *Super Dario Land* title, and Mike became a regular face on

Gresty Road. He knew his football, would happily stand chatting to anyone prepared to voice an opinion, and loved to continue the dialogue after the game when we all gathered in the club bar for the essential post-match analysis. He enjoying talking about the Alex so much I often wondered how he managed to sell any fanzines!

Still, it was more about making his mark, playing a part in the grander scheme of things that constituted the Alex matchday experience. With his fanzine he became embedded in that culture, just as I always hoped to with *SDL*. He belonged, and despite being a fiercely independent guy I think he needed that, being part of the Alex brotherhood. After a couple of years, realising that producing a monthly issue was a significant drain on his college time, he joined our band of writers. He was a fantastic addition, and for the next few years, into those unforgettable seasons in the Championship, I think his contributions made our humble rag a much better read.

The fanzines were often sold in the pubs, and the regular matchday gathering was in full swing by now. So with the new century came the desire to expand the whole Alex experience within our burgeoning group of mates. Progress up the leagues was fantastic, but I think we all accepted that we'd never see our team playing in mainland Europe. We decided to do something about that. Mike, one of the youngest of the group, loved to travel, and when someone suggested a few lads' footy weekends abroad to fill blank dates on the football calendar a huge smile spread across his face. Glasses were raised and plans were made.

The Czech Republic's wonderful Prague was one of the first destinations that saw us all together, enjoying a spectacular city, beers aplenty and grabbing some magical photos of ten lads sporting Alex tops from various seasons. There were snaps sitting by monuments, alongside the river, with locals and around the historic streets. Mike always stood out, wearing his blue Alex hat in all weathers!

But it was Tallinn, the capital of Estonia, which sticks out for many reasons. We flew from East Midlands airport, the now predictable gaggle of excitable young men, all Alex fans, chomping at the bit to experience another major European destination. We had been chatting about potential reinforcements to the Alex squad before take-off, how to improve the team, the usual stuff. Phones were switched off during the flight, but as we emerged from the plane at the Lennart Meri airport every mobile chimed in unison.

'Bloody hell,' declared the blunt Yorkshireman within our ranks, 'we've signed Craig Hignett. We've got Higgy back!'

Mike said it, and then we all checked to see if this news was correct. It was true; one of Dario Gradi's early exports was back at Gresty Road. Everyone danced and cavorted like big kids on the back of this exciting snippet of transfer news. Those gathered in the arrivals lounge looked on bemused, unsure of the idiots that had invaded their space. It was akin to opening a Christmas present, an Alex legend that had played in the top flight back to help the cause, and the news was relayed to tourists and locals alike as we toured the bars and restaurants that evening. Higgy, it turned out over the next few months, was a flop!

I've always enjoyed spreading the Alex word, doing my best to recruit new followers wherever my travels have taken me, be it at home or abroad. So after far too many steins of strong lager I found myself toe-to-toe with a huge German fella, another football fan determined to recount every kick of his side's recent match. It didn't come to blows, but it got heated. He was six feet five inches tall, as wide as a house and very loud. St. Pauli, from Hamburg, was his team and he chanted the club's name relentlessly, even in the gents' toilets. I'd had enough by now, but Mike stepped in. A sensible head on his young shoulders, he discreetly led me away from the monster German and forced me to drink a couple of coffees. Bizarrely, we met the German and his mates at the airport two days later. There was no animosity, just a realisation that we are all passionate about our teams. Mike just shook his head as I asked if I'd said anything out of turn.

You take so many things in life for granted, so finally realising that Mike's illness was increasingly serious took us all by surprise. We knew that he'd been sick, but by his accounts all was okay and the treatment had progressed well. Then his doctor dropped a bombshell and revealed that further treatment was pointless. The cancer was too aggressive, too advanced. He was told to visit as many friends and family as he could over the next few months. That's a real conversation stopper, and yet he always wanted to carry on regardless, for us to treat him as we always had. There has been so much to admire about Mike, but his bravery and determination to go about life and football during his final months were an inspiration to us all.

The final months can't have been easy for his family, but even when his body started to fail his mind was on football. In October 2010 we all met up in Burton, for the many pubs, microbreweries and another new stadium for the ground spotters amongst us. It was apparent that Mike was struggling, that walking more than a few yards was a challenge. So we grabbed a taxi, onwards to the next pub.

Then at Chesterfield, another new stadium, he was there. It wasn't the Mike of old, as despite the relentless flow of goals and the memorable 5-5 scoreline, he remained seated throughout, no celebrations, just a smirk on his face as the Alex came within seconds of being the first away team to win at the B2net Stadium. Mike was getting weaker but didn't want any fuss. He was happy watching us go mad, remonstrating with the stewards, cursing the referee and bemoaning the Alex players at their ability to throw away three points.

At home to Stockport, the penultimate game of the 2010-11 season and Mike's last Alex match, he arrived with his dad in the car. The train journey was likely to sap too much of his energy, what with changing trains at Manchester and getting from the station to the ground. He was on crutches and had a backpack containing his medication. We were all there, some a little sheepish, almost embarrassed to meet his gaze, not sure what to say under the circumstances. But Mike always broke the ice, lifted the mood and told us to get him a pint and just get on with it. His dad didn't watch the game; that was Mike's time with his mates. But he did join us in the Alex lounge beneath the main stand after the match, proud as punch that his son was amongst friends who obviously cared a great deal about him.

With the season over, two weeks later we all travelled to Leeds to visit Mike at home. He was wheelchair bound by now; only lucid for a few hours of each day, such was the strength of his increased medication. We took a trip to one of his favourite pubs and talked about the Alex and our hopes for the future. It wasn't likely to involve Mike, but he still gave us his opinion. It was always good comment, whatever he said. And he was usually right.

The next time the lads met up, there was no Mike. It was a solemn drive to Leeds, handshakes and nods as we arrived. Andy, Darren, Paul, Shaun and Steff, Richie and Emily, Dave, Alan, Simes, me, Ray and Marie, all numb, looking to each other for the right words. Then we received some advice from the funeral directors, who showed us how to carry the coffin and the first tears started. It didn't feel real, and even now I find it hard to accept that's he's gone.

Dario G's '*Sunchyme*' played as everyone took their places in the chapel, one of his favourite tracks. Then we sat there, in a daze, listening to some beautiful words from his family, classmates from school, university friends and recent work colleagues. The key theme that connected them all was Crewe Alexandra. It was one of Mike's passions, and he loved to tell them all about his beloved club.

And then he was gone. Two more tunes belted out from the chapel's speakers; Powderfinger's '*These Days*' and Ian Brown's '*Stellify*' as we made our way outside. Not everyone's cup of tea, but it was Mike's music. That was good enough for us.

There's no doubt that our group will continue to follow the Alex, home and away when we can, but there will always be someone missing – on the train, in the pubs and in the grounds. Mike and others like him are the reason so many of us continue to enjoy the matchday experience. It's the camaraderie, the unique banter only exchanged before games, and the euphoria of celebrating with friends when we score and occasionally win. Conversations will be poorer without Mike's spiky observations; incorrect statistics spouted by drunken fools like me will go uncorrected. We've lost someone special, but it's even sadder that the Alex as a club will not miss him. He was just one supporter, another anonymous face in the crowd. He paid his money but couldn't take his business elsewhere, no matter how bad things got. He was a dedicated supporter who should be properly recognised. We will never forget him.

JUST GOOD FRIENDS

In early July, the directors of Crewe Alexandra appealed to supporters in the pages of one of the local newspapers, pleading with them to buy season tickets. The following week, a reply in the letters page asked why should the fans put money into the club when players had been sold and no suitable replacements found? The irate writer went on to say that the club had no ambition. The letter in question was written in July 1902, but over a century later I suspect that many share the same sentiments.

***

'Why do you put yourself through it?' a good friend asked one afternoon.

The Alex were losing, away at Swindon on the opening day of the 2011-12 season. I couldn't go, as I'd just paid the balance on the family holiday. At long last the priorities had been stacked in the right order. Friends had come round for a late summer BBQ, but I was indoors listening to the radio commentary, and it was driving me crazy. In the space of three minutes I'd punched the air thinking that we'd scored, banged my head on the door frame in disgust when Lee Bell gave away possession, screamed at the commentator, berated the referee when he was conned into booking one of our players, and finally taken a swing at the cat as the Alex conceded the opening goal seconds before the interval. I was fuming, and very bad company. It was just another Saturday; the wife had seen it all before. Helen thought I was mad and went back into the garden.

The new season started on a depressing note, much as the last few chapters of this story have been particularly downbeat. But that's life. A series of ups and downs, happy and sad, occasionally more dips than troughs. Football is no different, but the current decline at Gresty Road seems particularly severe because we have fallen from such a great height. It's been a shit five years... and counting!

The term broken is a little dramatic, but I am an angry man when I think about the club. Much of it has been self-inflicted, but in many ways I feel that football in general has taken me for a fool. So now I've removed the rose-tinted spectacles that I wore for so many years, always defending the club, its players and other personnel. They are just people, passing through, doing a job, some moving on quicker than others. They are close to something that many of us covet, but that is no reason to place them on a pedestal.

What actually matters is the fans, the real people who pay hard-earned money to stand and sit together, week after week, from one year to the next. My good friend Andy Scoffin is one of them, someone who has supported the Alex through thick and thin for nearly half a century. He's fallen out with the club, argued toe-to-toe with other fans about managers, tactics and players, and like numerous others he has despaired at the club's recent tumble down the divisions.

But he's a fighter, and one bright spot was seeing him recover from cancer. You're never completely clear, as he told me recently, but he won't give in. That stubborn refusal to roll over mirrors his time as a supporter, and it's great to see him behind the microphone on matchdays, now the Tannoy Man, talking about the club he loves.

The big question is why put pen to paper and leave *She Wore A Scarlet Ribbon* hanging by a thread, mid-season, when nothing has been decided? Dario Gradi asked me the same question when we sat together at the Reaseheath training ground over a decade ago. *The Gradi Years* weren't over, he suggested. In fact, we were still flying high in the Championship, the most successful era in the club's history. He was right back then, but there was an unspoken understanding between us that surviving at that level was as good as it was likely to get for Crewe Alexandra. That was the case, it transpired, despite a gallant effort by all concerned.

This time, I can't see much changing as the latest season plays out. Pursuing a policy of youth is admirable, but a lack of experience and continued inconsistency is likely to see the Alex finish mid-table. If we're lucky, we might flirt with the play-off places, but only if we retain two or three of the up-and-coming stars for more than a season. Money talks, and I suspect that some of our prized assets will be gone sooner rather than later.

We are what we are, a modest sized club that will do well to stay afloat and preserve its league status. And to be honest, anything worse, like dropping out of the Football League, well, I'd rather not commit such misery to these pages. Consigning the club's downfall to print would be like plunging the knife of decline still deeper. I couldn't do that to Mistress Alexandra, no matter how she has treated me over the years.

You see the temptress is always forgiven. She's like a vampire that never ages, sucking the life from me, as I grow older sat up in the stands. But I always go back for more, unable to resist her. I am her slave, but I know that I'm not that special to her. She scours the area for fresh blood, and I often see new victims with that glazed look, hopelessly in love with her and everything she represents. They'll understand, in a few years.

I thought that I could break the habit, hide away and hope that I'd be forgotten, casually reading Internet reports or glancing at the sports pages. Not so. It's impossible; she still calls me, but now it feels like a dirty secret, something that I should lock away in the closet with other skeletons. But if I miss a game I find myself tucked away in the garden, still desperate to track her progress and keep in touch, but with the radio hidden behind cans of paint and general DIY disorder as I pretend to tidy the shed. I can't switch off and forget. And yet I want those around me to think I'm almost cured, that my obsession is under control, that I won't one day abandon the family for my mistress as I have so recklessly done in the past.

I can't deny that there have been some magical moments, and like so many others I wouldn't want to wind the clock back. Watching former players represent the national team, beating Stoke (twice in one season), winning at Wembley, topping the division, listening to opposition fans sing our club's praises, chanting deliriously with thousands of Alex fans, seeing Shaun Smith score from the halfway line and shaking hands with the manager… all highlights for me.

Despite all of those great times, things are not the same. The flame of passion that once burned bright is just a flicker, a lingering light that can't be extinguished. I still love her, with all of my heart, but I'm no

longer in love, if that makes sense.

That teenage infatuation has gone. I've been let down too many times. I suppose we're just good friends. She's a pair of old slippers that will never be discarded. My head tells me to sever all ties, properly move on, just as I have changed jobs and careers over the years. That, as any football fan will tell you, is impossible.

She will never allow me to move on. She's part of me, no matter what clever manoeuvres I employ to break free. Like thousands of others, I can't shake the disease. I suppose we're like a massive extended family; we all love each other, we argue and fight, disagree and vow to never speak with each other again. Then, at Christmas, we come together to kiss and make up. Everything is forgotten, temporarily, until the next bust up. That's football all over.

It's been a fantastic journey, and I will forever be glad that I bought a ticket to ride. My lads, well, I hope they catch the bug eventually, as there is so much to celebrate and enjoy about the beautiful game. Whether their love affair is with Mistress Alexandra remains to be seen. I'd never force the issue, as some things need to be discovered under your own steam.

If they do, I'll be there, sat next to the old girl, just not holding hands any more. Then the scarlet ribbon that dangles from her hair will flutter seductively in the breeze that drifts across the top of the main stand. I'll reach out, still tempted as I was so many years ago. Well, what else would I do with my Saturday afternoons?

ACKNOWLEDGEMENTS

Thanks to Mark Potts, Tony Marks, Adam Breeze, Ray Belcher, Andy Scoffin, Simon Welch, Tim Robinson, Helen Moss, Andy Howarth, Colin Higginson, Ian Affleck, Rob Wilson and Alison Bowler. To Rachel, Jacob and Leon for putting up with my post-match moods, and of course to mum and dad who tolerated me for many years.